FORENSIC ASSESSMENT WITH THE MILLON INVENTORIES

Forensic Assessment with the Millon Inventories

JOSEPH T. McCANN
FRANK J. DYER

Foreword by
Theodore Millon

THE GUILFORD PRESS
New York   London

© 1996 The Guilford Press
A Division of Guilford Publications, Inc.
72 Spring Street, New York, NY 10012

Printed in the United States of America

This book is printed on acid-free paper.

Last digit is print number: 9 8 7 6 5 4 3 2 1

Library of Congress Cataloging-in-Publication Data

McCann, Joseph T.
   Forensic assessment with the Millon inventories / Joseph T.
McCann, Frank J. Dyer.
      p.   cm.
   Includes bibliographical references and index.
   ISBN 1-57230-055-8
   1. Psychology, Forensic.   2. Millon Clinical Multiaxial Inventory.
I. Dyer, Frank J.   II. Title.
[DNLM: 1. Personality Inventory.   2. Personality Assessment.
3. Mental Disorders—diagnosis.   4. Psychology, Clinical.
5. Jurisprudence—United States.   BF 698.5 M478f 1996]
RA1148.M33   1996
614′.1—dc20
DNLM/DLC   96-7349
                                                              CIP

To my loving wife, Michele,
for every reason imaginable.
—J. T. M.

To Lois, Abigail, and Lisbeth,
for their support and encouragement.
—F. J. D.

Foreword

The Lord Chancellor of England commented in the 1920s that "psychology is a most dangerous science to apply to practical affairs." This so-called danger is no more evident than in the realm of forensics where psychologists and psychiatrists are questionably invited guests. Despite these restrictions, mental health professionals who have worked in the legal system find that the opportunities for clear thinking and precise recommendations are as challenging as they are in any area of psychology. Bringing the worlds of law and psychology together is a complicated task. Moreover, there are all sorts of professional liabilities, including experiences which can prove demeaning, if not humiliating, as when lawyers do their best to "unsettle" or "expose" the psychologist undergoing a cross-examination. Here, the psychologist must justify the legitimacy of his/her methods as a basis for arriving at psychological conclusions which have significant judicial consequences.

This sophisticated piece of work has been undertaken by two respected and knowledgeable *practicing* clinicians, one a lawyer, as well as a highly competent psychologist, the other a highly experienced psychological professional with a thorough grounding in psychometrics and a full-time clinical practice devoted mainly to forensic work. Both authors have been major contributors to the psychological literature on the MCMI and MACI: both have been unusually skilled presenters at informative workshops that illustrate their sophistication, not only with regard to the theoretical and clinical grounding of these instruments, but to their direct forensic utility. It would be difficult to find a better pair of scholars and practicing clinicians to undertake this task.

What makes this text by McCann and Dyer so useful is that they recognize that the primary task of the forensic psychologist is not primarily one of assigning an Axis I diagnosis, such as depression or anxiety; rather, the job is most often that of clarifying the personality characteristics of the individual being examined. This focus on understanding the person who has been charged with a crime, or is a participant in a complicated civil suit, is essentially that of appraising traits and characteristics, not symptoms or disorders. It is in this realm that the authors have made a most significant contribution. They focus on the MCMI and the MACI to achieve such goals, given the special utility of these two instruments in discerning the psychological features of clients.

The richness of this text is exemplified by the case histories describing the personality characteristics of clients seen in our legal system. These cases will be illuminating to the experienced hand, but will be especially valuable to the novice who is only beginning to learn about the utility of instruments such as the MCMI and MACI. Moreover, the book is replete with well-presented tables and figures that make the information necessary to assuming the role of an expert witness highly accessible.

This text brings together a wide range of significant forensic topics under a single cover. Especially fruitful to those clinicians who wish to understand the personality makeup of the clients under review are the many subtypes of each of the different possible MCMI codes. There is no simple one-to-one assignment of a diagnostic description, such as implied by a "pure" narcissist or a "prototypal" antisocial, or a "singular" borderline. Rather, there is a refinement and distinction process that the authors illustrate with the MCMI. No self-respecting clinician would assert that a client evidences a single personality pattern or style. Rather, they know and are led to demonstrate, that most clients show combinations or mixtures of several styles or patterns. It is in this realm that the McCann/Dyer book goes beyond that of any other text that seeks to strengthen the perspicacity of psychologists in assessing forensic clients.

Owing to their experience and knowledge, the authors discuss at length a wide range of relevant and practical topics, for example, overviewing case law and providing a basis for expert testimony. Several chapters deal with the utility of the MCMI and the MACI in assessing various criminal populations, for example, sex offenders, domestic violators, juvenile delinquents, malingerers, as well as issues related to the insanity defense and dangerousness. Similarly, issues that pertain to civil jurisprudence are covered incisively, for example, personal injury, disability determination, child custody, and so on. Thoughtful chapters helpful to the clinician who may use the MCMI or MACI deal with matters concerning: the preparation of testimony, the use of computerized reports in the courts, and an "interpretive strategy" for employing these instruments.

Throughout the text there is a sensitive awareness of the conflicting roles that psychologists must assume in working within the judicial system. There are ethical issues that must be considered in the role of a forensic assessor; for example, learning to abdicate the position of advocate for one's "patient". Similarly, the forensic clinician must learn to be comfortable with the role of being explicator of human behavior, rather than the role of a change agent. At this time when our profession is being assaulted by the limitations imposed on it through managed care, numerous psychologists are searching for new directions to expand their practice and to apply their skills and compassion. The role of psychologists in the courts is one that is not likely to diminish, as are so many other significant professional activities in our field.

There is no other book like the McCann/Dyer text available in our current literature. As noted above, what is especially attractive is that so much that can be useful in preparing for trials employing instruments such as the MCMI and the MACI is available in a single volume. Here you will find information on the several versions of these tests, detailed discussions of validity and reliability, as well as a preparatory checklist to ensure an adequate stance when deposed or cross examined. Whatever role one might be asked to assume with these tools are well organized, not only for the experienced user of self-reports, but for all those who may first be considering the MCMI or the MACI in the courtroom. In this regard, this text can serve as a useful companion volume to guide the use of the MMPI, the MMPI-A, or the 16PF in court settings. Together with these other inventories, the clinician can come well prepared to deal with the courtroom experience. In our judgment, of course, we believe that the MCMI and MACI provide especially clear explications of a client's personality characteristics.

As the primary author of the MCMI and MACI, I am heartened that the authors have undertaken the task of approaching their book in an even-handed and critical fashion. There are legitimate weaknesses and criticisms of the Millon Inventories. Although I believe their utility and strengths far outweigh these limits, I am delighted that the authors have not used this text as an opportunity to trumpet the superior value of the MCMI and MACI for forensic assessment. Among the elements which make this text so valuable are its integrity and its unwillingness to present the overly enthusiastic support that a test author might very much have enjoyed. It is a straightforward, honest, and balanced work, not loaded with the fluff of irrelevant details, nor crammed with obscure clinical issues and a pretense of scientific credibility in realms that have no bearing on the tasks of being a forensic psychologist. Any psychologist who is interested in expanding the range of his/her competencies will find this to be a clinically sound, eminently well written, and extremely useful and practical forensic text.

THEODORE MILLON

Preface

We originally met at a workshop led by Ted Millon and sponsored by NCS Assessments, which served as training for our future work providing continuing education workshops to other mental health professionals who use the Millon inventories. Through this experience, we discovered that our mutual interests in forensic psychology were based on similar values. That is, we have continuously searched for the best tools for conducting forensic psychological evaluations. As a result, our search led both of us to the Millon Clinical Multiaxial Inventory–II (MCMI-II), which we feel has been one of the most scientifically adequate instruments in terms of psychometric and theoretical sophistication. However, our intention in writing this book is not only to assist in more effective use of the Millon inventories, but also to improve forensic evaluations overall.

In our forensic work, the Millon inventories have shown themselves to be of great practical utility. In fact, recent trends in psychological testing among clinical psychologists reveal that the Millon inventories have grown in their popularity and stature among psychologists (Watkins, Campbell, Nieberding, & Hallmark, 1995). Forensic evaluations present many challenges and the Millon inventories, although by no means serving each and every assessment need, have certainly made many diagnostic and psychometric issues much easier in complex cases.

Thus, our purpose is to outline specific methods for utilizing these tests in forensic contexts. Moreover, through a combination of reviewing published research, summarizing clinical experiences, and providing in-depth case studies, we hope to make the forensic use of these instruments ethical, more accessible, and practical. The reader will note that our coverage deals primarily with the MCMI-II and the Millon Adolescent Clinical Inventory. Some attention is given to the new MCMI-III, but as stated in the text, we recommend that the MCMI-II be used for most forensic cases because "the jury is still out," if you will, on the newest version. Also, neither one of us has any experience with the Millon Behavioral Health Inventory, so we have not covered that particular instrument in this volume.

In no small terms, we both owe a great deal of gratitude to Ted Millon. Not only is he responsible for our meeting, but he has provided, in our opinion, some of the most incisively accurate and enlightening theoretical work ever to come out of the field of psychology. Not only are his influences felt in clinical practice, but his work has great use in forensic evaluation and consultation, as the following pages illustrate. Though issues are dealt with differently in this book than they are in more clinically oriented texts, this represents our forensic perspective.

Also instrumental in the completion of this work was the helpful and critical reading provided by M. George Feeney, Ph.D., and James F. Suess, Ph.D., at various stages of writing. The staff at NCS Assessments, especially Scott Allison, Terri Foley, Kristi Everson, and Patricia Elias, has been extremely helpful. Their professionalism and support has been of great service to the advancement of the Millon inventories. Moreover, their permission to reproduce selected items and materials to help illustrate important aspects of the tests is greatly appreciated.

At Guilford, Seymour Weingarten has been extremely helpful and his openness to the idea for this book made us approach the work with enthusiasm. In addition, we are grateful to Jeannie Tang, production editor; Keisha Simmons and Lori Frucht of the marketing department; and Lori Jacobs, copy-editor. The professionalism of the Guilford staff has made it a pleasure for us to work with them on this project.

Finally, the support and encouragement of our spouses, Michele Ries McCann and Lois Dyer, and family, Abigail and Lisbeth Dyer, have been perhaps the greatest resource available to us. Without them, this work might never have come into being. We are eternally indebted to them.

Contents

ONE

An Overview
of the Millon
Inventories

At one time, the assessment of personality and
psychopathology with an objective personality inventory was limited primarily to the Minnesota
Multiphasic Personality Inventory (MMPI). Over the past several years,
however, a number of personality inventories have been developed,
each with its own set of unique features. In addition to new tests being
developed, more established instruments have undergone revision to
reflect changes in diagnostic terminology and definitions, incorporate
innovative psychometric approaches to test construction, and update
normative data. In some instances, two different objective assessment
inventories can be used to obtain different pieces of information (e.g.,
Axis I vs. Axis II pathology) or to serve complementary functions (Antoni, 1993).

Objective psychological tests are especially suited for forensic practice because of the primary emphasis on nonambiguous stimuli (i.e.,
written test questions), clear-cut administration and scoring procedures,
and the availability of quantitative analysis of test results. In fact, even
ardent critics of psychological science in courtroom settings recognize
some of these benefits of objective instruments (Ziskin & Faust, 1988).

In this volume, we outline various applications and uses of one
particular set of psychological tests, the Millon inventories. This group
of tests includes the Millon Clinical Multiaxial Inventory (MCMI; Millon, 1983, 1987, 1994a) and the Millon Adolescent Clinical Inventory
(MACI; Millon, 1993), including its predecessor, the Millon Adolescent
Personality Inventory (MAPI; Millon, Green, & Meagher, 1982a). Each
of these instruments has been developed to provide diagnostically per-

tinent information across a wide range of clinical and forensic populations. For adults, the MCMI represents an instrument that has undergone several revisions and is designed to measure personality disorders and clinical symptomatology in adults. For adolescents, the MACI represents the most recent version of an instrument that has been developed to assess and measure personality styles, psychological concerns, and clinical disturbances in teenagers.

Several factors distinguish the Millon inventories from other personality instruments. Unlike most empirically derived tests, the Millon inventories are based on a comprehensive theory of personality and psychopathology formulated by the test developer (Millon, 1969, 1981, 1986a, 1986b, 1990). In addition to being theory based, each of the Millon inventories was also developed using a rigorous three-stage approach to test construction that is more elaborate and extensive than the purely empirical approach from which other instruments are derived. The procedures for developing and revising the MCMI and MACI involved substantive-theoretical, internal-structural, and external-criterion considerations. Such an approach to test construction incorporates modern psychometric theory and technology.

Perhaps one of the major distinguishing features of the Millon inventories, which has made the tests very popular among clinicians, is the coordination of scales with the current official diagnostic system in the *Diagnostic and Statistical Manual* revisions (DSM-III, DSM-III-R, DSM-IV; American Psychiatric Association, 1980, 1987, 1994). Each subsequent version of the MCMI and MACI has maintained close adherence to DSM criteria. Thus, the MCMI-III, for example, is closely aligned with current DSM-IV criteria and terminology. Consistent with the multiaxial approach to diagnosis outlined in the DSM-IV, the MCMI-II, MCMI-III, and MACI all have separate groups of scales to facilitate differential diagnosis between more enduring personality characteristics or trait features that are found on Axis II and the more transient and changeable state features associated with Axis I clinical syndromes. Different scale groups on these instruments also distinguish the severity level of pathology exhibited. Therefore, the Millon inventories have wide clinical and forensic applications because of their adherence to a model of psychopathology that reflects the current status of the field.

In order to develop a more adequate appreciation of how the Millon inventories can be applied in a legal context, it is necessary first to have an understanding of some of the basic principles that guide usage of these tests. This chapter therefore provides a brief overview of Millon's theoretical model, which forms the foundation for these instruments, followed by a discussion of test construction procedures that guided development and subsequent revisions; also provided is a description of the scales that make up the MCMI-II, MCMI-III, and MACI. In addition, the chapter discusses the changes that have taken place in revising the MCMI-II into the current MCMI-III. Given the lack of validity data on the MCMI-III and the relative newness of this test, the chapter focuses on the MCMI-II as the best choice for many forensic applications at this time. Information on the MCMI-III is provided to keep the reader abreast of developments with the MCMI and the current directions being taken to refine its properties. This chapter provides an overview of the Millon theory, test construction procedures, and scale descriptions. Those readers wishing to have more in-depth coverage of these issues are referred to the test manuals (Millon, 1987, 1993, 1994a), as well as to other interpretive texts (Choca, Shanley, & VanDenburg, 1992; Craig, 1993a, 1993b).

MILLON'S THEORETICAL MODEL OF PERSONALITY

The Millon inventories are based on the comprehensive model of personality and psychopathology outlined by Theodore Millon (1969, 1981, 1990). Although this model is not one that directly guided development of all DSM-IV classifications, Millon was on the Personality Disorder Work Group for DSM-III and DSM-IV. As such, his influences are seen in the resulting criteria. Moreover, DSM-IV criteria were utilized to validate the MCMI-III and MACI. Therefore, criticism of the original MCMI that it failed to correspond to DSM-III criteria (Widiger, Williams, Spitzer, & Frances, 1985) has been addressed in subsequent revisions of the tests.

To understand the meaning of various Millon inventory profile configurations, the best place to begin is with the underlying model. Three basic polarities form the foundation for the theory, which is based on the premise that humans are naturally driven to maximize pleasurable experiences and to minimize unpleasant or painful circumstances. Each dimension defines a different aspect of this principle. One dimension describes the nature of reinforcement, that is, the *pain–pleasure* polarity. A second dimension defines where reinforcing experiences take place, either in self-gratification or in relationships with others; this is the *self–other* polarity. Finally, a third dimension defines how one goes about seeking reinforcement by either actively manipulating and interacting with the environment or passively accepting and adapting to life experiences, the *active–passive* polarity.

In addition to the underlying reinforcement motivations that guide human behavior, Millon's biopsychosocial model holds that individuals also develop instrumental strategies for attaining reinforcing experiences. Specifically, people can engage in pursuit of pleasurable and life-enriching experiences by interacting with the environment and generating activity that leads to reinforcement. Likewise, people can passively accept various life experiences and wait for pleasurable or life-enhancing experiences to arise. Such passivity leads to the individual accommodating to and following the direction provided by the environment.

Eleven basic personality patterns are defined by examining active and passive personality types that develop a primary reliance on one of five sources of reinforcement. Individuals may develop disturbances in the pain–pleasure polarity such that individuals become *detached,* withdrawing from reinforcing or potentially rewarding experiences because of a general failure to experience pleasure or an extreme sensitivity to painful experiences. The passive subtypes of the detached type are the schizoid and depressive personality disorders, whereas the active subtype of the detached style is the avoidant personality disorder.

Other personality types are defined by the reversal of pain and pleasure, such that those experiences generally considered rewarding and pleasurable become associated with pain, discomfort, or other unpleasant feelings. In the same way, negative or painful events become associated with pleasure and gratification. These are *discordant* types and are represented by the passive (self-defeating) and active (aggressive/sadistic) variants.

Still other personalities develop an excessive focus on reinforcing experiences based almost exclusively on self-gratification and fulfillment of the needs and desires of one's self. These *independent* types look only for experiences that will gratify their own self-centered needs. Such personality types are represented by the passive (narcissistic) and active (antisocial) subtypes.

Two other personality types develop an overreliance on reinforcement which arises within the context of relationships with others. That is, pleasure and satisfaction are obtained by having other people involved in one's life. If others are responsive, attentive, and available, these *dependent* types derive a great deal of gratification in life. Again, there are active (histrionic) and passive (dependent) variants to the dependent personality pattern.

Finally, there are those styles that become conflicted over whether to attend to and follow their own needs or whether they should comply and follow the needs and wishes of others. These subtypes are referred to in the theoretical model as *ambivalent,* and they may take the form of an active (negativistic) and passive (compulsive) variant. Table 1.1 illustrates the relationship between active and passive instrumental styles and the disturbances in experiencing or seeking reinforcement, accounting for the 11 basic personality disorders.

Based on this model of basic personality disturbance are some general principles that serve to distinguish pathological patterns from more normal patterns. First, there is assumed to be a degree of flexibility among individuals such that a mix of personality traits may exist but the individual can adopt particular characteristics as situations demand. For example, greater assertiveness can be seen when the situation calls for it, whereas personal restraint is possible in other circumstances. When character patterns become rigid and inflexible and perpetuate repetitive and disruptive patterns (e.g., relationships break up for similar or recurring reasons, such as the person's casual infidelity), personality is said to become more pathological. In addition, people can be more prone or susceptible to severe disruptions in their psychological stability, as in tendencies toward erratic behavior, intense moods, or disturbed self-image.

In more extreme instances, some personality styles develop more severe disturbances such as confused thought processes, bizarre thought content, emotional instability, and marked interpersonal maladjustment. Thus, some personality structures are more prone to brief psychotic episodes and severe mood disruption. Three severe personality disorders defined in the theoretical model are viewed as extensions of the 11 basic personality disorders and these are represented in Table 1.1. The schizotypal personality, best conceptualized as an extension of the detached personality types, is characterized by vague, diffuse, and autistic thought processes, social withdrawal, and oddities in behavior and appearance. The borderline, viewed as a severe variant of dependent and ambivalent types, is defined by erratic and unstable interpersonal relationships, lability of mood, self-destructive and impulsive behavior, and widely fluctuating feelings toward others. The paranoid personality, an extension of independent and ambivalent types,

TABLE 1.1. Millon's Theoretical Model for Personality Disorders

Domain of pathology	Instrumental style		Severe variant
	Active	Passive	
Nature of reinforcement			
Discordant	Sadistic	Self-defeating	Borderline/paranoid
Detached	Avoidant	Schizoid/ depressive	Schizotypal
Source of reinforcement			
Independent	Antisocial	Narcissistic	Paranoid
Dependent	Histrionic	Dependent	Borderline
Ambivalent	Negativistic	Compulsive	Borderline/paranoid

is identified by intense suspiciousness, rigid defensiveness against being controlled or influenced by others, and a tendency to read into situations to perceive potential threats to one's integrity or autonomy.

The 14 personality disorders provide the basis for understanding a number of aspects about the individual. By recognizing the person's ingrained, long-standing ways of behaving, coping with stress, viewing the world, and interacting with others, the clinician is in a better position to view the context in which clinical symptoms arise. Thus, the theoretical model demands that depression, anxiety, somatic concerns, substance abuse, and other clinical symptoms be viewed differently, depending on the individual's personality style. For example, depression in a dependent individual may represent loss or abandonment, whereas in a compulsive individual it may represent a feeling of having lost control over one's life. A multidimensional approach to examining and assessing psychopathology guided the development of a major group of psychometric tests.

DEVELOPMENT OF THE MILLON INVENTORIES

Construction Procedures

A major distinguishing characteristic of the Millon inventories is the three-stage approach to test construction that guided their development. Despite the differences in item content and normative samples that exist across all three versions of the MCMI and the two adolescent versions, this three-stage process has been utilized for developing and revising each instrument.

As outlined in the test manuals (Millon, 1983, 1987, 1993, 1994a), the selection of items and construction of the scales were carried out in three stages. The first of these stages was a substantive-theoretical process of selecting items which adequately reflected the constructs being measured. Therefore, both prototypical theoretical descriptions of personality disorders and DSM criteria served as the substantive material from which items were derived. The second stage involved an internal-structural analysis of the psychometric properties of each scale. In this step, such information as the internal consistency of scales, item endorsement frequencies, and correlations between each item and the scale scores was calculated to determine whether items were functioning as would be expected according to both theoretical and substantive diagnostic expectations. The third stage involved external-criterion studies to assess the validity of each scale. During these procedures, item responses and scale scores were correlated with such external-criterion measures as clinician ratings of pathology and scores from other standardized tests to make sure that items and scales had a meaningful relationship to external diagnostic information.

Base Rate Scores

Another major distinguishing feature of the Millon inventories is the fact that the profiles utilize a base rate (BR) score to translate raw scores into an interpretively meaningful scale. Unlike such norm-referenced measures as the T-score, which is used on many psychological tests, the BR score does not assume a normal distribution of the various traits and syndromes being measured. For example, the MMPI, MMPI-2, and MMPI-A all utilize T-scores to convert raw scores into distributions where the mean scale scores are assigned a score of 50 and a standard deviation of 10 (Archer, 1992; Graham, 1990). Moreover, the MMPI-2 and MMPI-A have utilized uniform T-scores, with the result being equivalent percentile ranks across different scales at the same T-score cutoff.

The Millon inventories go in the opposite direction. The assumption is that various diagnostic categories and symptomatology are not normally distributed in any given population. That is, one personality disorder or clinical syndrome may be more or less prevalent than another. Base rate scores are based on the conversion of raw scores into a standardized scale that reflects these varying percentages or prevalence rates of disorders in the population against which an individual's scores are compared. By reflecting the different prevalence rates of various disorders, the Millon inventory profiles are a diagnostically useful representation of those attributes that are of most importance in the evaluation process.

The particular method by which BR score transformations were developed for all the Millon inventories is fairly straightforward. First, the prevalence rates for each personality disorder and clinical syndrome were established in the normative sample for each particular test. Next, the raw score frequency distributions were plotted for each scale. An arbitrary set of three anchor points was assigned at BR scores of 0, 60, and 115, with a BR of 0 corresponding to a raw score of 0, a BR of 60 corresponding to the median raw score for each scale, and a BR of 115 corresponding to the maximum raw score possible for a particular scale (see Millon, 1993, 1994a, for a further discussion of BR scores). Table 1.2 reflects these BR anchor points and their meaning.

Also noted in the table are two other BR score anchor points which were selected at 75 and 85. A BR score of 75 represents the raw score for a particular scale which corresponds to the percentile of patients in the normative sample that was deemed to have a personality trait/dis-

TABLE 1.2. Meaning of Millon Inventory BR Scores

BR score	Raw score equivalent	Descriptive meaning
0	Raw score of 0	
60	Median raw score	Average among patients
75	Raw score corresponding to % of sample with disorder rated as present	Trait/syndrome/concern present
85	Raw score corresponding to % of sample with disorder rated as prominent	Trait/syndrome/concern prominent
115	Maximum raw score on scale	

order or clinical syndrome as being "present" by collateral rating. A BR score of 85 corresponds to the raw score reflecting the percentile of patients who were deemed to have the disorder or syndrome rated as prominent.

Once the five anchor points were established at BR 0, 60, 75, 85, and 115, algebraic interpolation was used to fill in the BR conversions for all raw scores in the distribution for each scale. This process resulted in the BR conversion tables in the manual (Millon, 1987, 1993, 1994a).

Although the MCMI-II, MCMI-III, and MACI all have different normative samples, and thus different prevalence rates for each disorder, syndrome, or expressed concern, the BR scores were developed according to those same procedures for all the Millon instruments. Therefore, this discussion of the meaning of different BR scores applies to each test.

THE MCMI-II AND MCMI-III SCALES

The MCMI is a 175-item inventory consisting of statements that are read by the individual taking the test and responded to as being either true or false. It is designed for adults, age 18 and older, and requires an eighth-grade reading level.

Items are keyed in such a way that scores for 26 scales are obtained on the MCMI-II and for 28 scales on the MCMI-III. Tables 1.3 and 1.4 present the names and number of items for each scale, as well as sample items from the MCMI-II and MCMI-III, respectively. The scales are broken down into five general groupings which are plotted in profile form, as the examples in Figures 1.1 and 1.2 illustrate.

TABLE 1.3. MCMI-II Scales

Scale		No. of items	Sample item
Modifier indices			
V	Validity	4	I flew across the Atlantic thirty times last year.
X	Disclosure	N/A[a]	N/A
Y	Desirability	23	I think I am a sociable and outgoing person.
Z	Debasement	46	I always feel I am not wanted in a group.
Clinical personality patterns			
1	Schizoid	35	I've always found it more comfortable to do things quietly alone instead of with others.
2	Avoidant	40	I am a quiet and fearful person.
3	Dependent	37	When I run into a crisis, I quickly look for someone to help me.
4	Histrionic	40	It is very easy for me to make friends.
5	Narcissistic	49	I know I'm a superior person, so I don't care what people think.
6A	Antisocial	45	Punishment never stopped me from doing what I wanted.
6B	Aggressive/ sadistic	45	I believe in being strong willed and determined in everything I do.
7	Compulsive	38	I keep very close track of my money so I am prepared if a need comes up.
8A	Passive–aggressive	41	I often let my angry feelings out and then feel terribly guilty about it.
8B	Self-defeating	40	I often feel I should be punished for the things I have done.
Severe personality pathology			
S	Schizotypal	44	I believe there are people who use telepathy to influence my life.
C	Borderline	62	Other people seem more sure than I am of who they are and what they want.
P	Paranoid	44	I protect myself from trouble by never letting people know much about me.
Clinical syndromes			
A	Anxiety	25	Lately, I get butterflies in my stomach and break out in cold sweats.

(continued)

TABLE 1.3. *(cont.)*

Scale		No. of items	Sample item
H	Somatoform	31	I have a hard time keeping my balance when walking.
N	Bipolar: Manic	37	There are many times, when for no reason, I feel very cheerful and full of excitement.
D	Dysthymia	36	For the past few years even minor things seem to depress me.
B	Alcohol dependence	46	I have a drinking problem that I've tried unsuccessfully to end.
T	Drug dependence	58	My drug habits have often gotten me into a good deal of trouble in the past.
Severe syndromes			
SS	Thought disorder	33	Ideas keep turning over and over in my mind and they won't go away.
CC	Major depression	31	In the last few weeks I begin to cry even when the slightest of things goes wrong.
PP	Delusional disorder	22	Many people have been spying into my private life for years.

Note. Sample items are from the *Manual for the Millon Clinical Multiaxial Inventory–II,* by Theodore Millon, 1987, Minneapolis, MN: National Computer Systems. Copyright 1987 by Theodore Millon. Reprinted by permission.
*"*Disclosure is calculated based on the raw score sum of Scales 1 through 8B.

Scale Descriptions

Modifier Indices

The modifier indices consist of the Validity index (V), Disclosure (X), Desirability (Y), and Debasement (Z) scales which are all measures designed to assess the individual's general test-taking attitude and response biases and the general validity of test results. Specifically, these measures are sensitive to the degree to which an individual misrepresents or otherwise provides an inaccurate picture of his or her problems.

Scale V. This is a four-item scale on the MCMI-II and a three-item scale on the MCMI-III. It consists of items with bizarre content which are designed to assess the individual's tendencies to respond with random, oppositional, or other response sets that reveal a failure to accurately read the test items or to otherwise ignore item content. Also

TABLE 1.4. MCMI-III Scales

Scale		No. of items	Sample item
Modifier indices			
V	Validity	3	I flew across the Atlantic thirty times last year.
X	Disclosure	N/A[a]	N/A
Y	Desirability	21	I think I am a sociable and outgoing person.
Z	Debasement	33	Things that are going well today won't last very long.
Clinical personality patterns			
1	Schizoid	16	When I have a choice, I prefer to do things alone.
2A	Avoidant	16	I avoid most social situations because I expect people to criticize or reject me.
2B	Depressive	15	I've had sad thoughts much of my life since I was a child.
3	Dependent	16	I am a very agreeable and submissive person.
4	Histrionic	17	I like to flirt with members of the opposite sex.
5	Narcissistic	24	I know I'm a superior person, so I don't care what people think.
6A	Antisocial	17	As a teenager, I got into lots of trouble because of bad school behavior.
6B	Aggressive/ sadistic	20	I often criticize people strongly if they annoy me.
7	Compulsive	17	I think highly of rules because they are a good guide to follow.
8A	Negativistic/ passive– aggressive	16	I often let my angry feelings out and then feel terribly guilty about it.
8B	Self-defeating	15	I seem to choose friends who end up mistreating me.
Severe personality pathology			
S	Schizotypal	16	People make fun of me behind my back, talking about the way I act or look.
C	Borderline	16	I feel pretty aimless and don't know where I'm going in life.
P	Paranoid	17	Sneaky people often try to get the credit for things I have done or thought of.

(continued)

TABLE 1.4. (*cont.*)

Scale		No. of items	Sample item
Clinical syndromes			
A	Anxiety	14	I've become very jumpy in the last few weeks.
H	Somatoform	12	I very often lose my ability to feel any sensations in parts of my body.
N	Bipolar: Manic	13	There are many times, when for no reason, I feel very cheerful and full of excitement.
D	Dysthymia	14	I've become quite discouraged and sad about life in the past year or two.
B	Alcohol dependence	15	I have an alcohol problem that has made difficulties for me and my family.
T	Drug dependence	14	My habit of abusing drugs has caused me to miss work in the past.
R	Posttraumatic stress	16	Years later I still have nightmares about an event that was a real threat to my life.
Severe syndromes			
SS	Thought disorder	17	Lately, I have to think things over and over again for no good reason.
CC	Major depression	17	I feel terribly depressed and sad much of the time now.
PP	Delusional disorder	13	Many people have been spying into my private life for years.

Note. Sample items are from the *Millon Clinical Multiaxial Inventory–III Manual*, by Theodore Millon, 1994, Minneapolis, MN: National Computer Systems. Copyright 1994 by Theodore Millon. Reprinted by permission.
^aDisclosure is calculated based on the raw score sum of Scales 1 through 8B.

picked up by this scale are difficulties in concentration, low reading level, problems with reading comprehension, or extreme mental confusion that can impair an individual's ability to read items.

Scale X. The Disclosure index is not a true scale in the sense that it is composed of a discrete set of items; rather, it consists of the differentially weighted raw scores of the basic personality scales (Scales 1–8B). The Disclosure index is designed to measure general openness to revealing personal aspects about one's self. Low scores reveal a general tendency to be secretive and defensive, as well as an unwillingness to

MILLON CLINICAL MULTIAXIAL INVENTORY-II
FOR PROFESSIONAL USE ONLY

```
ID NUMBER = 1131                  VALID REPORT
PERSONALITY CODE = 3 7 5 ** 4 * 8A 6A 2 8B 6B 1 + - " - '' // P ** - * //
SYNDROME CODE = - ** - * // PP ** - * //
DEMOGRAPHIC = 1131      /ON/F/22/W/S/H9/--/--/--/30390/07/10/30190/  627000021
```

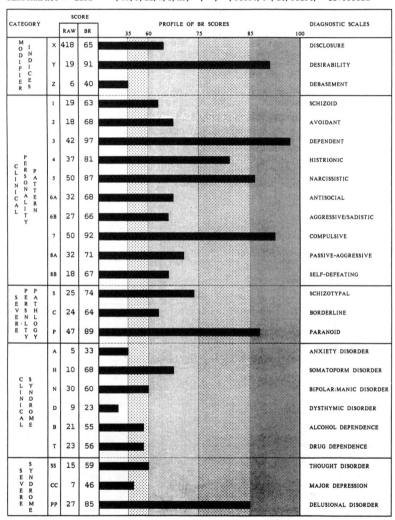

FIGURE 1.1. Sample MCMI-II profile. MCMI-II/Copyright 1987 by Theodore Millon. Reprinted by permission.

MILLON CLINICAL MULTIAXIAL INVENTORY - III
CONFIDENTIAL INFORMATION FOR PROFESSIONAL USE ONLY

ID NUMBER: 3341   Valid Profile
PERSONALITY CODE: - ** 2A * 2B 5 3 + 8B 4 7 1 " 6B 8A 6A ' ' // - ** - * //
SYNDROME CODE: - ** A * // - ** - * //
DEMOGRAPHIC: 3341/OP/M/56/O/D/12/--/--/-----/09/-----/

CATEGORY		SCORE		PROFILE OF BR SCORES					DIAGNOSTIC SCALES
		RAW	BR	0	60	75	85	115	
MODIFYING INDICES	X	76	50						DISCLOSURE
	Y	12	55						DESIRABILITY
	Z	2	38						DEBASEMENT
CLINICAL PERSONALITY PATTERNS	1	3	36						SCHIZOID
	2A	8	77						AVOIDANT
	2B	7	74						DEPRESSIVE
	3	6	60						DEPENDENT
	4	15	48						HISTRIONIC
	5	18	73						NARCISSISTIC
	6A	2	15						ANTISOCIAL
	6B	3	26						AGGRESSIVE (SADISTIC)
	7	14	47						COMPULSIVE
	8A	3	22						PASSIVE-AGGRESSIVE
	8B	3	59						SELF-DEFEATING
SEVERE PERSONALITY PATHOLOGY	S	3	59						SCHIZOTYPAL
	C	3	29						BORDERLINE
	P	13	72						PARANOID
CLINICAL SYNDROMES	A	6	80						ANXIETY DISORDER
	H	0	0						SOMATOFORM DISORDER
	N	1	12						BIPOLAR: MANIC DISORDER
	D	4	64						DYSTHYMIC DISORDER
	B	1	15						ALCOHOL DEPENDENCE
	T	1	15						DRUG DEPENDENCE
	R	8	67						POST-TRAUMATIC STRESS
SEVERE SYNDROMES	SS	3	45						THOUGHT DISORDER
	CC	0	0						MAJOR DEPRESSION
	PP	4	65						DELUSIONAL DISORDER

FIGURE 1.2. Sample MCMI-III profile. MCMI-III/Copyright 1994 by Theodore Millon. Reprinted by permission.

reveal aspects of one's private life. High scores suggest the individual uses little discretion when making self-reports and he or she may be looking to others for attention, sympathy, or some support by being overly revealing of personal difficulties or concerns. This scale, unlike the Debasement or Desirability scales, strives to be neutral as to whether a positive or negative impression is being created. However, this scale does correlate highly with the Debasement scale.

Scale Y. The Desirability scale consists of items contained on several other scales that are sensitive to a social desirability response set. High scores on this scale are indicative of a respondent's attempt to present him- or herself in a favorable light. Also revealed by high scores is the attempt to minimize and downplay personal faults and to hold unrealistically positive attitudes about one's stability and psychological well-being. This scale can often be elevated when the respondent has some secondary gain that can be achieved by being viewed as having positive rehabilitative and treatment potential.

Scale Z. Response sets that involve a tendency to magnify and overreport problems and personal faults are the main attributes assessed by this scale. Elevated scores are found in individuals who have some motivation, either psychological or material, to overreport problems or other forms of psychopathology. In other words, this scale is useful in assessing tendencies toward malingering, psychological "cries for help," or other instances of unrealistic overreporting of problems.

Basic Personality Scales

The basic personality scales are designed to measure more stable and long-standing characteristics of the individual. Though they are meant to reflect more enduring aspects of the person's psychological and interpersonal style, they are also affected by such transient states as depression or anxiety. The following descriptors represent features that guided formal development of the scales and that characterize high scorers.

Scale 1. This scale was designed to assess characteristics associated with the schizoid personality disorder in DSM-IV. Therefore, high scores reflect such symptoms as emotional blandness, lethargy, social withdrawal and isolation, indifference to praise or criticism, and a lack of interest in personal relationships. Thought processes may be restricted and lacking in detail. This scale can be elevated in cases in which these symptoms also reflect a dysphoria or general emptiness in the person's life. Overall, there is a passively detached personality pattern in relationships.

Scale 2A. The characteristics associated with avoidant personality disorder in DSM-IV are revealed in elevations on this scale. As such, the major traits assessed include social anxiety and fear, withdrawal from others, expectations of ridicule and rejection, low self-image and feelings of inadequacy, and excessive rumination and worry over potential injury. Persons scoring high on this scale experience very few pleasures in life and they remain on constant guard against possible hurt or injury from others.

Scale 2B. This scale appears only on the MCMI-III and was not included on the MCMI-II. It is a new scale which measures characteristics associated with the depressive personality disorder, found among the criteria sets needing further study in DSM-IV. The pain of life's experiences is taken to be a permanent part of existence. High scores reflect a prominent pessimism, a sad and gloomy mood, a hopelessness about the future, and a general feeling of emptiness and a lack of connectedness to others. In addition, the inner thoughts of these individuals are marked by dysphoria.

Scale 3. The characteristics associated with DSM-IV dependent personality disorder are measured by high scores on this scale. Particular features include lack of initiative, passivity, placing others' needs before one's own, and seeking out the nurturance of and attachment to others. These individuals lack the security in their own self-assurance to take a more assertive and autonomous approach to life. Therefore, these individuals passively accept what comes their way, though they remain oriented toward closeness and dependence on others.

Scale 4. This scale corresponds to the histrionic personality disorder in DSM-IV. Major features of high scorers include excessive display of emotion, a dramatic need for attention, manipulation of others and events to satisfy their need for affection and approval, and an extreme concern with physical appearances and self-presentation. The individual scoring highly also tends to be quite dramatic and theatrical, often exaggerating displays of emotion in order to obtain the attention from others that is so important. Sometimes the dramatic behavior can become erratic and impulsive.

Scale 5. Characteristics of DSM-IV narcissistic personality disorder are measured by this scale. As such, the major attributes of high scores include a grandiose and egocentric self-image, extreme confidence and overvaluing of personal achievements, arrogance and exploitative intentions in interpersonal relationships, and a lack of empathy or sensitivity to the needs of others. This scale often reflects a sensitivity to personal slight and injury such that the person reacts angrily when others attempt to confront the overly confident self-image that narcissistic individuals have.

Scale 6A. This scale corresponds to the antisocial personality disorder in DSM-IV. It reflects the traits commonly associated with that pattern, including involvement in illegal activity, a history of childhood and adolescent conduct disturbances, impulsivity, inability to form meaningful attachments, and exploitation of others and circumstances to meet one's own self-centered needs. When confronted with their actions, antisocial individuals feel justified in having manipulated or conned others, as they feel it is best to take from others rather than wait for others to take advantage of them. They lack sensitivity and can be quite ruthless.

Scale 6B. Although the sadistic personality disorder was deleted from diagnostic nomenclature in DSM-IV, this scale was retained and has utility in MCMI assessments. Major characteristics revealed in this scale include an aggressive and hostile style. These individuals can derive a great deal of gratification from either causing or observing the humiliation or suffering of others. In relationships they can be combative and strive for power and control. Also characteristic of high scorers are tendencies toward abusive, brutal, and malicious intentions and actions.

Scale 7. The obsessive–compulsive personality disorder of DSM-IV is represented by this scale. High scores are reflective of moralistic and perfectionistic thinking, as well as public displays of compliance and strict adherence to rules. Emotionally, there may also be evidence of a restriction in the display of feelings and there is often intense underlying conflict over the need for autonomy versus the need to conform and follow others. This scale is also sensitive to socially desirable response sets.

Scale 8A. This scale measures what was the passive–aggressive personality disorder in DSM-III-R and is now referred to as the negativistic personality in DSM-IV. High scores on this scale are associated with irritable mood, oppositional behavior, negative and pessimistic thinking, and a general stubbornness in relationships. Individuals with high scores are also prone to express contrary and negative sentiments that ruin periods of joy or happiness for others. When anger and hostility are expressed, a short-lived period of guilt and shame often follows.

Scale 8B. Although the self-defeating personality disorder was deleted from DSM-IV, this scale has been retained on the MCMI-II and MCMI-III. It measures characteristics associated with this personality style, including self-sacrificing behaviors, poor self-image, and excessive focus on unfortunate and painful experiences. High scorers find comfort in personal suffering and they feel deserving of the shame and humiliation they have experienced. In social settings, there is a tendency to be self-effacing and to feel inferior to other people.

Severe Personality Scales

The severe personality scales comprise three measures that assess more maladaptive levels of functioning. As a group and individually, these scales often reflect severe problems in the area of affect management, coherence and rationality of thinking, and interpersonal relationships. Because the scales measure more pathological variants of basic personality styles, other basic personality scales will generally be elevated when one or more of the severe personality scales is high.

Scale S. This scale is designed to measure features associated with the schizotypal personality disorder of DSM-IV. Characteristics associated with elevations on this scale include social isolation and withdrawal, vague or confused thought, paranoid ideation, autistic reasoning, and oddities in behavior and self-presentation. Brief psychotic episodes may be manifest, particularly when stress levels increase.

Scale C. The traits associated with this scale correspond to those found in the borderline personality disorder of DSM-IV. As such, this scale measures lability of emotions, self-destructive and self-mutilating behavior, intense and volatile relationships, and such disturbances in identity as a lack of clarity as to one's interests, goals, and long-term plans. Close relationships are marked by extreme conflict and ambivalence and can often precipitate intense cycles of rage, depression, and anxiety.

Scale P. This scale measures features associated with the paranoid personality disorder of DSM-IV. High scores on this scale are indicative of extreme defensiveness and excessive concern that others are attempting to control the person. There is vigilance and mistrust toward others and there is excessive rigidity in one's feelings and attitudes to the point that the individual expends a great deal of energy resisting external influences. There is also hypersensitivity to personal attacks and the constant questioning of the sincerity and motives of others is ever present.

Clinical Syndrome Scales

The next section on the MCMI profile comprises the clinical syndrome scales. They are designed to measure more transient symptomatology that manifests as DSM-IV Axis I disturbances. On the whole, the stability and reliability of these scales are somewhat lower than that of the personality disorder scales, primarily because of the changeable nature of the phenomena being measured.

Scale A. This scale is designed to assess symptoms associated with anxiety. High scores reflect tension, nervousness, worry and rumination, social fears and discomfort, and indecisiveness. Some physical signs of anxiety may be present, such as muscular tension, fidgety movements, and perspiration.

Scale H. High scores on this scale are associated with physical complaints and difficulties that are often a means of expression for underlying psychological conflict. Associated with elevations on the scale are fatigue and weakness, vague and nonspecific pains, loss of feeling in parts of the body, and tingling in the senses. Also, high scores usually reveal a tendency to dramatize ailments and overinterpret physical symptoms as evidence of more serious disease and attempts to utilize physical complaints to obtain sympathy and attention from others.

Scale N. This scale is designed to assess aspects of a bipolar mood disorder. High scores often reflect agitation, pressured speech, grandiose thought content, excessive energy, and irritability. In addition, impulsive actions, poor planning, and the setting of unrealistic goals for one's self are features found in high scorers. Labile mood, difficulty concentrating, and flight of ideas are also present.

Scale D. This scale is designed to measure depressive symptomatology that has been present for a relatively long time. Also, the scale is one of the most sensitive for measuring depression overall. The characteristics of high scorers are chronic depressed mood, apathy, guilt, suicidal ideation, hopelessness and pessimism about the future, a lack of interest in activities, and other symptoms associated with clinical depression.

Scale B. High scores on this scale reflect difficulties with controlling alcohol use. Primarily, this scale measures problems with work and family that are related to alcohol use and difficulties in controlling or stopping alcohol consumption.

Scale T. This scale is designed to assess recurrent problems with drug abuse. In addition, this scale is often associated with impulsivity, resistance to having limits placed on behavior, and an inability to recognize the negative consequences of one's impulsive acts.

Scale R. This scale was not included on the MCMI-II profile and appears only on the MCMI-III. It is designed to measure features associated with the DSM-IV diagnosis of posttraumatic stress disorder. High scores reflect excessive rumination and preoccupation with unpleasant events that were threatening to the individual. There may be frequent flashbacks, intrusive memories, or upsetting reminders of trauma that can trigger anxiety, nightmares, hopelessness, or other signs of distress.

Severe Clinical Syndrome Scales

In keeping with the MCMI's focus on distinguishing various levels of severity in pathology, the three severe clinical syndrome scales are designed to measure more pathological and debilitating symptomatology.

Scale SS. High scores on this scale are often indicative of more severe levels of pathology such as schizophrenia or other psychotic disturbances. Individuals showing elevations on this scale tend to exhibit disoriented thinking, delusions, hallucinations, and fragmentation in their thinking. Some social withdrawal and behavioral isolation may also be present.

Scale CC. This scale is sensitive to the more severe symptoms associated with major depression. Elevations reflect severely depressed mood, hopelessness, suicidal ideation or intent, loss of appetite, weight loss, worthlessness, fatigue, and rumination.

Scale PP. This scale measures acute paranoid ideation that may rise to the level of delusional content. There tends to be ideas of reference, hostile moods, feelings of persecution, hypervigilance, and alertness to being the object of ridicule or scorn.

THE MCMI-II VERSUS MCMI-III
FOR FORENSIC PRACTICE

When selecting the proper test for a particular application, a psychologist considers such issues as the similarity between the individual being assessed and the normative sample, overall reliability, and validity of the test for measuring the constructs of interest. Current revisions of tests have the advantage of updating scales and correcting problems that may have been present when using earlier versions of the test.

In forensic work, it is recommended that for the time being, practitioners use the MCMI-II, rather than the MCMI-III, for most applications. The reason for this recommendation is based on our analysis of the current validity data on the MCMI-III in light of the need for strong scientific and empirical research to support techniques in court-room settings. The MCMI-II has extensive internal-structural and factor-analytic data published in the manual, as well as studies that support the convergent, discriminant, and construct validity of the scales (McCann, 1990, 1991). Moreover, the MCMI-II manual demonstrates good external criterion validity against clinical ratings with the Millon Personality Disorder Checklist (Millon, 1987). The MCMI-III, although showing good content validity in being coordinated with DSM-IV criteria, is not currently at a stage where factor-analytic and adequate external criterion validity studies have been conducted. Therefore, the MCMI-II has several advantages over the MCMI-III when the specific applications may require defending the validity of the MCMI under direct or cross-examination. The body of MCMI-II research is more substantial (Craig, 1993b) than the MCMI-III research at this particular time.

The MCMI-III holds promise, given the distinct advantages it has in having its content validity firmly established in DSM-IV criteria (see Millon, 1994a, Appendix A). Therefore, it may have some use in forensic settings when defending the test on cross-examination is not required (e.g., treatment planning evaluations and presentencing assessments). As a general guideline, the MCMI-II is firmly established and should continue to be used, with the MCMI-III gradually becoming the preferred test as sufficient data are accumulated and published that support its construct validity, criterion validity, and diagnostic predictive power.

THE MACI SCALES

The MACI is a 160-item inventory composed of statements that are read by the teenager taking the test and require him or her to respond either true or false to each statement. Designed for adolescents age 13 through 19, the MACI requires a sixth-grade reading level.

The items are scored in such a manner that 31 scales make up the MACI profile. Table 1.5 outlines the scales, their corresponding names, the number of items on each, and a sample item. There are four general groups of scales which are plotted in profile form, as Figure 1.3 demonstrates. A brief description of each scale follows.

Scale Descriptions

Modifier Indices

The MACI modifier indices are the same as those found on the MCMI, namely, the Reliability (VV), Disclosure (X), Desirability (Y), and De-

TABLE 1.5. MACI Scales

Scale	No. of items	Sample item
Modifier indices		
V Validity	2	I flew across the Atlantic thirty times last year.
X Disclosure	N/A[a]	N/A
Y Desirability	17	I always try to do what is proper.
Z Debasement	16	So little of what I have done has been appreciated by others.
Personality patterns		
1 Introversive	44	I don't need to have close friendships like other kids do.
2A Inhibited	37	I often feel that others do not want to be friendly to me.
2B Doleful	24	It's not unusual to feel lonely and unwanted.
3 Submissive	48	I worry a great deal about being left alone.
4 Dramatizing	41	I seem to fit in right away with any group of new kids I meet.
5 Egotistic	39	Some people think of me as a bit conceited.
6A Unruly	39	Punishment never stopped my from doing whatever I wanted.
6B Forceful	22	I sometimes scare other kids to get them to do what I want.
7 Conforming	39	I always try to do what is proper.
8A Oppositional	43	I often resent doing things others expect of me.
8B Self-demeaning	44	I guess I'm a complainer who expects the worst to happen.
9 Borderline	21	I seem to make a mess of the good things that come my way.
Expressed concerns		
A Identity diffusion	32	I often feel as if I'm floating around, sort of lost in life.
B Self-devaluation	38	I see myself as falling far short of what I'd like to be.
C Body disapproval	17	Most people are better looking than I am.
D Sexual discomfort	37	Thinking about sex confuses me much of the time.

(continued)

TABLE 1.5. (*cont.*)

Scale	No. of items	Sample item
E Peer insecurity	19	Most other teenagers don't seem to like me.
F Social insensitivity	39	Becoming involved in other people's problems is a waste of time.
G Family discord	28	I would rather be anyplace but home.
H Childhood abuse	24	I hate to think about some of the ways I was abused as a child.
Clinical syndromes		
AA Eating dysfunctions	20	Although people tell me I'm thin, I still feel overweight.
BB Substance abuse proneness	35	I used to get so stoned that I did not know what I was doing.
CC Delinquent predisposition	34	I'm no different from lots of kids who steal things now and then.
DD Impulsive propensity	24	As soon as I get the impulse to do something, I act on it.
EE Anxious feelings	42	I often fear I'm going to panic or faint when I'm in a crowd.
FF Depressive affect	33	Things in my life just go from bad to worse.
GG Suicidal tendency	25	More and more often I have thoughts of ending my life.

Note. Sample items are from the *Millon Adolescent Clinical Inventory Manual,* by Theodore Millon, 1993, Minneapolis, MN: National Computer Systems. Copyright 1993 by Theodore Millon. Reprinted by permission.
*a*Disclosure is calculated based on the raw score sum of Scales 1 through 8B.

basement (Z) scales. These four scales are also designed to assess overall test-taking attitude, response biases, and general validity of the results. Specifically, these measures are sensitive to the degree to which an individual presents an inaccurate picture or representation of his or her problems.

Scale VV. This is a two-item scale on the MACI. It also consists of items with bizarre content which are designed to assess the individual's tendencies to respond with random, oppositional, or other response sets that reveal a failure to accurately read or comprehend the test items. Difficulties in concentration, low reading level, and extreme mental confusion can be revealed through this scale.

PERSONALITY CODE: 2B**-*8A38B5//-**GHB*-//FF**-*EE//

VALID REPORT   DATE: 4/07/95

CATEGORY		RAW	BR	PROFILE OF BR SCORES	DIAGNOSTIC SCALES
MODIFYING INDICES	X	377	62		DISCLOSURE
	Y	17	94		DESIRABILITY
	Z	9	70		DEBASEMENT
PERSONALITY PATTERNS	1	20	47		INTROVERSIVE
	2A	17	49		INHIBITED
	2B	35	90		DOLEFUL
	3	55	73		SUBMISSIVE
	4	48	59		DRAMATIZING
	5	45	61		EGOTISTIC
	6A	28	48		UNRULY
	6B	2	5		FORCEFUL
	7	52	58		CONFORMING
	8A	32	74		OPPOSITIONAL
	8B	32	67		SELF-DEMEANING
	9	15	47		BORDERLINE TENDENCY
EXPRESSED CONCERNS	A	16	50		IDENTITY DIFFUSION
	B	36	76		SELF-DEVALUATION
	C	6	23		BODY DISAPPROVAL
	D	18	37		SEXUAL DISCOMFORT
	E	8	46		PEER INSECURITY
	F	22	45		SOCIAL INSENSITIVITY
	G	21	84		FAMILY DISCORD
	H	19	81		CHILDHOOD ABUSE
CLINICAL SYNDROMES	AA	10	27		EATING DYSFUNCTIONS
	BB	27	59		SUBSTANCE-ABUSE PRONENESS
	CC	21	44		DELINQUENT PREDISPOSITION
	DD	9	27		IMPULSIVE PROPENSITY
	EE	31	68		ANXIOUS FEELINGS
	FF	28	88		DEPRESSIVE AFFECT
	GG	17	54		SUICIDAL TENDENCY

Profile of BR Scores axis: 0   60   75   85   115

CONFIDENTIAL INFORMATION FOR PROFESSIONAL USE ONLY

FIGURE 1.3. Sample MACI profile. MACI/Copyright 1993 by Theodore Millon. Reprinted by permission.

Scale X. Comprising the total of weighted raw scores from the basic personality scales (Scales 1–8B), this scale is designed to measure a teenager's openness to revealing personal aspects. Low scores reveal a general tendency to be secretive and defensive, whereas high scores are indicative of teenagers who can be overly self-disclosing. The adolescent may be looking to others for attention, sympathy, or some support by being overly revealing of personal difficulties or concerns.

Scale Y. The Desirability scale consists of items contained on several other scales that are sensitive to a social desirability response set. High scores on this scale are indicative of a teen who is attempting to present him- or herself in a favorable light or attempting to minimize personal faults. This scale is often elevated when the adolescent has some secondary gain that can be achieved by being viewed as having positive rehabilitative and treatment potential.

Scale Z. Response sets that involve a tendency to magnify and over-report problems and personal faults are the main attributes assessed by this scale. Elevated scores are found in teenagers who have some motivation to overreport problems or other forms of psychopathology. In other words, this scale is useful in assessing tendencies toward malingering, psychological "cries for help," or other instances of unrealistic reporting of problems.

Personality Scales

The personality scales are similar to those on the MCMI, except for changes in scale names. The reason for changing names is to make the MACI less pathological while still emphasizing the clinical nature of adolescent disturbances. Moreover, the name changes acknowledge that while personality disturbances can develop in the adolescent stage of life, room for changes still exists as the individual enters adulthood. Thus, the scale names reflect general personality styles without necessarily implying a personality disorder diagnosis.

Scale 1. This scale corresponds to the schizoid personality in DSM-IV and reflects propensities to keep a distance in relationships. Adolescents who score high on this scale often appear quiet, unemotional, apathetic, uninvolved, and they prefer solitary activities to those that involve other people.

Scale 2A. Corresponding to the features of the avoidant personality, the inhibited scale reflects a shy, ill-at-ease teenager. Such an adolescent shows a preference for avoiding others because of fear of hurt or rejection. These adolescents are lonely, lack self-assurance, and anticipate ridicule and rejection from others.

Scale 2B. This scale is a measure of chronic dysphoric and gloomy mood that corresponds to the DSM-IV depressive personality. Low self-esteem, worthlessness, and inadequacy are all prominent features in high scorers. Adolescents with elevations on this scale are also prone to worry and experience excessive guilt.

Scale 3. The submissive scale corresponds to the dependent personality in DSM-IV. Those individuals who score high on this scale are found to be passive and submissive in relationships. They avoid taking a leadership role and tend to cling to others. Fearful of separation, these adolescents downplay their own achievements and abilities and go to great lengths to obtain the care and affection they need.

Scale 4. This scale corresponds to the DSM-IV histrionic personality. Characteristics of the high scorer include tendencies toward excessive emotionality, talkativeness, sociability, and the seeking of excitement. These adolescents become bored with routine and stable relationships and are overly concerned with their physical appearance to draw attention from others.

Scale 5. The egotistic scale corresponds to the narcissistic personality. Teenagers scoring high on this measure are overly confident in their abilities and are seen as conceited and self-centered by their peers. They require much admiration and they have little or no sensitivity to the needs of others. They may also have periods of preoccupation with fantasies of unlimited success and power.

Scale 6A. This scale is the MACI equivalent of the antisocial personality scale on the MCMI. This scale measures features of conduct disturbance. High scorers are difficult to manage, excessively autonomous, and prone to seek revenge for perceived injustices or abuses they have experienced. Their behavior is often impulsive and irresponsible, they are insensitive toward others, and they can be quite ruthless.

Scale 6B. This scale is designed to measure features associated with the sadistic personality. These teenagers are strong-willed, tough-minded, and in constant conflict with authority. They derive much satisfaction from humiliating and violating the rights of others. They are hostile and combative when confronted with the consequences of their actions.

Scale 7. The conforming scale is designed to assess features associated with the compulsive personality in DSM-IV. High scorers are found to be compliant with rules and they see themselves as industrious and proper. They show constricted and inhibited expression of emotion, and in social situations they expect that others should conform to their particular beliefs and values.

Scale 8A. This scale is the MACI equivalent of the passive–aggressive/negativistic personality scale on the MCMI. The features characterizing teenagers with elevations on this scale include intense resentment and irritability over having demands placed on one's self by others. Strong negative and oppositional attitudes prevail and there is a stubborn resistance to doing things that others ask of the adolescent.

Scale 8B. The self-demeaning scale corresponds to the self-defeating personality, which was removed from DSM-IV. The major features of high scorers on this scale are self-effacing patterns of behavior, feelings of unworthiness, putting the needs of others ahead of one's own needs, and hopelessness about the future. There is excessive focus on personal faults, chronic expectation of disappointment, and frequent complaining.

Scale 9. Though the MACI does not assess the range of severe personality pathology as postulated in the underlying theory developed by Millon, there has been sufficient research and clinical attention paid to borderline personality disorder in adolescence to warrant inclusion of such a scale on the MACI. High scores are associated with disturbances in identity, characterized by an inability to formulate long-term goals, labile and unstable moods, conflicted interpersonal relationships, and impulsive self-destructive acts. This scale reveals a greater level of personality disturbance and disruption in life.

Expressed Concerns Scales

The expressed concerns scales are designed to measure those difficulties or issues that are of most concern to the adolescent. Examination of these scales often reveals what is, from the particular teenager's perspective, of greatest importance in his or her life at a particular point in time.

Scale A. Elevations on the identity diffusion scale reveal concerns over the general direction in which one's life is heading. There are unclear goals about one's future career or education, a feeling of being lost in life, and a general inability to fit one's needs or interests into any meaningful framework.

Scale B. The self-devaluation scale measures adolescent concerns over the fact that one's achievements have fallen short of one's goals.

There is a general feeling of inadequacy and fears of taking on demands because of the self-perception of inadequacy, worthlessness, and weakness.

Scale C. Though all adolescents have concerns about the physical changes that may be occurring during their growth, elevations on the body disapproval scale reveal a prominent concern that one's growth and physical maturation are abnormal. Such adolescents fear that they do not look attractive to their peers and feel shame or embarrassment over perceived physical faults.

Scale D. High scores on the sexual discomfort scale reveal the adolescent's concern with his or her development of sexual feelings and impulses. This scale is sensitive to uncertainty and discomfort with how the adolescent views his or her developing sexual self and high scores are indicative of anxiety and tension over issues of a sexual nature.

Scale E. The peer insecurity scale is designed to measure anxiety and apprehension over peer rejection. High scores indicate a heightened level of fear and concern that one's peers will find fault and that because of this rejection, there will be little acceptance by one's social group.

Scale F. High scores on the social insensitivity scale reveal a tendency to view others with little or no empathy. The adolescent fails to see that other people have needs and feelings and the rights of others are readily ignored.

Scale G. This scale indicates a concern over family tension and discord that is brought about either by perceived rejection by one's parents or because of one's inability to accept parental limits and direction. When scores are elevated, they suggest that an adolescent is in a family situation that is marked by strife, turmoil, strained relationships, and conflicted interaction.

Scale H. High scores reflect a concern over intrusive thoughts and memories about being the victim of physical, sexual, or emotional abuse. The abuse can be either recent or remote, but intrusive and recurrent thoughts are the major concern.

Clinical Syndrome Scales

The clinical syndrome scales were designed to measure those problems that may reach the level of requiring mental health intervention. They are often helpful in the diagnosis of clinical syndromes and each scale can take on different significance, depending on the configuration of the personality and expressed concerns scales.

Scale AA. High scores on this scale reflect specific problems with bulimia, anorexia, or overeating. There is significant concern over body image and the adolescent may be highly driven to achieve a thin, idealized weight.

Scale BB. This scale measures tendencies in the adolescent to abuse alcohol and drugs. High scores are generally indicative of problems in school, relationships, or work that are due to substance abuse. Also, the teenager usually endorses attitudes and beliefs that make him or her highly susceptible to substance abuse.

Scale CC. The delinquent predisposition scale reflects behavioral patterns that demonstrate a general disregard for societal conventions and norms. There is little empathy or consideration for the rights of others and the adolescent who scores high on this scale either has or is at risk of getting into legal troubles because of illegal or rule-violating behavior.

Scale DD. High scores on this scale reflect a proclivity toward erratic, impulsive actions that often lead to negative outcomes. Adolescents generally react to their impulses before thinking about the consequences of their actions. Impulsive acts can be found in any one of several activities, including sexuality, substance abuse, fighting, sensation seeking, and risky behaviors.

Scale EE. The anxious feelings scale measures general feelings of nervousness, tension, and worry. There is evidence in high scorers of social anxiety, specific fears, or physical agitation and arousal. In addition, the adolescent is prone to rumination and worry.

Scale FF. This scale measures symptomatology that is present in clinical depression. High scores reflect a sad mood, psychomotor retardation, hopelessness about the future, decreased appetite, lethargy, and difficulty sleeping. There also tend to be periods of restlessness, rumination, and suicidal ideation.

Scale GG. The suicidal tendency scale provides a more focused assessment of the adolescent's tendencies toward self-destructive or self-injurious behavior. High scores reflect suicidal ideation, hopelessness,

and either a pattern of consistent ideation or a history, either recent
or more remote, of suicidal behavior in the form of attempts or gestures.

CODING PROFILES

At the top of each Millon inventory computer printout from National
Computer Systems (NCS; see Figures 1.1, 1.2, and 1.3), there is a "personality code," "syndrome code," or "profile code." Thus, for example,
an MCMI-III profile code might read: 2A 2B 8B ** 3 1 8A * 7 5 + 4
" 6A 6B // C ** - * // A D ** R H * // - ** CC * //. If deciphered properly,
such a code allows one to construct a general profile that represents
the individual's elevations on each scale. This method of coding results
is used in later chapters to summarize Millon inventory profiles for
specific case examples. Thus, a brief overview and referral to Table 1.6
allows the reader to quickly understand the individual's Millon inventory code.

According to Millon (1987, 1993, 1994a), the sections of the MCMI-
II, MCMI-III, and MACI profiles are divided by double slash marks (//),
so that, for example, basic personality and severe personality scales on
the MCMI are separated by this mark. Scales with a BR score of 85 or
higher are followed by a double asterisk (**), whereas those scales falling in the BR 75–84 range are followed by a single asterisk (*). Those
scales in the BR 60–74 range are followed by a plus sign (+), scores
from 35–59 have quotation marks that follow ("), and scales in the BR
34 and below range have no symbol to the right except the section mar-
ker (//). When no scales are elevated in a particular range, a hyphen
(·) is entered in the appropriate space. Table 1.6 summarizes these rules
for quick reference. It is important to note that generally only the basic personality scales on the MCMI are reported across the entire range
of BR scores (0–115). Only BR scores greater than or equal to 75 are
reported for the severe personality, clinical syndrome, and severe clinical syndrome scales on the MCMI-II and MCMI-III and for all the MACI
scales.

Thus, the sample MCMI-III profile above could be read as follows.
Scales 2A (Avoidant), 2B (Depressive), and 8B (Self-Defeating) are all
above a BR of 85, with 2A the highest and 8B the lowest of the three.
The scales elevated between BR 75 and 84 are 3 (Dependent), 1 (Schizoid), and 8A (Negativistic), again in that order. Scales 7 (Compulsive)
and 5 (Narcissistic) are elevated between BR 60 and 74, followed by
Scale 4 (Histrionic) in the BR 35–59 range. Only two scales are lower
than a BR score of 35, those being Scales 6A (Antisocial) and 6B (Ag-
gressive/Sadistic). Among the severe personality scales, only C (Border-

TABLE 1.6. Key to Profile Codes

Code symbol	Meaning
//	Separates sections of the profile.
**	Separates BR ≥ 85 from BR 75–84.
*	Separates BR 75–84 from BR 60–74.
+	Separates BR 60–74 from BR 35–59.
"	Separates BR 35–59 from BR ≤ 34.
·	Indicates no scales in that range.

line) is elevated and the magnitude of its elevation is greater than BR 85. The clinical syndrome scales show a prominent (BR ≥ 85) elevation on A (Anxiety) and D (Dysthymia), whereas R (Posttraumatic Stress) and H (Somatoform) are clinically elevated in the BR 75–84 range. On the severe clinical syndrome scales, CC (Major Depression) is elevated, but only in the BR 75–84 range. Given a particular profile code, each Millon inventory can be roughly plotted into a meaningful and easily interpretable format.

A BRIEF NOTE ON INTERPRETATION

In the last few years, a number of interpretive guides have been published on the MCMI (Choca et al., 1992; Craig, 1993a, 1993b). For the MACI, the manual currently provides information on interpretation of the test (Millon, 1993). However, a full discussion of interpretive strategies is beyond the scope of this chapter and text. Millon inventory interpretation is a multifaceted procedure that involves (1) the examination of individual scale elevations; (2) sectional analysis of the profile to assess relative severity of pathology; (3) differential interpretation of single scales depending on other elevations in the profile; (4) interpretation of two-, three-, and four-scale configurations; (5) effects of response style on profile interpretation; and (6) the effects of various demographic, contextual, and other similar factors on profile meaning. Proper interpretation requires familiarity with the literature on these instruments, experience with using the tests in appropriate settings, and a good working theoretical knowledge of personality and psychopathology, as well as experience in the practice of clinical diagnosis and evaluation. In Chapter 9, we outline a general strategy for interpreting the Millon inventories in forensic settings.

The purpose of the intervening chapters which follow is to provide clinicians with information that will facilitate application of the

Millon inventories in forensic settings. This initial chapter is only meant to introduce these tests and to serve as a quick reference to basic information. Proper forensic practice also requires that the material in each test manual be familiar to those practitioners who make use of the information in the pages that follow.

The Role of Psychological Testing in Forensic Assessment

Psychologists who appear as expert witnesses in forensic matters assist the court in deciding ultimate legal issues by giving expert opinions on the stand. An expert opinion is one that is based on a level of expertise beyond that of the average juror. This expertise implies grounding in some type of objective scientific or technical discipline guided by empirical research rather than mere subjective speculation. Unfortunately, mental health practitioners who assume the witness stand often fall short of this ideal and offer testimony that amounts to little more than subjective opinion and personal preference dressed up in scientific jargon. One of the most egregious examples of this type of testimony occurred in *United States v. Hearst* (1976) (the Patricia Hearst case), in which opposing psychiatric experts traded speculation as to the defendant's mental state during the offenses with which she was charged. Public reaction to this spectacle was extremely negative and set the stage for an erosion of confidence in mental health experts who testify in criminal and other matters.

Psychological testing, when properly employed as a basis for expert testimony, has the capacity to elevate the expert's opinions beyond the limitations of individual subjectivity by providing a grounding in objective empirical research. Thus, an opinion as to whether a defendant is capable of rehabilitation, has suffered from diminished capacity to form the requisite mental state at the time of the offense, or suffers from a personality disorder is much more scientifically acceptable when based in part on an objective personality test's diagnosis than when based on the expert's number of years of experience in working with that particular type of client.

In fact, Dawes (1989) cites research demonstrating that years of clinical experience have no correlation with the accuracy of clinical judgment. He identifies a fundamental flaw in the concept that a clinician's years of experience improve diagnostic accuracy, namely, that in order to learn by experience one must be exposed to cases in which one's diagnostic hypothesis is proven to be wrong as well as to cases in which the diagnosis is found to be correct. It is the negative feedback that really accelerates learning; however, this type of feedback is almost never available to clinicians. Thus experience, instead of being the best teacher, is actually a rather poor teacher in this particular area. Dawes also observes that among the many topics in their field, psychologists often testify in court as to content areas in which they have the least theoretical knowledge. He further states that the best predictions are made on an actuarial basis using well-validated tests. Also, there have been studies in which clinicians' interview findings actually decrease predictive accuracy in situations in which they are weighted over objective predictors with empirically demonstrated validity. Thus, although an expert's testimony as to having worked for a number of years in a particular field is impressive to a jury, the reality, contraintuitive as it might be, is that this variable is unrelated to the witness's accuracy and, in fact, the expert is most likely testifying in an area of psychology in which theoretical knowledge is sparsest.

The use of psychological test data, especially when the instrument has been studied as to its validity for a particular class of situations or psychological diagnoses, provides a genuinely scientific foundation for the expert's opinions. Such testing meets Dawes's criterion for negative feedback as an essential aspect of developing diagnostic accuracy, as criterion-related validity studies include cases in which subjects do and do not have the target trait (or have greater or lesser degrees of it); these studies also compare the presence or absence of the trait with the test's assessment. In fact, criterion-related validity studies that present operating characteristics (discussed in Chapter 6) lay out in great detail how often the test is right or wrong in identifying the target trait in terms of various percentages of "hits" and "misses."

Courts look to experts for well-grounded opinions based on scientific neutrality rather than disguised personal preferences or speculation. The appropriate application of well-constructed psychological tests provides a safeguard against the powerful temptation for experts to confuse personal biases with objective conclusions. Over their years in practice, individual clinicians may have developed an excessive reliance on their own particular diagnostic "indicator" that is actually just the result of being exposed to a restricted range of cases in which that particular feature is coincidentally present. Or, clinicians may have assimilated such interpretive fallacies from their graduate school training. The clinician's perception of a relationship between the "indicator" and a target trait or diagnosis is therefore illusory. Such biases are minimized when psychometric instruments, validated on a number of cases that are much greater than what an individual diagnostician would ever see, are given substantial weight in formulating conclusions, especially when clinical hypotheses are cross-checked against the results of these procedures. Similarly, clinicians tend to confuse what is speculative with conclusions that rest on a more secure foundation of empirical results. Without the objective balance that psychometric testing brings to an assessment, the distinction may be lost entirely, with potentially grave consequences for expert witnesses and the litigants or criminal defendants about whom they offer such opinions in courts of law.

Most psychologists have been trained in psychological assessment from the perspective of a clinical model, with the focus on developing an understanding of the test subject's capacities, personality characteristics, current problems, strengths, and vulnerabilities for the purpose of specifying appropriate therapeutic interventions. In this soft use of testing, the payoff matrix is typically structured to reward comprehensiveness and generation of clinical hypotheses that are useful in guiding treatment. Clinicians are particularly sensitized to picking up aspects of pathology that may not be apparent and that, although requiring therapeutic attention for treatment to be successful, may be heavily defended against by the patient. The most skillful clinical diagnosticians are those who are able to draw tentative conclusions from nuances of subjects' test performance and explore these in treatment, often with striking results. Clinicians who possess advanced capability in this area typically describe their inner reasoning process as an intuitive one that resists quantification and explicit articulation. Indeed, the research of Goldberg (1965, 1970), Sawyer (1966), and other investigators suggests that replacing actual clinician judgments with multiple regression models would result in more accurate assessments because of enhanced reliability in cue utilization. This research provoked a backlash among practitioners who feel that such thinking is both heretical and scientistic. Clinicians, including those who train young clinical psychologists, place a premium on experience based on clinical intuition of the type that often results in striking breakthroughs in treating psychotherapy patients.

This type of clinical wisdom has actually come to be revered as the ideal in psychological assessment, where the goal of the evaluation is to determine what type of intervention is most appropriate for the patient and to provide a road map for the treating clinician into the patient's inner world. Indeed, there are individual psychologists who have attained a seemingly superhuman capacity for incisive understanding of patients based on intuitive methods. Reik (1948), for example, reports a case in which his intuitive interpretation of two consecutive associations of a young female analysand led him to the correct conclusion that she once had an abortion, when neither association had any obvious connection with that theme.

Another well-known anecdote concerns Rorschach expert Samuel Beck and his capacity for blind diagnosis of Rorschach protocols. Beck was asked to determine the site of a patient's brain lesion solely on the basis of the patient's Rorschach record. He retired to his office with the protocol in hand and emerged a half hour later with the correct conclusion as to the locus of the lesion. He was unable to articulate the precise basis for the determination but merely cited the fact that he had analyzed tens of thousands of Rorschach records.

This type of approach, although undeniably impressive and dramatically valid in certain instances, is inappropriate in a forensic context because it is impossible to articulate the specific reasoning processes leading to intuitive conclusions. It is also impossible to replicate or cross-validate such methods, which are entirely dependent on the subjectivity of an individual evaluator. Any examination method or reasoning process that leads to an expert conclusion must be capable of being subjected to analysis via cross-examination, permitting weak links to be identified and challenged. Expert opinion, without such an explicit basis, will be thoroughly impeached upon cross-examination regardless of its validity in terms of the proverbial true state of nature. Such reports are characterized as "conclusory" by attorneys and are not persuasive to the trier of fact, who is confronted with a mere authoritative assertion rather than a reasoning process that can be subjected to logical analysis.

ADMISSIBILITY OF EXPERT TESTIMONY

The forensic psychologist who testifies as an expert witness is held to a higher standard of scientific rigor than is the clinician who is called upon to offer conclusions in a treatment setting. In many venues this more stringent standard is termed "reasonable psychological certainty or probability." Although it is routine in many jurisdictions for attorneys and judges to inquire of experts as to whether their conclusions are couched in terms of such certainty, in practice, definitions of this standard vary considerably. For trial purposes, the reasonable certainty standard has been variously defined by attorneys as "ninety percent certain" and as "more likely than not." These formulations are analogous to the "clear and convincing" and "preponderance of evidence" standards, respectively. The New Jersey Board of Psychological Examiners, for example, has defined reasonable psychological certainty as requiring that expert conclusions be based on substantive clinical observations, empirical research findings, well-accepted theoretical propositions, or an integration of these; moreover, the conclusions must not be speculative (New Jersey State Board of Examiners, 1993). The reasonable certainty standard necessitates that the reasoning processes leading to experts' conclusions be capable of precise articulation, which permits each element of the process to be examined through questioning. Thus, the brilliant intuitive interpretation of Reik and the precise determination of the locus of the brain lesion by Beck would not pass muster as expert opinions under this standard if either were to testify in a court of law.

Expert testimony is also governed by the recent United States Supreme Court opinion in *Daubert v. Merrell Dow Pharmaceuticals* (1993). In this decision, the issue before the Court was the appropriate standard for admissibility of scientific testimony. The two child plaintiffs alleged that they had suffered brain damage as a result of their mothers' having ingested during pregnancy a medication developed by the defendant company. Merrell Dow presented scientific studies employing a human epidemiological model purporting to show that there were no instances of brain damage associated with administration of the drug. The plaintiffs countered with a statistical reanalysis of the Merrell Dow studies and animal test results that demonstrated tissue damage resulting from chemicals with a structure that closely paralleled that of the medication that had been administered to the children's mothers. The lower court ruled that plaintiffs' evidence was inadmissible because it did not meet the standard outlined in *Frye v. United States* (1923) of "general acceptance in the scientific community." That ruling was upheld by the appeals court as well.

The United States Supreme Court, citing the liberalization of evidentiary standards that characterizes the revised Federal Rules of Evidence, overturned the *Frye* test and emphasized the role of the trier of fact as arbiter of what is admissible scientific evidence. The Court enumerated criteria by which trial judges were to assess the admissibility of evidence, including several that are of obvious interest to psychologists, namely, reliability, validity, and error rate. This dovetails with efforts within the profession to ensure that forensic evaluations employ instruments of demonstrated reliability and validity. For example, the *Specialty Guidelines for Forensic Psychologists* (Committee on Ethical Guidelines for Forensic Psychologists, 1991) and the *Guidelines for Child Custody Evaluations in Divorce Proceedings* (American Psychological Association, 1994) both admonish psychologists to use the most appropriate methods available and to obtain information from multiple sources so as to achieve greater reliability and validity of conclusions that are drawn.

The *Daubert* opinion adds that liberalization of admissibility criteria will be counterbalanced by aggressive cross-examination of expert witnesses. This procedural tactic necessitates an increased level of scientific rigor to be required of expert testimony that is based, in part, on results of psychometric procedures and inferences derived from psychological theory.

Another criterion for admissible evidence set forth in the *Daubert* decision, that of helpfulness to the trier of fact in resolving the ultimate legal issue, is of particular importance to users of the Millon inventories. These instruments, with their emphasis on personality disorders, assess characteristics that have been argued to have little relevance in determining mental state and other ultimate issue questions. The historical emphasis has been on DSM-IV (American Psychiatric Association, 1994) Axis I disorders, or clinical syndromes, as the determining factors in deciding mental state and related questions. As Millon (1994b) points out, however, current thinking stresses the importance of personality disorders in achieving a comprehensive understanding of an individual's behavior, Axis I symptoms, and many important domains of intrapsychic functioning.

A recent court decision in New Jersey, *State v. Galloway* (1993), reflects the growing acceptance of diagnostic statements regarding personality disorders in forensic settings. The defendant in this case, Galloway, admitted to the police that he had shaken his girlfriend's baby in order to make the child stop crying. The child presented at the emergency room with cerebral bleeding as a result of the shaking and subsequently died. During his interrogation, Galloway also stated to the police that he was aware that this child was the product of a rape by his girlfriend's previous partner and that he had been thinking about killing the child. He was charged with first-degree murder and found guilty. The defense introduced expert testimony that Galloway suffered from borderline personality disorder and that, because of this disorder, he had suffered a severe regression at the time of the offense that resulted in a diminished capacity to form the requisite knowing and purposeful mental state for first-degree murder under New Jersey statutes. The lower court held that borderline personality disorder was not a mental disorder and that it therefore could not be regarded as a factor in producing diminished capacity. This was also the opinion of the intermediate appellate court. The New Jersey Supreme Court, however, found that the testimony offered by the defendant's expert to the effect that he suffered from borderline personality disorder was acceptable and of clear relevance to the court's determination of his mental state. The court explicitly stated that borderline personality disorder falls within that class of mental disorders that affects an individual's cognitive capacities, with ramifications for the capacity to form the knowing and purposeful mental state required for murder under state law. Thus, the area in which the Millon inventories are recognized as being particularly strong, that is, diagnosis of personality disorders, has been explicitly recognized as being helpful to the trier of fact in determining whether a defendant possessed the requisite *mens rea* for a first degree homicide. Therefore, the Millon inventories clearly meet the helpfulness standard under the United States Supreme Court *Daubert* decision in this important area of criminal law.

PSYCHOLOGICAL TESTING AND EXPERT TESTIMONY

In a comprehensive review of psychological testing in forensic assessment, Heilbrun (1992) stresses the issue of relevance of test findings to the determination of the ultimate legal issue before the court. He states that psychological testing typically does not yield information that is of direct relevance to the ultimate legal issue but addresses the threshold issue of mental or emotional disturbance. The causal connection between these conditions and legally relevant behavior must be assessed by different means. As self-evident as this may seem, it bears repeating that the test results on which experts rely simply provide data for a further process of inference in which connections are drawn between conditions diagnosed by the test and the particular facts of the case. These connections are most helpful to the trier of fact and most resistant to cross-examination when based on solid theoretical propositions. Kurt Lewin's remark that there is nothing so practical as a good theory is especially relevant to the complex process of making legally relevant sense out of litigants' or defendants' behavior in expert testimony.

Heilbrun lists seven standards for applying psychological tests to forensic assessment cases. The first requirement is that the instrument be commercially available (NCS Assessments for the Millon inventories), accompanied by an adequate technical manual (Millon, 1987, 1993, 1994a), and reviewed in the *Mental Measurements Yearbook* (Widiger, 1985) or a similar source. Although not specifically mentioned in Heilbrun's article, *Test Critiques* is another valuable source for critical reviews of psychometric tests.

A second requirement cited by Heilbrun is a reliability figure of .80 as being the minimum standard for psychological tests used in court. Unfortunately, he makes the statement that this criterion would refer primarily to test–retest data in the case of trait measurement with objective tests. This pronouncement ignores the issue of internal consistency, an absolute necessity for estimating true scores on the basis of a one-time administration of a psychometric instrument. The belief that test–retest reliability can substitute for internal consistency is a common one among practitioners who are not well versed in the essentials of psychometric theory, and this topic is taken up in greater detail in Chapter 6.

Heilbrun explicitly lists relevance to the ultimate legal issue as one of the seven standards for forensic psychometric tests. The discussion of this standard is couched in terms of the relevance of the psychological construct measured by the test to the issue before the court.

Standardized administration and use of tests that are applicable to a forensic population also appear as standards. Caution is made against the forensic use of tests that have been standardized on groups whose characteristics differ significantly from those of the litigant or defendant to be assessed. Heilbrun further cautions against using test findings for purposes for which the instrument was not developed, as, for example, making inferences as to psychopathology from intelligence test findings.

Another standard expressed by Heilbrun is a strong preference for objective testing and actuarial prediction methods for which a suitable formula exists based on outcome data. He cites literature that explodes the myth of clinical accuracy in making complex configural judgments weighting multiple data sources with limited reliability (such as projective test response patterns).

Finally, Heilbrun (1992) proposes a standard that mandates explicit assessment of response style to identify malingering, defensive, or irrelevant response sets in subjects. Remarkably, he asserts that the only psychological test with extensive empirical support in measuring response style is the MMPI. This assertion is simply false, as numerous empirical studies have investigated the various validity and modifier indices of the MCMI-II, with generally favorable results (see Chapter 4 for a full discussion).

DIAGNOSIS, EXPERT TESTIMONY, AND THE MILLON INVENTORIES

DSM-IV is a document that has come to dominate the forensic arena as the ultimate "learned treatise" with which experts are expected to be familiar. It is of interest in that in addition to being regarded as the standard by which expert diagnoses are judged, the document itself is actually a diagnostic instrument. DSM-IV has demonstrated reliability, although the adequacy of its reliability is a matter of continuing professional debate, and validity based on the criteria of a blue-ribbon panel of expert judges. It is routinely cited in court cases in which any of the ultimate legal questions relate to a psychological diagnosis; experts are routinely cross-examined as to whether their diagnoses of litigants or criminal defendants are consistent with DSM-IV. Thus, whether or not the expert's own particular frame of reference for psychological assessment agrees with the DSM medical model, experts are saddled with the burden of squaring their test findings with the DSM system. Experts who ignore this convention do so at the peril of being considered unsophisticated, uninformed, or excessively radical in their approach to forensic assessment.

For users of the Millon inventories, this burden can actually be an advantage, because these instruments are intimately linked to DSM-IV as are virtually no other broad-band self-report personality measuring instruments. From the initial stages of development of the original MCMI, the Millon inventories were planned and researched according to specific DSM diagnostic criteria, or closely related criteria based on Millon's theory of personality. Indeed, the MCMI's underlying conceptualization of psychological disorders is the same as the DSM multiaxial system. In the case of the MCMI-III, the content of more than half the items has been revised to conform literally to the criteria of DSM-IV (Millon, 1994a). Thus the optimal strategy for forensic experts to cope with courts' reliance, for better or worse, on DSM-IV is to employ an instrument that is grounded in both theory and research on that document. To date, only the Millon inventories fill the bill.

Finally, it is stressed that the role of psychological testing in court is subordinate to the role of the expert as one who thoroughly understands the psychometric characteristics of the test instruments forming the basis for opinions. Although it is perfectly appropriate to place great weight on psychological tests as scientifically grounded methods for generating valuable assessment data, it is inappropriate—to the point of verging on malpractice—to place great weight on the psychological test as constituting the opinion as though the expert were merely a recorder and not an interpreter of test data. One of us (F. D.) recalls a particularly absurd courtroom experience while waiting to testify at a workers' compensation hearing. In an unrelated case, a psychiatrist was testifying about his examination of a petitioner to whom he had administered an MMPI as part of the assessment. His testimony as to the MMPI results was based entirely on the computerized narrative report and he was unable to give any independent opinions regarding the meanings of elevations on certain scales. The psychiatrist appeared to be vaguely familiar with the L scale or the MMPI. However, when cross-examined in regard to the client's response set, he cited a test item that very obviously was not an L scale item as belonging to that scale and as indicating the petitioner had been responding truthfully to all the test items. This led to a lengthy exchange between the witness and the cross-examining counsel in which all the questions and answers were predicated on the erroneous assumption that the item in question belonged to the L scale. The absurdity of that exchange was compounded by the psychiatrist's refusal to submit to the court the actual test booklet containing the test items, although the psychiatrist was more than willing to supply the computerized answer form, with items omitted, to the court. His rationale for refusing to submit the actual test questions was that if he were to testify on the results of a CAT scan, it would be ridiculous for the court to require him to bring in the apparatus when the resulting scanned images were all that was necessary. Thus, it was unnecessary for the judge to have access to the test items on which he had been testifying.

Another case in which a forensic expert relied in an extremely concrete manner on the computerized narrative of a psychological test led to the loss of his New Jersey psychologist's license. The expert in question rendered opinions in dozens of divorce/custody cases based on a psychological examination that included the MMPI as the only instrument. The psychologist did not have an independent capacity to interpret the scales of the test but simply incorporated the statements of the computerized interpretive report into his final conclusions and made recommendations accordingly. When interviewed by the State Board of Psychological Examiners, this expert attempted to defend what were wildly absurd conclusions and recommendations by citing the MMPI printout quite literally and in isolation from other facts of the particular case that would call into question some of the computer-generated statements regarding the litigants. It is of more than passing interest that in this particular case it was the State Board of Psychological Examiners, rather than the family court, that put an end to this practice.

CONCLUSION

Although the use of psychological tests in forensic settings can offer numerous advantages in terms of objectivity and empirical grounding, their indiscriminant use is not without potential difficulty. Practitioners must be mindful of rules of evidence so that the use of psychological tests is in conformity with legal standards. Moreover, psychologists should be aware of the ethical guidelines that require tests to be reliable and valid but also only one part of an overall evaluation. Finally, given the requirements for appropriate use of psychological tests in forensic assessment, the Millon inventories meet each ethical, legal, and professional standard. They are objective methods for assessing clinical symptomatology and personality disorders that have direct bearing on many legal issues. We next turn to a more detailed examination of how these instruments have been viewed by the courts.

THREE

Case Law and
the Millon Inventories

The goals and values that guide procedures and practice are quite different in the fields of law and psychology. Whereas the mental health professional seeks to employ effective assessment and treatment techniques that will, it is hoped, alleviate human suffering, the law strives for truthful determination of facts that will lead to the equitable resolution of conflict. In addition, it can be fairly stated that the professional atmosphere in mental health settings is one of a collaborative effort, whereas the legal arena is characterized by its adversary nature. Consequently, a lawyer or judge is likely to appraise and value facts and information quite differently from a mental health professional.

Much can be learned by examining how various courts interpret psychological tests as pieces of evidence. Some attorneys and judges may be very accepting of test results because such data offer quantitative and concrete findings that can be more easily viewed as "solid evidence." In fact, some psychologists find that their services are sought specifically to provide test results. On the other hand, some lawyers and judges tend to view psychological tests with skepticism or disdain. Tests may be viewed as unreliable, invalid, and a source of confusion that only blurs the legal issues being litigated. Therefore, it is not unusual for psychologists who engage in extensive forensic work to find their use of psychological tests accepted with respect at one time and rejected with derision at other times.

In order for the results from psychological testing to be admissible as evidence, they are required to meet certain levels of reliability. According to Rule 703 of the Federal Rules of Evidence (FRE; 1992), opinions that are expressed by expert witnesses must be based on facts or data that are "of a type reasonably relied upon by experts in the particular field" for which the witness holds him-/herself out as an expert. To determine whether a particular test meets this requirement, many courts look to see how other judicial bodies have viewed the admissibility of evidence of that particular type.

Courts take direction on the admissibility of psychological tests based on specific rules of evidence. Although each state derives its own set of rules or body of common law for dealing with evidence and the federal courts adopt the FRE, there is often great overlap between federal and state rules. Therefore, the FRE are particularly useful as a model for examining relevance of psychological test data in general. Rules 401, 402, and 403 generally govern the relevance of evidence. Rule 401 states that evidence is relevant if it makes "the existence of any fact that is of consequence to the determination of the action more probable or less probable than it would be without the evidence." Thus, relevant evidence must have some direct bearing on an issue that is part of the litigation. In addition, according to Rule 402, relevant evidence is generally admissible, whereas irrelevant evidence is deemed inadmissible. Note that relevant evidence is *generally*, but not always, admissible. Rule 403 of the Federal Rules of Evidence states that some relevant evidence may be deemed inadmissible if it results in prejudice, confusion, or waste of time in court proceedings. Therefore, the Millon inventories must be examined within the context of these provisions.

In order to further explore how various courts have viewed the Millon inventories, in terms of their relevance to particular issues being litigated, a comprehensive computer search was carried out to identify all published judicial opinions that cited at least one of these instruments. The search was carried out on the computerized legal database LEXIS by identifying various word roots (e.g., "MCMI," "MAPI," "MBHI," "Millon Clinical Multiaxial Inventory," etc.) which might have been used to describe the tests in a court opinion that had been published in any legal source contained in the data bank. This search yielded 22 court opinions that cited one of the instruments through 1994. This chapter presents an overview and discussion of the results of this search, as well as their implications for forensic practice.

OVERVIEW OF CASES

The cases that have involved the use of the Millon inventories address a wide range of issues in a rather wide range of forensic settings. (Table 3.1 provides a brief description of these issues and their relevance to the final disposition of the case. Several factors of interest have emerged from the various holdings in these opinions.) Indeed, the range of applications of the inventories includes cases of child sexual abuse, emotional stability to testify as a witness, insanity evaluations, attempts to present evidence of nonviolent propensities to mitigate sentences, treatment/rehabilitation potential, and disability hearings. Moreover, courts have recognized the Millon inventories as standard assessment procedures that are of the type reasonably relied on by professionals in the field. In addition, results from these tests have been used to support various expert opinions, but these opinions have either been accepted or rejected by courts based more on how Millon test results are used, rather than because of the particular nature of the tests themselves.

Admissibility of the Tests

The leading case on the admissibility of psychological tests, and the MCMI in particular, is *People v. Stoll* (1989), summarized in Table 3.1. This case has been recognized in several other court opinions, including *People v. Ruiz* (1990) and *United States v. Banks* (1992), as legal precedent that upholds admissibility of the MCMI. Particularly important are the facts that specific language used by the court in *Stoll* has acknowledged the MCMI as having achieved widespread acceptance in the field of clinical psychology and that the test is a standard part of the psychologist's testing battery.

The facts and legal holding in *Stoll* warrant further detailed discussion because of their significance. The case involves an appeal of four defendants who were jointly tried and convicted of sexual molestation ("lewd and lascivious conduct" in the court's language) of seven young males. One of the major issues raised on appeal was that the trial court had committed prejudicial error in not permitting the defendants to offer the opinion of a psychologist that they displayed no signs of "deviance or abnormality," thus supporting their claim that the alleged behavior never occurred. More important, the defendants argued that "special restrictions governing admission of new, novel, or experimental scientific techniques not previously accepted in the courts did not apply to the professed testimony [of the psychologist]" (*Stoll*, 1989, p. 698).

In holding that the trial court had committed prejudicial error in refusing such testimony, the court in *Stoll* focused extensively on the status of the MCMI in current clinical practice. Direct testimony was obtained from the psychologist during an offer of proof on the nature of the testimony which defendants' counsel sought to provide during the direct case. An offer of proof is a legal mechanism in a trial or hearing whereby one party can indicate on the record, and outside the presence of the jury, what particular testimony will be offered when

TABLE 3.1. Summary of Case Law Citing the Millon Inventories

Case name	Fact pattern	Test cited	Specific test application
1. *Taylor v. Heckler* (1984)	Disability claim	MBHI	To support opinion of unemployability; court did not reject diagnosis and results, just opinion rendered as to employability.
2. *McGee v. Bowen* (1986)	Disability claim	MCMI	To explain mental illness that can cause pain to exceed actual injury.
3. *United States v. Dennison* (1986)	Motion to transfer juvenile to adult court and prosecute for murder	MAPI	Psychological maturity of defendant assessed, which was one of six key factors to consider.
4. *Garibaldi v. Dietz* (1988)	Termination of parental rights	MCMI	Issue of parent's bipolar illness being controlled was assessed.
5. *In re Subpoena Issued to L.Q.* (1988)	Motion to quash subpoena served on sexual assault victim	MAPI	Assessment of witness's emotional stability, relevant to testifying.
6. *Haywood v. Sullivan* (1989)	Appeal of denial of SSI/SSD	MCMI	Part of posthearing evaluation to support opinion that claimant could not work.
7. *People v. Stoll* (1989)	Appeal of conviction for lewd conduct with minors	MCMI	Used to support no sign of deviance or abnormality. Testimony stated test had achieved "widespread acceptance" and court felt testimony would assist jury.
8. *In re Marriage of L.R.* (1990)	Termination of father's visitation based on mother's allegation of sexual abuse of child	MCMI	Used in investigation by psychologist. Court held usage "questionable" because psychologist lacked experience in administration and interpretation of test and its "clinical rather than forensic" focus.
9. *People v. Ruiz* (1990)	Appeal of conviction for lewd conduct with child	MCMI	Test used to support opinion of defendant being unlikely to commit particular acts. Court ruled this admissible as character evidence.

(continued)

TABLE 3.1. **(cont.)**

Case name	Fact pattern	Test cited	Specific test application
10. *Bankston v. Alexandria Neurosurgical Clinic* (1991)	Action for medical malpractice	MCMI	Test records were allegedly destroyed, but plaintiff's claim was held to be frivolous.
11. *Iwanski v. Streamwood Police Pension Board* (1992)	Disability claim	MCMI-II	Results support evidence of severe depression leading to disability.
12. *Johnson v. Sullivan* (1992)	Disability claim	MCMI	Supports finding of anxiety and personality disorder, but judge ruled no substantial evidence of disability.
13. *United States v. Banks* (1992)	Appeal of conviction for rape and sodomy of child	MCMI	Court did not view MCMI results as admissible if they were used to support opinion that defendant did not have pedophilic "profile."
14. *Brooks v. White* (1993)	Appeal of sodomy conviction	MAPI	Used to assess victim with borderline IQ; jury accepted results showing victim's strong needs for acceptance and emotional maladjustment.
15. *CDI v. McHale* (1993)	Worker's compensation award upheld	MBHI	Used to support key opinion that a causal connection existed between psychological problems and work-related injury.
16. *May v. S.E. Wyoming Mental Health Center* (1993)	Dismissal of action for false sex abuse report	MCMI	Used by neutral court-appointed investigator to evaluate alleged perpetrator.
17. *Gustafson v. State* (1993)	Appeal of murder conviction	MCMI	Part of presentence evaluation showing defendant wasn't violent. Court rejected opinion because it relied solely on test results and failed to also consider police reports, collateral evidence, etc., suggesting otherwise.

(continued)

TABLE 3.1. (*cont.*)

Case name	Fact pattern	Test cited	Specific test application
18. *In re A.V.* (1993)	Mother's petition granted to terminate father's rights based on sexual abuse of child	MCMI	Used in overall assessment of perpetrator. Report admitted without objection.
19. *Nebraska v. Tlamka* (1993)	Appeal of conviction of sexual assault of child	MCMI-II	Test viewed as "generally accepted," but its use in this case didn't pass admissibility test because of use in attempt to show defendant was "normal heterosexual," not likely to commit sexual acts against children.
20. *Tyler v. State* (1993)	Conviction for murder upheld on appeal	MCMI	Part of insanity evaluation; results showed no evidence of psychosis.
21. *In re Donald C.H., Jr.* (1994)	Delinquency hearing to determine whether minor should be tried as adult for burglary and arson	MAPI	Used to make treatment recommendations of long-term structured setting; court accepted opinion and kept minor within juvenile justice system.
22. *In re Woodward* (1994)	Disbarment of attorney for substance abuse and mismanagement of client funds	MCMI-II	Supported position of expert that defendant had propensity to abuse substances again and that supervision would be needed.

the opposing side has objected to such testimony and the court has sustained the objection, thus refusing to allow the proffered testimony (*Black's Law Dictionary,* 1990). In this way, an appellate court then has the record available with which to determine whether the trial court made either a correct or a prejudicial exclusion of the testimony.

In *Stoll* (1989), the psychologist whose testimony had been excluded was able to testify during the offer of proof on the MCMI: "[the MCMI] was copyrighted in 1976, and had achieved wide spread acceptance in the three or four years preceding trial. It is widely used in Kern County, but less frequently at the national level" (p. 705).

Based on its interpretation of existing case law, the court concluded that "diagnostic use of written personality inventories such as the

MMPI *and* *MCMI* has been established for decades" (p. 711, emphasis added). Thus, the court held that the MCMI could be viewed as an established psychological test that withstands the level of acceptance required under state evidentiary laws (in this case, California).

Despite its acceptance of the MCMI, the court was able to provide a realistic appraisal of the potential value of the psychological test results in the case. Specifically, as outlined later, there are problems in providing testimony on psychological and personality characteristics that are consistent with the defendant's not having committed an alleged act. The court therefore emphasized that even though a test may be admissible, psychological tests such as the Millon inventories are not necessarily sources of "infallible truth on issues of personality, predisposition, or criminal guilt" (p. 712). In addition, the court held that because the MMPI and MCMI are not diagnostically accurate 100% of the time, "issues of test reliability and validity may be thoroughly explored on cross-examination at trial" (p. 712). There can also be cross-examination into the expert's reliance on other pieces of information, such as interviews, case history, and past professional experiences, in forming an opinion. In other words, the court in *Stoll* views tests such as the MCMI acceptable and admissible, but the particular manner in which the test is used and the degree of reliance on test results are subject to cross-examination and careful scrutiny. As the next sections illustrate, many problems can arise when the Millon inventories are used improperly.

Problematic Applications

Despite the recognition afforded the Millon tests themselves, courts have still rejected reports or opinions based, in part, on these tests. The principal reason cited has been the way the results were used rather than the actual test itself. For instance, in *Gustafson v. State* (1993), a psychologist administered the MCMI to a 19-year-old male who was convicted of second-degree murder after he fired a rifle into a car he mistakenly believed had attempted to sideswipe the truck in which he was a passenger. The gunshot hit a passenger in the car, killing him instantly. The psychologist who administered the MCMI did so as part of a presentencing evaluation, after the defendant had already been tried and convicted. Based on an MCMI profile indicative of deeply ingrained narcissistic and obsessive–compulsive traits, an interview, and MMPI results, the psychologist concluded that the defendant was not a violent person. In spite of these results, the court rejected this opinion based on police records, grand jury evidence, and other records that pointed to an extensive history of violent criminal behavior. In other words, the MCMI, although recognized as a generally accepted technique in the field of clinical psychology, was inadequate by itself to support the expert opinion in this case.

It is interesting to note that the profile achieved by the defendant in *Gustafson,* revealing prominent narcissistic and obsessive–compulsive traits, is consistent with a standard fake good profile in which the individual seeks to distort self-report test results in a manner that underreports pathology and presents a favorable overall impression (Retzlaff, Sheehan, & Fiel, 1991). Clearly, because the results of the psychologist's evaluation would be introduced at the penalty phase of the trial, the defendant had adequate motive to be seen in a positive way in order to achieve a reduced sentence from the court. More important, *Gustafson* illustrates an issue that is common among the cases in which expert opinion that is supported by Millon inventory results has been ignored or rejected by judges. That is, the testimony and test results are not given weight due to the examiner's failure to consider alternate sources of data and information.

Other cases reveal additional problems with the ways in which these tests have been administered and used in forensic settings. Problems are cited with the examiner's lack of experience in administering and interpreting a test, the inability to associate the test with a standard profile for sexual offenders or pedophiles, and the general tendency to view ultimate issue testimony (i.e., test results support the finding that the defendant did not commit the crime) with skepticism.

For example, in the case of *In re Marriage of L.R.* (1990), a psychologist administered the MCMI to evaluate a father who had been accused by the mother of sexually abusing his child. The court ruled that the psychologist's reliance on the MCMI was "questionable" (p. 788) because of her own admission that she was inexperienced with how the test was administered and scored and her lack of experience with interpreting the profile. In fact, during cross-examination of her methods, the psychologist admitted that "she had yet to receive formal training in its [MCMI] administration" (p. 784). As a result, the judge disregarded the psychologist's testimony. This case illustrates the need for professionals to be familiar with materials in the manual and to have experience with interpreting the results before venturing into the forensic arena. If the expert witness does not have sufficient experience with the test, he or she should read additional sources (e.g., Choca et al., 1992; Craig, 1993) and obtain formal training through supervised experience or professional workshops and conferences.

Profile Evidence

Some expert witnesses have attempted to use the MCMI profile results to determine whether or not a particular defendant fits the "profile"

of a pedophile, sex offender, "normal heterosexual," or other classification. As Chapter 4 reveals, research demonstrates that no standard
profile of a rapist, pedophile, or other sex offender can be found. Instead, MCMI profiles can be used to classify subtypes of known sex
offenders, each with varying characteristics; more important, however,
it must be noted that these profiles are also found in other diagnostic
groups of non-sex offenders.

Such profile evidence, as it has sometimes been called, was at issue
in *People v. Ruiz* (1990), *United States v. Banks* (1992), and *Nebraska v. Tlamka* (1993). In *Ruiz,* for instance, the defendant was convicted of lewd
conduct with a child in which he engaged in illegal sexual touching
with the child. On appeal, the defendant's major argument was that
he was denied a fair trial because of the trial court's refusal to permit
him to introduce as character evidence the opinion of a psychologist.
The psychologist was to testify that the defendant showed personality
characteristics that were not commonly associated with individuals who
are pedophiles. In the *Ruiz* holding, the appellate court ruled that the
defendant had been denied a fair trial by the exclusion of such evidence.

Despite the appellate court's ruling, several important issues were
raised in the opinion. The *Ruiz* court held only that such evidence
should be permitted by allowing "[the] defendant the opportunity to
make the appropriate showing necessary for allowing the expert witness' testimony" (1990, p. 1241). This means that the psychologist's opinion would be subjected to cross-examination during an offer of proof,
similar to the procedure in *Stoll* (1989), to determine the relevance of
the proposed testimony. The appellate court in *Ruiz* acknowledged explicitly that "the reliability of the material upon which [the psycholo-
gist] based his opinion seems questionable, as does its relevance to the
issue of guilt" (1990, p. 1245).

We learn from the holding in *Ruiz* that psychologists who offer
MCMI results to support an opinion that states that a particular individual was or was not likely to have committed an alleged act will
have this opinion questioned usually before it ever is presented to a
jury. Strong research findings will be necessary to support such an opinion. The psychologist will not find such profile evidence easily accepted; rather, he or she will merely have an opportunity to try to
demonstrate the reliability and relevance of the opinion.

In *Nebraska v. Tlamka* (1993), the court is more clear as to how Millon inventory results and the opinions supported by the tests are to
be viewed:

> . . . it is not the acceptance in the psychological community of the
> tests that [the psychologist] administered which must withstand the

[court's] standard of reliability. We acknowledge that the battery of tests administered are standard and accepted tests. Instead, we believe it is the *use which [the psychologist] seeks to make of those tests* which must have an evidential underpinning of acceptability in order to pass the *Frye* test of reliability for admission. (p. 141, emphasis added)

In this particular case, the court had difficulty seeing the reliability in a conclusion based on MCMI-II, MMPI, and other test results, as well as an interview, that found the defendant to be "a normal heterosexual not likely to commit sexual acts with a 4-year-old child" (*Tlamka*, 1993, p. 141).

The court in *United States v. Banks* (1992) is more explicit in clarifying when profile evidence based on psychological tests such as the MCMI is admissible. In *Banks,* the defendant was convicted in a military trial by general court martial of raping and sodomizing his 7-year-old stepdaughter. Again an issue was raised as to the admissibility of profile evidence and the court provided a clearer demarcation of when such testimony is appropriate. According to the *Banks* court:

. . ."profile" evidence is admissible — but only in narrow and limited circumstances. First, it is admissible as purely background material to explain sanity issues. . . . Second, it is admissible as an investigative tool to establish reasonable suspicion. . . . Third, it may be admitted in rebuttal when a party "opens the door" by introducing potentially misleading testimony. (1992, p. 162)

Therefore, the introduction of profile evidence will have some relevance to forensic matters, but the applications, as outlined in *Banks,* are narrow. Psychologists will usually be called upon to perform evaluations that fall under the first (sanity issues) and third (rebuttal witnesses) categories outlined in *Banks.* It is rare that psychological evaluations will be conducted in the second (investigatory) form of profile evidence because criminal defendants are generally not evaluated until after their arrest and/or incarceration, when a major portion of the investigation has been conducted.

An example of an appropriate use of the MCMI to support expert opinion on sanity issues is found in *Tyler v. State* (1993). In this case, the MCMI was used to support a conclusion that the defendant, who had been convicted of murder after an unsuccessful insanity plea, showed no evidence of psychosis. This profile evidence was then interpreted with respect to other information from the evaluation to arrive at the conclusion that the defendant was not insane at the time he committed the crime.

Although many courts have either disregarded or refused to admit profile evidence in cases involving the prosecution of child sexual abuse perpetrators, unfortunately some trial courts have admitted such testimony. Principles G1, G2, and G3 of the *Standards for Educational and Psychological Tests* (American Psychological Association, 1974) require a psychologist to be familiar with the general knowledge and research that support a test. Moreover, Principles 1.15 (Misuse of Psychologist's Influence), 2.02 (Competence and Appropriate Use of Assessments and Interventions), and 7.02 (Forensic Assessments) of the *Ethical Principles of Psychologists and Code of Conduct* (American Psychological Association, 1992) are particularly relevant to the use of psychological tests in forensic evaluation. The ethical principles call for psychologists to exercise care and sound professional skill when reporting on test results in a forensic setting. Therefore, when presenting results from the Millon inventories in the evaluation of alleged or known sex offenders, familiarity with the research on this population is of great importance. The psychologist must rely on his or her professional skill and judgment when making statements about a particular profile, rather than leaving it to the judge to decide what is and is not acceptable.

Disability Claims

Several cases have cited the use of Millon inventory results in supporting expert opinion pertaining to whether or not a claimant is disabled and/or unable to work. The cases summarized in Table 3.1 reveal that not many problems have arisen in this particular area. In disability cases, the applicable legal procedures are different than those in a criminal trial. Disability claims generally arise within the context of an administrative hearing in which a government agency board or administrative law judge (ALJ) will hear evidence from opposing sides. The standard of review for these cases is such that "substantial evidence" must exist to support a particular ruling.

Because of this standard, disability claims frequently involve mental health professionals for the claimant and ones for the government offering conflicting testimony which must be weighed by the ALJ under the substantial evidence standard. The various cases that have cited use of the Millon inventories have not found any problem with the use of these tests; rather, an expert's opinion has usually been accepted or rejected based on the strength of the clinical reasoning used to arrive at a particular opinion.

For example, in *Iwanski v. Streamwood Police Pension Board* (1992), an appeal was made from the denial of an officer's application for disability benefits. The appellate court reversed the decision, finding that the officer had indeed been disabled due to a severe depression and that he was entitled to a non-duty-related pension. In part, the ruling was based on direct testimony of a psychologist who utilized the MCMI-II to evaluate the claimant officer's functioning. From the results of a comprehensive evaluation performed by the psychologist and several other mental health professionals, the court found that there was sufficient evidence to reverse the pension board's initial denial of benefits.

On the other hand, in *Johnson v. Sullivan* (1992), the MCMI was utilized to support a finding that a disability claimant had suffered anxiety and depression. However, no causal connection could be drawn from the other data sources between the claimant's anxiety/depression and his inability to work. Therefore, his claim was denied. This case illustrates the importance of establishing a causal connection between any psychological disturbance revealed on the Millon inventory results and the actual disability that is claimed.

Matters Involving Juveniles

The computer search on legal citation of the Millon inventories yielded four cases, summarized in Table 3.1, pertaining to the MACI's precursor, the MAPI. Although the legal posture and factual patterns vary across these cases, the psychological issues being evaluated are similar and involve the overall level of psychological stability of juveniles in various roles in court proceedings.

In *United States v. Dennison* (1986), a 16-year-old male with a history of juvenile delinquency was accused of stabbing a 20-year-old male to death. The government moved to transfer the juvenile to adult status in order to prosecute him for first-degree murder. In making a motion to dismiss the prosecution's petition and thus avoid transfer to adult status, the defense offered the testimony of a psychologist who had evaluated the defendant with an interview and a battery of tests which included the MAPI. The evaluation revealed several areas in which treatment of the teenager was warranted, including the need for inpatient treatment for alcohol abuse, violence potential, and the need for long-term structured rehabilitation; the expert felt that given the lack of any treatment in the past, the juvenile showed some potential for benefiting from some form of treatment. In adopting the opinion of the expert, the court held that it would be in the interest of justice and the juvenile's best interests to keep him within the juvenile justice system. The government's motion to transfer to adult status was denied.

A similar finding was held in *In re Donald C.H., Jr.* (1994), in which MAPI results were used to evaluate potential treatment and rehabilitative needs in a juvenile charged with burglary. The state attempted to have the juvenile court waive its jurisdiction to allow the juvenile to be tried as an adult. Although the trial court originally waived jurisdiction, the appellate court in *Donald C.H.* reversed, holding that there was insufficient evidence to support the petition to waive jurisdiction.

In another criminal matter, this time involving a juvenile victim, the adult defendant filed a *habeas corpus* petition in *Brooks v. White* (1993) in which he claimed that there was insufficient evidence to support his conviction for sodomy of a minor with borderline intellectual functioning. The court opinion in *Brooks* cites use of the MAPI in the initial stages of the trial to evaluate the victim's personality style and his emotional adjustment to being victimized. A major issue raised during trial was the victim's interpretation of his interaction with the perpetrator. Because the victim was 17 years old but had intellectual deficits, the prosecutor argued that the victim was emotionally less mature than a typical 17-year-old in order to combat a potential defense argument that the victim was more of a willing participant. The MAPI confirmed, as did collateral data, that the victim was a compliant and submissive teenager who was more likely to be influenced by adults. Although not bearing directly on the issue of guilt or innocence, the MAPI was useful in *Brooks* to clarify the context in which the abuse occurred by revealing aspects of the psychological maturity level of the victim.

Another case involving use of the MAPI to evaluate a victim of sexual abuse is *In re Subpoena Issued to L.Q.* (1988). The facts involve a minor who was the victim of a sexual assault. Her parents sought to have the court quash (i.e., annul or void) a grand jury subpoena to have the girl testify against the perpetrator. Her parents felt she lacked the current emotional stability to testify and that forcing her to do so could be psychologically and emotionally damaging. On the trial level, the court refused to quash the subpoena, but the appellate court reversed, stating that although the victim had no qualified privilege to prevent her from testifying, she should be permitted a hearing on her level of mental and emotional stability and physical health. The MAPI was used as part of an evaluation that revealed that the victim was strongly motivated by conventional behavior and strong moral convictions that would lend her strength when testifying.

Some important trends can be observed in these court proceedings involving juveniles that may have bearing on use of the MACI and MAPI in forensic cases. Although no court has commented directly, it appears that the admissibility of these adolescent versions of the Millon inventories is not a focus of challenge and that they are generally accepted by juvenile courts. Moreover, it appears that these tests are useful in evaluating the psychological maturity, sophistication, and stability of adolescents in a variety of legal contexts. Psychological factors that have an impact on the adolescent's status as a victim, offender, and witness are issues in which the MACI and MAPI may be extremely useful. Finally, it appears that in many of these cases the test results have not been seriously challenged, primarily because the tests are applied to answer questions that are specific, narrow, and for which the MACI and MAPI can offer some useful information.

CONCLUSION

Case law can shed much light on more effective applications of a particular test in forensic settings. Generally, courts have viewed the Millon inventories as a standard part of the clinician's assessment procedures and have not looked upon the tests with skepticism. When courts have rejected or ignored the results, they have done so primarily because of the manner in which the results were used by the professional rather than because of any questions about the soundness of the tests. This chapter discusses ways in which forensic psychologists can make more effective use of the Millon inventories by (1) being familiar with the manual and research literature, (2) obtaining experience in using the instruments, (3) basing interpretation on research findings, (4) integrating test results with other sources of information obtained throughout the assessment, and (5) focusing conclusions on answering the specific questions that prompted the original referral. If the Millon instruments are used with research, ethical standards of practice,

TABLE 3.2. The Millon Inventories in Legal Contexts

Application	MCMI	MACI
Evaluation of sex offenders	×	×
Evaluation of juvenile victims		×
Mental status at time of offense	×	×
Treatment/rehabilitation potential	×	×
Sentencing	×	×
Violence potential	×	×
Personal injury	×	
Capacity to testify		×
Disability determination	×	
Juvenile delinquency hearing		×
Termination of parental rights	×	
Emotional maturity related to competencies	×	×

and comprehensive, multimethod assessment procedures in mind, forensic practitioners are less likely to confront major obstacles to getting their testimony heard. In addition, the testimony that is offered will be more likely to stand up on cross-examination. Table 3.2 describes potential applications for these instruments found within the existing case law. This list is not exhaustive but merely summarizes current case law trends. The next chapter examines these and other applications in greater detail.

FOUR

Criminal Applications and Issues

There are several institutions in American society that provide the authority to prohibit specific forms of human behavior, rendering certain acts unacceptable for various ethical, moral, religious, or legal reasons. In the judicial system, some forms of conduct are punished because of laws that make them criminal. According to *Black's Law Dictionary* (1990), a crime is defined as: "any act done in violation of those duties which an individual owes to the community, and for the breach of which the law has provided that the offender shall make satisfaction to the public" (p. 370). Although many crimes such as murder, robbery, and assault have their origins in common law, today crimes are defined by statute according to enacted federal and state law.

Those mental health practitioners who offer their services in the legal arena will quickly realize that there are differences between the ways in which disputes are resolved in criminal versus civil matters. Whereas criminal cases involve adversary battles between the public (usually represented by a district attorney or federal prosecutor) and an accused citizen, civil actions involve disputes between a private citizen, government agency, or corporation and another private citizen. Because of this dichotomy in the way legal disputes are resolved, there are differences in the legal principles which apply in each type of case. Specifically, criminal as opposed to civil disputes emphasize different rules of evidence or discovery and different presumptions or burdens of proof. In addition, there are other significant distinctions between the two. As a result, it is not uncommon to see lawyers specializing in either civil or criminal litigation. Therefore, it makes sense to treat these two types of legal matters in separate chapters.

In addition to legal concerns, there are issues found in the behavioral sciences that make it important to examine various specific applications of the Millon inventories in such specialized contexts. Because parameters of a specific setting and features of a particular diagnosis (e.g., sex offender and malingering) may affect test performance, a discussion of the utility of these measures in specific groups and settings is important. Experienced clinicians recognize that there is a large degree of variability among individuals presenting with similar types of problems. Hence, it is rare that a specific diagnosis or trait can be characterized completely by a single pattern of test results. Rather, the various possible configurations on a test instrument reveal important insights into the person's behavior, affect, methods of relating interpersonally, and cognitive style of processing information. Scales from a particular test can take on different meaning, depending on the particular setting or population under consideration.

The purpose of this chapter is to outline some ways in which the Millon inventories may be applied with individuals who are evaluated at various points in the criminal justice system. A forensic practitioner may be called upon at any time in the process, including during pretrial hearings (e.g., competency to stand trial), trial preparations (e.g., mental state at time of offense), presentencing phases (e.g., sentencing recommendations), and postconviction evaluations (e.g., treatment progress). Those areas addressed in this chapter include (1) classification of sex offenders; (2) domestic violence; (3) evaluation of juvenile delinquency and other status offenses; (4) malingering and deception; and (5) evaluation of criminal defendants for such issues as criminal responsibility, voluntariness of confessions, competence to stand trial, mitigation of criminal intent, sentencing, and the prediction of dangerousness. Although these particular areas represent a broad range of applications for the Millon instruments, these applications do not represent the complete range of potential uses in criminal cases. These topics were selected based on the amount of attention given to each in the literature, as well as the relative importance of these issues in forensic practice generally. Selected case examples are also included to illustrate some of the issues and principles discussed.

CLASSIFICATION OF SEX OFFENDERS

Langevin et al. (1988) found that the MCMI was not successful in predicting sex offender status. Moreover, the instrument appears to have little empirical support for being a *predictor* of who is or will become a sex offender. However, there is evidence obtained with the MCMI-I that may be extrapolated to the MCMI-II, MCMI-III, and MACI, suggesting the latter's utility in *classifying* various subtypes of known sex offenders. Nevertheless, a particularly enlightening and clinically useful analysis of sex offenders has been conducted by Bard and Knight (1987). These investigators developed an empirically derived typology of sex offenders who were deemed "sexually dangerous persons" as exhibited by repetitive, violent, and compulsive sexual offenses. The following descriptions were synthesized from these findings, yielding four distinct clusters of known sex offenders.

Perhaps the most important conclusion to be drawn from the work of Bard and Knight is that no single "sex offender profile" exists on the Millon inventories. Rather, several subtypes appear to exist and can be differentiated based on interpretation of the profile.

Detached Type

These individuals can be identified by elevations on Scales 1 (Schizoid), 2 (Avoidant), and 3 (Dependent). Overall, there is a low level of social interaction with others, as these individuals are isolated, detached, and show poor independent functioning. No particular sexual offense characterizes this subtype; there are often equal numbers of rapists and child molesters. The likelihood of offenders in this subtype having themselves been the victim of sexual assault as a child is greater than for the other subtypes. Drug and alcohol use is not frequently found. The offenses of these individuals tend to be impulsive, with little or no planning involved. Social skills are poorly developed and if mental retardation is present, there is an increased chance that the person will fit the prototypical pattern of this subtype.

Criminal Type

Elevations on Scales 4 (Histrionic), 5 (Narcissistic), 6A (Antisocial), or 6B (Sadistic) identify this subtype of sex offender. The typical offender in this category is likely to be a rapist. A strong history of psychopathology in the parents is common and only a small percentage of these individuals complete high school. Few ever obtain the status of a skilled worker. Given the elevations present, these individuals see themselves as highly sociable, outgoing, and independent. They detest having limits placed on their actions and their offenses can be characterized as aggressive. Of all offenders, this group tends to be the most malicious, not because of the sexual nature of their offenses but because of their need to exert power and control over others, including their victims. This group has the lowest incidence of psychosis.

Negativistic/Angry Type

Principal MCMI-II elevations are found on Scales 6A (Antisocial), 6B (Aggressive/Sadistic), and 8A (Passive–Aggressive/Negativistic). A general feeling of resentment over the way they have been treated by society is characteristic of this group of offenders. They remain angry, caustic, and mean around others; however, this group has the lowest percentage of offenders who were abused as children. Moreover, there is a low incidence of family psychopathology and low numbers of such "nuisance" offenses as exhibitionism. A large number of offenses committed by these individuals involve victims, but these acts tend not to be sexual in nature. There is a low percentage of sexual psychopathology (e.g., paraphilias). Substance abuse often plays a role in the aggressive actions of these individuals, and although they may not have extensive criminal histories, their offenses are generally aimed at others rather than victimless crimes. They have difficulty forming positive relationships with others and their offenses are often a way of acting out anger.

"Healthy" Type

Deriving their name from the fact that these individuals yield profiles that are "within normal limits" (i.e., all BR scores less than 75) or have subtle elevations on Scales Y (Desirability), 7 (Compulsive), and, to a lesser degree, 4 (Histrionic) and 5 (Narcissistic), these individuals are far from well adapted. Although there tends to be a low prevalence of family psychopathology and substance abuse, these individuals often assault their victim to compensate for their own inadequacies. The offenses are reported to be thought out and planned, not impulsive. Nevertheless, clinical records usually reveal a history of deviant sexual arousal patterns and tendencies toward psychotic thinking. A history of incestuous relationships is often present and the serious sexual offender falls within this group. The history of apparent family stability, along with the appearance of adequate childhood and adolescent adaptation, gives way to increasing emotional and psychological demands in adulthood for which the person is ill-prepared to handle. As an adult, these individuals have bizarre ideas about sexuality and interpersonal relationships in general.

CASE 4.1. JUVENILE PERPETRATOR OF SEXUAL ABUSE

The case of Jerry is an example of Bard and Knight's (1987) *criminal type* in an adolescent. Jerry, a 14-year-old white male, was hospitalized for treatment after his family discovered that he had been repeatedly coercing his younger siblings, a 7-year-old brother and 11-year-old sister, to engage in oral and anal sex with him. He threatened them with killing the family pet and other acts of aggression if they told anyone. In addition, Jerry exhibited excessive sexual preoccupation by simulating intercourse with the family dog and asking his parents inappropriate details about their sexual relationship. Jerry's sexual abuse of the younger children necessitated their undergoing treatment for traumatic responses to his coercive abuse.

Generally, Jerry had a long history of defiant and acting-out behavior for which he showed no remorse. He engaged in such ritualistic compulsions as pinching his lip until he developed blood blisters. He had no history of psychosis or suicidal ideation and no prior psychiatric admissions. His mother had been hospitalized for a bipolar disorder and his father was undergoing outpatient treatment for alcoholism. Jerry had a history of shoplifting, truancy, and fighting in school but no involvement with the legal system. On interview, he was indifferent to being hospitalized and he exhibited no motivation for change. There was no psychotic symptomatology and no evidence of mood disturbance. In addition, Jerry denied being the victim of physical or sexual abuse. His diagnosis was conduct disorder and obsessive–compulsive disorder.

The MACI was consistent with the "criminal" type sex offender described earlier. A valid profile was obtained (BR X = 35; BR Y = 64; BR Z = 35) and the codetype was as follows: - ** 6A 4 * - // - ** G * F // - ** CC * DD //. Like the type described, Jerry saw himself as sociable, outgoing, and independent (Scale 4, Dramatizing). His peers on the unit saw him as manipulative, superficial, and difficult to engage (Scale 6A, Unruly). They were often angry because they felt Jerry offered little about himself while they worked on difficult personal problems. He placed the "blame" for his problems on family members (Scale G, Family Discord) and rejected any limits on his behavior (Scale CC, Delinquent Predisposition).

As would be predicted from Bard and Knight's typology, Jerry was not psychotic, there was a family history of psychopathology, he exerted control and power over peers and siblings whom he saw as weaker than himself, and he made malicious verbal attacks on staff and peers when limits were placed on him. He responded poorly to acute inpatient treatment and with agreement from the family he was referred for longer-term care.

DOMESTIC VIOLENCE

The social problem of domestic violence, and spousal abuse in particular, has received much attention in recent years. Descriptions of the personalities of men who commit violent acts against their spouses add insight into the psychological factors that contribute to or maintain abusive patterns as well as being useful for designing and planning treatment programs. The MCMI has been used in a number of studies on males who have histories of abusing their spouses and who subsequently presented for treatment (Hamberger & Hastings, 1986, 1989; Lohr, Hamberger, & Bonge, 1988). From these studies, one major finding has been the lack of a typical MCMI profile pattern that characterizes the abusive male; rather, factor-analytic studies have yielded eight subgroups of male batterers, each with their own characteristic features (Hamberger & Hastings, 1988). Table 4.1 outlines the profile elevations and some emotional indicators that have been found to occur in each subtype (Hamberger & Hastings, 1986).

Individuals in Group I can be described as withdrawn, isolated, and sensitive to rejection and slights. They tend to be moody and irritable, and their anger tends to be explosive and volatile. Often, guilt and remorse follow angry or violent outbursts, as these individuals attempt to remain calm and controlled. However, they anger quickly and present with a "Jekyll-and-Hyde" type of personality. Emotional discomfort is moderate and occurs in the form of depression and anxiety. Alcohol is often used as a method for coping with these feelings. The violence exhibited is usually explosive and unexpected. If an alcohol problem exists, it should be treated first because such a difficulty may lead to premature termination from treatment for the domestic violence.

Group II contains individuals who are very narcissistic and self-aggrandizing. They often have firm convictions about how life should be approached in general and feel others should adopt the same beliefs, values, and ideals that they have. A strong sense of entitlement exists and violence is usually in response to others having failed in their "obligation" to treat them well. As such, they see abuse as punishment for their spouse's shortcomings; thus, they experience little anxiety, worry, or guilt. In fact, their entitlement often leads these men to feel as though it is their responsibility to show their spouse the "error of her ways."

Individuals in Group III are generally seen as dependent and rigid in their interpersonal relationships. They experience anxiety and worry over a fear of abandonment and feel highly insecure in their attachments to others. Contributing to their insecurity is a low self-image and

TABLE 4.1. MCMI Subtypes of Male Spouse Abusers

Group	Typical high scales	Depressive symptomatology	Anger proneness
I	1–2–8A–8B	Moderate	High
II	5–6A–6B	Low	Low
III	3–7	Moderate	Low
IV	4–5–6A	Moderate	High
V	1–2–3–8A–8B	High	High
VI	3–4–5	Low	Low
VII	3–8A–8B	High	Moderate
VIII	Flat/normal limits	Low	Low

Note. Data from Hamberger and Hastings (1986).

general feeling of ineffectiveness in getting one's needs met. Angry and abusive outbursts are uncharacteristic of the general demeanor in these individuals; however, unlike Group I, the aggression usually has an identifiable set of precipitants which involve heightened frustration from ineffective attempts at getting dependency needs fulfilled. Although aggressive or hostile fantasies may arise, a strong sense of guilt usually strives to keep these feelings in check. When these defenses break down, aggressive and abusive outbursts result, followed by extreme guilt and remorse.

The males in Group IV can be characterized as having the pathology exhibited by the first two groups. Not only do they display highly narcissistic and self-centered tendencies, they also exhibit periodic depression, irritability, and a high degree of volatility. As such, they attempt to exert control over their spouse in an extremely aggressive and exploitative manner. Much of this lifestyle can be characterized as antisocial and highly refractory to intervention.

Group V represents a highly pathological group of abusive males who generally tend to exhibit symptomatology of depression and features of borderline personality. They have strong dependency needs, but they fear that their spouse may be rejecting or withholding. Thus, they approach their relationship with a large degree of ambivalence, associated with irritable, sullen, and anxious periods. In more severely disturbed individuals, episodes of labile mood swings or transient psychotic decompensation may be present. Although abusive behavior is generally in response to anger and resentment over unfulfilled dependency needs, these individuals have few resources for adaptively modulating their feelings.

The spouse abusers who constitute Group VI are generally seen by others as socially outgoing yet very superficial. They behave in a highly dramatic fashion to either encourage others to see them in a positive light or minimize and detract attention from problems in their family life. Because of a well-hidden insecurity and extreme sensitivity to rejection or personal slights, the males in this group react with sudden outbursts of hostility or aggression when they have been rejected or emotionally "injured." They will quickly return to their superficial appearance of emotional control and social charm to avoid dealing with the problems that remain.

Group VII consists of males who depend upon others and who experience chronic dysphoric mood. They are anxious and fearful of abandonment or rejection and will often cling to their spouse in a desperate attempt to avoid being left. Because they can almost never be appeased or comforted, they experience a variety of dysphoric moods which include irritability, depression, dejection, and futility. They may make futile threats of suicide to keep their spouse from leaving. When all else fails, they may respond with a brief, aggressive, and abusive outburst which is followed by self-loathing, guilt, and depression.

The profile that characterizes Group VIII is generally flat, with no personality scales above a BR of 75. These men present themselves as self-confident and assertive, yet not aggressive, and see their behavior as socially appropriate and guided by social norms. However, the most likely interpretation of this profile is that these men are guarded and defensive in their self-reports and they are unwilling to explore domestic problems. In the context of domestic violence treatment, these men are usually resistant to admitting any difficulties, much less open to any treatment recommendations.

JUVENILE DELINQUENCY AND STATUS OFFENSES

The role of mental health professionals in matters adjudicated in juvenile court continues to be quite influential (Melton, Petrila, Poythress, & Slobogin, 1987). One major reason for the importance given to the testimony of clinicians in such cases is the special consideration given to juveniles in court proceedings. For instance, juveniles who engage in criminal activity become involved in a legal system that asks such questions as: "To what extent should a child or teenager be treated the same as or differently from adults?" As noted by Mnookin and Weisberg (1989), the juvenile criminal process is affected by such factors as the parent–child relationship, a juvenile's level of maturity and competence, and the greater emphasis placed on the need for re-habilitation of juveniles.

Aside from the criminal process, juveniles are also subject to res-triction of certain rights and liberties as the result of legal proceed-ings that are found nowhere else in our legal system other than juvenile and family courts. For example, many states have legislation that per-mits the classification of status offenses (e.g., staying out late, defying parents, running away from home, and truancy). These offenses are deemed illegal for individuals under a certain age (often 16) who are frequently referred to as person in need of supervision (PINS), child in need of supervision (CINS, CHINS), or a similar descriptive name.

Because of the special questions raised in juvenile court proceed-ings, forensic evaluation is often a key portion of the testimony provid-ed. Therefore, psychologists are often called upon to answer questions related to the juvenile's amenability to treatment, various disposition-al or placement alternatives, the juvenile's interaction with family mem-bers, academic and vocational issues, and diagnostic questions (Melton et al., 1987). Given the wide range of potential questions likely to be asked, the MACI can be a particularly useful component of the overall assessment.

When using the MACI in juvenile court-referred evaluations the major considerations are guided by the particular questions asked of the examiner. Again, the clinician must rely on a broad-based approach to data collection; it is important to investigate behavior at school, home, social settings, and so forth. The MACI provides information related to personality style and disturbances, response style, expressed concerns as the adolescent sees them, and such major areas of clinical concern as eating disorders, anxiety, depression, impulsivity, delinquency, sui-cidal behavior, or substance abuse.

Though no research currently exists on the ability to predict vari-ous treatment outcomes, some MACI indicators can be useful. For in-stance, the expressed concerns scales (A through H) provide a reflection of those areas the adolescent views or sees as the problem. If, for ex-ample, Scale G (Family Discord) is high but no other expressed con-cerns scales are elevated, the adolescent may be projecting blame onto others while taking little responsibility for current problems.

Scale F (Social Insensitivity) also has some prognostic implications, particularly for antisocial or conduct-disordered teenagers. An eleva-tion on this scale suggests a willingness on the part of the teenager to admit that he or she violates the rights of others and takes advantage of those in weaker positions. With such a heightened level of openness, an adolescent with an elevation on Scale F *may* have some motivation to work on his or her socially insensitive or exploitative behavior, though this is not necessarily true in all cases. On the other hand, some socially insensitive teenagers may express no concern at all about their aggressive, mean, and insensitive actions; these low Scale F scores can also be interpreted as reflecting minimal insight. Thus, adolescents who have a history of social insensitivity but who have low Scale F scores will generally be difficult to treat with traditional therapies.

Case 4.1, presented earlier as an example of a juvenile sex offender, illustrates this principle. Jerry's low Scale F score (BR = 61) was indicative of his complete lack of concern over the degree to which his behavior was damaging and hurtful to others. Elevations on Scales 6A (Unruly, BR = 82) and CC (Delinquent Predisposition, BR = 82) were present and reflected his extreme disregard for the rights of others, rejection of external limits, and predatory sexual behavior. As the case history revealed, this adolescent was very difficult to treat and had a poor response to an extended inpatient hospitalization.

The following case demonstrates the utility of the MACI in diagnosing substance abuse and personality disturbance in a juvenile who was on a PINS petition and who was referred for an evaluation to determine an appropriate treatment plan.

CASE 4.2. SUBSTANCE ABUSE IN A PINS ADOLESCENT

Tony, a 14-year-old white male, was referred for an evaluation while he was in a detention facility after violating his PINS petition. He had expressed suicidal ideation and intent due to his recent incarceration. He had been placed on PINS for truancy, fighting in school, and general noncompliance at home. On interview, Tony showed no acute distress, he denied symptoms of psychosis and focused his thoughts on his anger at the legal system for treating him unfairly.

His history revealed extensive substance abuse, including regular marijuana use since the age of 13. He also inhaled butane on occasion and had been drinking alcohol heavily for several months. Tony admitted to frequent blackouts and he claimed that his use of alcohol had steadily increased over the last few months. There was no history of physical or sexual abuse. However, 3 years earlier, Tony's younger sister died after battling a lengthy illness. His mother "fell apart" emotionally, and she was psychologically unavailable to him. Tony had once tried to hang himself in response to a family argument and when speaking about his sister, he became deeply saddened but could not allow himself to cry.

The MACI yielded a profile of questionable validity (X = 75, Y = 42, and Z = 90), with a prominent self-debasing response style. The high Debasement scale raised a question of possible overreporting or malingering (see Table 4.5) to gain some treatment that would allow him to escape incarceration. The following code was obtained: 9 ** 6A 8A 2B 6B * 8B // G ** B A * - // BB DD FF ** GG * CC //. The major findings on the MACI reveal a personality style that is marked by a moderate to severe level of pathology. Tony appears to be a teenager with extreme anger and resentment toward others. He expects others to take advantage of him and he responds by adopting a caustic, negative, acting-out style. He exhibits instability in all areas, including his relationships, moods, and behavior. There is much impulsivity and his expressed concerns scales reveal that the only major problem he sees is the family discord that exists. The clinical scales reveal prominent difficulties with substance abuse and impulsive and reckless behavior, as well as depressive affect with suicidal preoccupation. Diagnostically, his MACI profile is consistent with the clinical diagnosis he was given, which included Conduct Disorder, Dysthymia, and Alcohol Dependence with Polysubstance Abuse.

Tony was somewhat open to discussing the loss of his sister and the subsequent emotional unavailability of his family. However, his insight was superficial and he maintained a manipulative interactive style with others. Based on the evidence of substance abuse that was found in his history and on the MACI, a recommendation was made that as part of his PINS, Tony be required to seek treatment "voluntarily" in a residential treatment program for adolescent substance abusers that had an average length of stay of 6 months. Tony was open to this suggestion, mainly because he viewed the program as more desirable than the possibility of spending extensive time in a juvenile detention facility. On 3-month follow-up, Tony was reported to be doing surprisingly well in the program and the staff expected that he would complete the program.

ASSESSMENT OF MALINGERING AND DECEPTION

The use of psychometric inventories to assess psychopathology depends greatly on the honesty, accuracy, and consistency of self-reports. Patients in all clinical settings may be motivated to distort their responses by either exaggerating or minimizing problem areas. The four validity scales on the MCMI-II and MACI were specifically designed to assess these tendencies. In forensic settings particularly, there is a large degree of motivation for individuals to distort their responses on psychological tests. A defendant in a murder trial might be prone to feign mental illness in an attempt to gain acquittal by reason of insanity; a parent in a child custody dispute may be prone to give an unrealistically favorable presentation in order to gain custody of the child; someone who suffered a personal injury may be motivated to exaggerate and magnify the severity of impairment to gain a higher monetary award as compensation. Whereas the assessment of malingering and deception is relevant to many clinical settings, it is particularly important in almost all areas of forensic practice. The issues discussed, however, apply for any setting in which deceptive response sets may be encountered.

There are a number of different response styles that define individuals who dissimulate, that is, people who deliberately distort or misrepresent their physical or psychological symptoms (Rogers, 1988). *Malingering* refers to the conscious and deliberate fabrication of physical and/or psychological symptoms to obtain some recognizable secondary gain, whereas *defensiveness* represents a conscious and deliberate denial or minimization of symptoms. *Inconsistent responding,* of which random responding is a subset, refers to a response set where the patient responds to items in a manner unrelated to content. Of course, the last response style is one of *honest responding,* where the individual makes an effort to be accurate and sincere in his or her responses.

Only a limited number of studies have examined the effectiveness of the Millon inventories in detecting dissimulation. However, there is good indication that these instruments are accurate in distinguishing between honest, fake good (defensiveness), and fake bad (malingering) response sets (McNiel & Meyer, 1990). VanGorp and Meyer (1986) used the original MCMI-I to assess the efficacy of Scale X (Disclosure) in detecting a variety of faking strategies. Their results showed that the MCMI-I was able to detect fake bad profiles but was unable to detect the fake good profiles accurately.

The MCMI-I and MAPI had only two validity indicators, the Validity index and Scale X (Disclosure). However, the MCMI-II and MACI introduced two new validity scales, Desirability (Scale Y) and Debasement (Scale Z). Bagby, Gillis, and Dickens (1990) examined the effectiveness of all four MCMI-II validity scales in distinguishing honest, fake bad, and fake good response sets using discriminant function analyses. Their results showed that the MCMI was capable of not only classifying fake bad profiles accurately but also identifying fake good and honest profiles with much accuracy. Nevertheless, the MCMI-II showed a slight tendency to identify fake bad profiles more accurately than honest or fake good profiles. A primary reason for this tendency appears to be the manner in which the MCMI-II was constructed. Because the instrument is theory based and was developed specifically to assess psychopathology in clinical samples, a number of the items are more subtle and do not appear to be related to obvious psychopathology (Bagby et al., 1990).

In clinical practice, the process of deciding whether malingering or defensiveness is reflected in the results of an objective personality inventory involves a number of sequential steps. Following the rationale outlined by Greene (1988) for the MMPI, the assessment of MCMI-II, MCMI-III, and MACI validity is discussed. To determine whether a particular profile is valid, the clinician must first determine whether the patient has provided enough information by answering a sufficient number of questions. Item omissions, as they are often called, refer not only to those items left blank but also to double-marked items (i.e., items marked both true and false). Once the number of items answered is deemed to be satisfactory, the next step in assessing validity is to determine the consistency of item endorsement. This refers to whether or not the individual has provided a reliable and consistent pattern of responses to the items. The last step in evaluating validity of the instrument involves the assessment of accuracy in item endorsement. Specifically, the accuracy of endorsement represents whether the individual responded in an honest fashion, a malingering response set, or with defensiveness and denial of problem areas.

The scales and indices that can be used to assess item omissions and the consistency and accuracy of endorsement are outlined in Table 4.2 in a manner adapted from Greene (1988). Whereas Greene proposes a statistically derived cutoff score for each scale or index based on frequency distributions and percentile scores, the values in Table 4.2 were synthesized from the MCMI-II, MCMI-III, and MACI manuals and from rational deduction based on the characteristics that define each of the validity indicators. Although statistical derivation of cutting scores is possible for each of the scales, at the present time there is no large body of data that would permit such developments.

The decision as to what constitutes an ideal cutoff for any validity indicator is a difficult one to make. Thus, a degree of flexibility must be allowed in determining appropriate decision points. For item omissions, each test manual provides the number of item omissions that invalidates the test when using computerized scoring and these are reported in Table 4.2. The marginal category in the table represents the number of item omissions that is less than the maximum required by the manual but constitutes 5% or more of the total test items. Although some item omissions may be expected, the number of omissions should be less than 5% of the total items, particularly as the relatively short length of the Millon inventories makes item responses a valuable commodity.

Table 4.2 also outlines two indices for assessing the consistency

TABLE 4.2. Cutting Scores for Determining Validity

Validity indicator	Acceptable	Marginal	Unacceptable
A. Item omissions			
MCMI-II	<8	8–11	12+
MCMI-III	<8	8–11	12+
MACI	<8	8–9	10+
B. Consistency of endorsement			
1. Validity Index			
MCMI-II	0	—	1+
MCMI-III	0	—	1+
MACI	0	—	1+
2. BR Y and BR Z ≥ 75			
MCMI-II	No	Yes	Yes
MCMI-III	No	Yes	Yes
MACI	No	Yes	Yes
C. Accuracy of endorsement			
1. Malingering/overreporting			
a. Scale X[a]			
MCMI-II	250–400	401–590	>590
MCMI-III	61–122	123–178	>178
MACI	260–419	420–589	>589
b. Scale Z			
MCMI-II	BR < 75	BR 75–89	BR ≥ 90
MCMI-III	BR < 75	BR 75–89	BR ≥ 90
MACI	BR < 75	BR 75–89	BR ≥ 90
2. Defensiveness/denial			
a. Scale X[a]			
MCMI-II	250–400	145–249	<145
MCMI-III	61–122	60–34	<34
MACI	260–419	201–259	<201
b. Scale Y			
MCMI-II	BR < 75	BR 75–89	BR ≥ 90
MCMI-III	BR < 75	BR 75–89	BR ≥ 90
MACI	BR < 75	BR 75–89	BR ≥ 90

Note. Format adapted from Greene (1988).
[a]All cutoffs for Scale X are based on raw scores.

of item endorsement. The cutoffs reported for the Validity Index (on the MCMI-II and MCMI-III) and Reliability (on the MACI), consisting of bizarre items with very low endorsement frequencies, are different than those outlined in the manuals (Millon, 1987, 1993, 1994a).

Whereas each manual suggests that profiles in which Scale V or VV values of 1 are considered of questionable validity and those with values of 2 as invalid, research has shown that Scale V values of 1 identify invalid profiles with more than 95% accuracy (Bagby, Gillis, & Rogers, 1991). Another measure of response consistency is the relative configuration of Scales Y (Desirability) and Z (Debasement). When Scales Y and Z are both elevated over a BR of 74, the patient has endorsed antithetical and inconsistent attitudes and self-reports which should lead one to question the reliability of his or her responses.

Finally, the indices for assessing malingering and defensiveness are provided in Table 4.2 as well. All cutoffs reported are based on the raw scores for Scale X. Values for Scale X (Debasement) are ones provided in the test manuals. The cutoffs for Scales Y (Desirability) and Z (Debasement) on the MCMI-II, MCMI-III, and MACI are such that the marginal and unacceptable categories are separated by a BR value of 90 whereas a BR score of 75 separates the acceptable and marginal categories.

The cutoff of 90 on Scales Y and Z is based on the observation that an individual is endorsing almost all the items on these scales in the affirmative when the BR score reaches 90. The exceptions to the rule of viewing the profile as invalid when the BR is ≥ 90 are if the profile is inconsistent with the response style (e.g., high levels of depression and anxiety when Scale Y ≥ 90) or if the resulting profile is consistent with the individual's psychosocial history or clinical presentation.

The test of further research and continued clinical practice will determine whether the cutoffs in Table 4.2 will remain useful. In addition, the base rates of malingering and defensiveness are likely to differ from setting to setting, and the differences in prevalence of these response styles have an effect on the predictive accuracy of these cutoff scores (Greene, 1988; Retzlaff & Sheehan, 1989). More important, it is hoped that the scales and indices utilized for assessing test validity will be expanded as clinicians and researchers develop clinically useful measures for the consistency and accuracy of item endorsement.

The following case illustrates issues involved with both disability evaluation (to be discussed in Chapter 5) and the assessment of malingering.

CASE 4.3. THE CHRONIC PAIN SUFFERER

Ms. H. a 46-year-old single, African American female, has an extensive history of physical problems which are well substantiated by medical records. She was evaluated on the referral of her attorney to assess her employability. As a young adult, Ms. H. incurred severe leg injuries in an automobile accident and has since experienced pain in her legs. She also has a history of hypertension, degenerative arthritis of the spine and hips, and glaucoma. Her activities showed a marked reduction and at the time of assessment she had not worked in 6 years. Prior to that time, she had worked steadily as a health care aide and secretary, with her longest job lasting 10 years. Ms. H. employed a number of procedures to reduce her pain, including heating pads and daily back rubs from her mother. Having never married, Ms. H. continued to reside in her parents' home. No drug or alcohol abuse was uncovered and she did not rely on analgesics for her pain.

In all other aspects, Ms. H. reported a relatively normal life. She denied any history of childhood difficulties and reported her upbringing as unremarkable. Though she had some friends, they were not particularly close and she did not date. She had discrete periods of intense anxiety characterized by feelings of panic and she reported poor sleep and appetite, with associated depressed mood every few days. In addition, Ms. H. engaged in periodic checking behavior and was often uncomfortable when leaving home. Her main reasons for this fear were a self-consciousness and embarrassment over the way her physical problems restricted her activity.

Results of the MCMI-II revealed a valid profile that showed Ms. H. to be very nondisclosing of problem areas. Her Desirability and Debasement scales were low (BR < 75) as well. Such a response set is inconsistent with malingering inasmuch as Ms. H. does not appear to be making a deliberate or conscious attempt to magnify or exaggerate problem areas. On the contrary, her response style shows her to be evasive and unwilling to disclose issues of a personal nature. Moreover, she appears to lack a curiosity about psychological matters and she utilizes defenses of denial and repression. Her personality code was as follows: 7 ** · * 1 4 + 3 5 6B " 8B 6A 2A 8A // · ** · * //. The clinical code was characterized by a spike-H configuration: · ** H * // · ** · * //. These results are consistent with Ms. H's history and clinical presentation. She lacks the willingness to explore issues of a psychological nature, preferring a physical cause for her difficulties. Physical symptoms are used to achieve a significant degree of secondary gain and attention from others, including her mother (i.e., daily back rubs) and five different physicians. Ms. H.'s characteristic personality style reveals that she has a rigid cognitive style and she wishes to appear as a moralistic person. Her relationships are distant and she has difficulties with intimacy.

The MMPI-2 was administered as part of her evaluation and yielded a profile highly congruent with that of the MCMI-II. A high degree of denial and a lack of openness were evident. The 1–3 codetype was obtained, with Scales 1 and 3 highly elevated and all other clinical scales, with the exception of Scale 2, falling below a T-score of 70.

Based on the findings, Ms. H. was not considered to be malingering in that her physical problems were substantiated by medical records and the psychometric instruments did not reveal a malingering response style. If Ms. H was attempting to deliberately fake her difficulties, she would be expected to exaggerate, rather than minimize, her problems. As such, although her test results would point to a somatization disorder, the history and medical records suggest that the diagnosis of psychological factors affecting physical condition was most accurate. The MCMI-II findings reveal that many of Ms. H.'s psychological conflicts were out of her awareness and were fairly ingrained in her character style. It was concluded that, at the present time, she was unable to work due to medical problems.

EVALUATING CRIMINAL DEFENDANTS

Competence to Stand Trial

The legal definition of "competence to stand trial" varies slightly from state to state, however each standard is a variation on that outlined in the United States Supreme Court decision in *Dusky v. United States* (1960): " . . . whether [the defendant] has sufficient *present ability* to consult with his attorney with a reasonable degree of rational understanding and a rational as well as factual understanding of the proceedings against him" (p. 402, emphasis added). Therefore, the specific task of the evaluator in competence to stand trial evaluations is to determine the defendant's ability to work with his or her attorney, to appreciate the charges and possible penalties faced, and to understand the legal process in which he or she has become involved.

According to Grisso (1988), the competence to stand trial evaluation must achieve five objectives. First, a functional determination must be made of the defendant's strengths and deficits in understanding trial and legal processes. Second, a causal explanation is sought, linking any mental disorder or other reason (e.g., malingering, intellectual deficits, and ignorance of the law) that can explain the defendant's deficits. Third, interactive issues are assessed to explain ways in which the defendant's deficits may be manifest in the specific nature of his or her trial. Fourth, a conclusion may be sought where the consultant comments on the "ultimate issue" as to whether or not the defendant is competent (Grisso does not favor such testimony, although other forensic practitioners do). Finally, prescriptive goals seek to identify the potential for remediation of deficits and restoration of the defendant's competence by highlighting treatment options directed at this goal.

Competence to stand trial differs from such other forensic evaluations as criminal responsibility in that, as the *Dusky* standard emphasizes, the focus is on present abilities. Thus, competence is always an issue during the trial process because a defendant's fluctuating mental state may interfere with the ability to comprehend legal procedures and to assist one's attorney at one time and not others.

Because of the focused and highly specialized abilities being assessed in a competence to stand trial evaluation, a complete personality profile such as the MCMI-II or MACI is rarely needed. However, there are some instances in which these tests may be useful. For example, malingering and dissimulation are important factors to consider in a competence evaluation. The section on malingering and deception in this chapter would be relevant in such cases. In addition, if the forensic consultant has questions as to the causes of the defendant's competence deficits revealed on interview, the MCMI-II or MACI may be of use in assessing possible clinical symptomatology such as extreme anxiety, dissociative processes, thought disturbance, or depression which can interfere with understanding the legal process or with relating to an attorney. For example, clinical depression scales on the Millon inventories may reveal a severe depression that leads to a defendant's self-defeating attitude which will prevent him or her from assisting with defense counsel in raising or preparing an appropriate defense. The forensic consultant is reminded, however, that personality tests such as the Millon inventories have a secondary role in competence to stand trial evaluations and must not replace a thorough clinical interview, mental status examination, record review, and specialized assessment instruments such as the Competency to Stand Trial Assessment Instrument or Competency Screening Test (Grisso, 1988).

Voluntariness of Confessions

Forensic evaluators who do extensive criminal work routinely encounter cases in which individuals accused of extremely serious offenses have given a statement to the police admitting the offense alleged against them. This phenomenon is seemingly in defiance of the dictates of reason that one in such a position should not make self-incriminating statements and, in a justice system that is based on the presumption of innocence, should allow the burden of proof to remain with the accuser. The frequency of such detailed self-incriminating statements is even more curious in light of the fact that since *Miranda v. Arizona* (1973), police officers have an affirmative duty to apprise criminal defendants of their constitutional right against self-incrimination and must follow detailed procedures in doing so. Nor is the individual's confession ever an insignificant factor in the case. As Kassin and McNall (1991) point out, the introduction of a confession has been deemed by legal authorities to be so persuasive a piece of evidence as to render other aspects of the trial superfluous.

Unless defendants are "Mirandized," their statements while under custodial interrogation are inadmissible in court. Further, even if they waive their Miranda rights after having had them read and explained to them, the waiver is only valid if it is "knowing, intelligent, and voluntary" (Melton et al., 1987). Although the "knowing" and "intelligent" requirements of a valid waiver of Miranda rights are issues of major importance to forensic evaluators, the voluntariness of the waiver is of greatest relevance to the use of the Millon inventories in such assessments. Speaking generally, criminal defendants whose Miranda waivers are questioned with respect to their having been made knowingly or intelligently function at too low a level intellectually, educationally, or in terms of basic personality integration to be appropriate subjects for an MCMI-II evaluation. Their needs are better served by the administration of other diagnostic instruments. However, several of the constructs assessed by the Millon inventories are highly relevant to the issue of voluntariness of waivers and the resulting self-incriminating statements.

Melton et al. (1987) cite instances of subtle psychological coercion applied by police to criminal defendants during interrogation. They note that the United States Supreme Court has considered the constitutionality of such coercive procedures from the standpoint of both the degree of objective pressure exerted by the interrogators (i.e., the strength of the "tug" on the suspect of confess, p.94) and the psychological capacity of the suspect to resist the coercion. These authors state: "Confessions—even if reliable—are seen as unfairly obtained if they were elicited in a situation in which the defendant's will was overborne" (p. 95). Among the questions that a forensic evaluator is to consider in such situations is: "Was it 'voluntary'; that is, was the situation in its totality—and in its interaction with the defendant's state of mind—so coercive that the defendant's will was overborne?" (p. 95). Melton et al. (1987) also label this issue the most problematic of the knowing, intelligent, and voluntary tests.

Wrightsman and Kassin (1993) cite a number of coercive and deceptive interrogation procedures culled from police manuals. One of these strategies is for the interrogator to reframe the subject's cognitions regarding the offense by minimizing its seriousness or to allow the suspect to save face by providing an external attribution of blame, such as an irresistible impulse to which the suspect momentarily succumbed. Often the interrogator suggests the possibility that the victim's behavior was actually responsible for the crime. Another tactic cited is for the interrogator to frighten the suspect into confessing. One method of accomplishing this is to exaggerate the seriousness of the offense through such techniques as falsely reporting the amount of the loss in theft or embezzlement cases. There is also the "knowledge-bluff" trick in which interrogators persuade the suspect that he or she has already been implicated by an accomplice, pretend to have strong circumstantial evidence, or have a police officer pose as an eyewitness and identify the suspect in a rigged line-up. A similar technique is falsely telling the suspect that he or she has failed a polygraph test. A third technique cited by these authors involves the development of a personal rapport with the suspect through sympathy, flattery, and such gestures as offering a drink. A common variant of this procedure is the "good cop–bad cop" routine in which one interrogator plays the role of friend and another the role of antagonist.

As would be expected, criminal suspects differ in their degree of susceptibility to these methods. Wrightsman and Kassin (1993) state that interrogative suggestibility appears to be mediated by anxiety. This has been demonstrated in research with laboratory subjects, as well as in field studies of actual criminal suspects who were able to resist police interrogation procedures and those who made a self-incriminating statement that they ultimately retracted. Gudjonsson (1992) finds that compliance is associated with a tendency to give in to pressure to confess and that this is mediated by eagerness to please and avoidance of controversy. Several of the items from Gudjonsson's Compliance Scale, which has been used in his study of voluntariness of confessions, closely resemble MCMI-II items that tap aspects of dependent personality disorder (Scale 3) and antisocial personality disorder (Scale 6A), the latter type of item being scored in the negative direction on the Gudjonsson Compliance Scale. This scale differentiated significantly between alleged false confessors and other criminal defendants charged with similar offenses (Gudjonsson, 1992).

In terms of practical application, the validity of a subject's assertion that he or she was coerced into making a false confession or coerced into waiving his or her Miranda rights is affected by personality characteristics assessed via the Millon inventories. Whereas this claim might be found to be more credible in an insecure individual with dependent personality disorder (Scale 3 elevations on either the MCMI-II or MACI) who claims to have succumbed to a strategy in which he or she was befriended by the interrogator, such an assertion by a defendant diagnosed as antisocial (MCMI-II/MACI Scale 6A), paranoid (MCMI-II Scale P), or passive–aggressive (MCMI-II/MACI Scale 8A) personality disorder would be viewed more skeptically. However, apart from the suggestive research by Gudjonsson noted above, there has not been any empirical study of the impact of personality disorder on the capacity to resist interrogation strategies and any expert conclusions ventured at this point must necessarily rest on a foundation of clinical theory and deductive reasoning.

Insanity and Criminal Responsibility

Most discussions on the interaction between mental health and the law quickly focus on the insanity defense. The reason for this is that few other areas of criminal law have generated as much controversy as whether or not a mentally ill criminal defendant should be held responsible for his or her behavior. In particular, when John Hinckley was found not guilty by reason of insanity for the attempted murder of then-President Ronald Reagan, there was great public outcry that eventually resulted in legislative changes in the legal definition of insanity in federal and many state statutes (Bonnie, 1994).

A detailed discussion of the history of the insanity defense in this country is beyond the scope of this chapter. However, it is helpful to recognize that states have different standards for defining the requirements necessary for a defendant to be held legally insane. In fact, some states, such as Montana, have abandoned the insanity defense and do not allow it to be raised in criminal trials (Bonnie, 1994). The Model Penal Code represents a general test for insanity from which many states have derived statutory definitions. According to this model, a defendant is considered to be not criminally responsible if, due to mental disease or defect, he or she lacked substantial capacity to appreciate the wrongfulness of his or her conduct or lacked substantial capacity to conform his or her behavior to what is required by law. Specifically eliminated from the requirements are those diseases or defects that are manifest by repeated criminal or antisocial behavior (e.g., antisocial personality disorder).

The process of evaluating a criminal defendant's responsibility is no small task. An adequate assessment involves extensive time spent researching police reports, physical evidence, and documents on the defendant, as well as numerous hours interviewing both the defendant and collateral informants and administering psychological tests. Shapiro (1985) has outlined a framework for organizing insanity evaluations. Several issues must be assessed because the difficult task is to reconstruct the defendant's mental state at some point in the past, namely, the time of the crime.

Within the framework outlined by Shapiro, nine major issues need to be evaluated when an insanity defense is raised. First, the events and circumstances surrounding the crime must be established. This can be done through interviews with the defendant, examination of police reports, and interviewing witnesses. Second, the consistency of the defendant's behavior and psychological functioning is established by taking a thorough psychosocial history and utilizing collateral resources to establish the defendant's life history. Third, malingering or other deceptive processes must be considered because a criminal defendant has a high degree of motivation to fake psychological disturbance. Fourth, delusional systems are often present in defendants alleged to be psychotic. The forensic examiner must determine whether the content of any delusion has a causal connection to the defendant's criminal behavior. Fifth, physical evidence from the crime is helpful in establishing the facts and in helping the examiner develop a re-creation of the defendant's version of the facts. Sixth, an insanity evaluation needs to consider the role of drugs and alcohol in influencing the defendant's behavior. Although many substances can induce psychotic symptoms, some state laws will not allow an insanity finding when the use of illegal substances has induced the symptomatology. Seventh, neurological causes for the defendant's actions must be ruled out as a physical basis for fluctuations in the defendant's mental state. Next, because most insanity statutes exclude from consideration those diagnoses characterized by repetitive antisocial behavior, the examiner must differentiate psychotic from psychopathic motives for the defendant's actions. Finally, some cases call for evaluating defendants when they are refusing to raise what might be a valid insanity defense. Some attorneys may ask a forensic practitioner to determine whether the defendant's refusal is due to manifestations of his or her mental illness.

This model for conducting insanity evaluations provided by Shapiro (1985) can serve as an outline for organizing data from the assessment. With respect to the Millon inventories, there are some issues, such as malingering, with which the tests can be quite helpful. For other issues, such as determining the facts of the case, the tests will obviously not be useful. Table 4.3 outlines the components of Shapiro's model and the relevant scales and indicators on the MCMI-II and MACI that can be used for particular assessment issues. A question mark is placed next to those scales that may have some utility for a particular factor but were not developed for the particular issue being assessed or do not bear directly on the specific factor listed. For example, the MACI expressed concerns scales were designed to provide a measure of specific problems from the adolescent's perspective. Elevations in these scales, however, are not indicative of delusional or psychotic thought. But, these scales may provide some insight into the thought content and preoccupations of those adolescents who have

TABLE 4.3. Components of an Insanity Evaluation

Issues to be evaluated[a]	Relevant scales/indicators	
	MCMI	MACI
1. Determining what occurred	None	None
2. Consistency of functioning	Unstable personality/ clinical patterns	
3. Malingering/deception	V, X, Y, Z	VV, X, Y, Z
4. Delusional systems	S, P, N, SS, CC, PP	Expressed concerns (?)
5. Physical evidence	None	None
6. Role of drugs and alcohol	B, T	BB
7. Neurological dysfunction	None	None
8. Psychosis versus psychopathy	6A, 6B, S, SS	6A, 6B
9. Refusal of valid defense	D, CC, 8A, 8B, SS (?)	8A, 8B, 9, B, FF (?)

[a]From Shapiro (1985).

been shown to have symptoms of psychosis through other assessment procedures.

It must be reemphasized that the Millon inventories add only one source of information in the evaluation of criminal responsibility. However, once all pieces of data are obtained, they must be organized and presented in a fashion that is of assistance to the court. This section is meant to serve as a model for facilitating organization of the Millon inventory data obtained in criminal responsibility evaluations.

CASE 4.4. MENTAL STATE AT THE TIME OF THE OFFENSE

Alice W., a 37-year-old African American female, was charged with first-degree homicide (requiring a knowing and purposeful mental state) in connection with the stabbing death of her boyfriend during an argument. She earned a high school equivalency diploma after dropping out of school and subsequently received training as a clerk–typist, data entry clerk, work processor, and telex operator at four different business schools. Her longest period of employment was 1 year as an administrative assistant at a drug rehabilitation program. Alice reported that during a period when she was living near a funeral parlor she developed hallucinations and delusions relating to ghosts. She was hospitalized at that time and subsequently qualified for Social Security benefits on the basis of her psychiatric illness. She was hospitalized a second time some years later when she developed hallucinations involving her niece.

Alice gave the following account of the incident resulting in the death of her boyfriend of 7 years. She and the boyfriend had been drinking alcohol since 2 o'clock that afternoon. They went furniture shopping and also bought a set of kitchen knives that day. That evening, while Alice was caring for her grandson, the victim commented, "You going to feed that motherfucking baby before you feed me? That baby don't give you nothing." Alice reported that she was upset by the victim's use of profanity in her home and replied, "You better watch your fucking mouth!" The victim left the house and subsequently kicked in her door, causing Alice to throw the baby, bottle and all, on the couch in order to eject the victim from her home. She then left the baby alone in the house, went to buy some more beer and wine, and warned the victim not to disturb her by ringing her doorbell. Later that night, the victim returned and rang her doorbell repeatedly. Alice stated that she gave the baby a bottle, selected a steak knife from the set that she had purchased with the victim, and went downstairs to confront him. The victim was hitting and kicking the door and then grabbed Alice, who retaliated by hitting and kicking him. The victim called her short, ugly, and fat, and received a fatal knife wound when he attempted to grab her.

Alice's MCMI-II record was as follows: 3 ** 2 4 * 5 8B 7 1 8A 6B 6B + · " · // · ** S * // · ** · * // · ** SS * //. These results, in conjunction with her history, indicate that Alice has schizophrenia and also a dependent personality disorder. Her thought processes, judgment, and impulse control are considerably more impaired by alcohol intoxication than would be true for a psychologically healthier individual. In reconstructing the subject's mental state at the time of the offense, it is important not only to consider these factors but also the fact that she was provoked and angered by the victim's behavior, which included insulting her and her grandson, incessantly ringing the doorbell, and physically assaulting her. The facts that this individual with a dependent personality disorder had been in a nonabusive relationship of 7 years with the victim, that she had just been out shopping with him that day, and that he had bought her furniture further suggest that this was not a case of specific intent to inflict grievous bodily harm. Rather, this is a case in which an intoxicated schizophrenic woman lashed out blindly after having been pushed past the limits of her tenuous controls in a tragically absurd drunken altercation.

———◆———

Mitigating Factors: Criminal Intent and Sentencing

Information yielded by both the personality disorders and clinical syndrome sections of the Millon inventories has been found in practice to be useful in a variety of criminal forensic contexts. Among these cases are those in which Millon inventory evidence is introduced to support a diminished capacity defense, which effectively lowers severity of a crime (e.g., voluntary manslaughter as opposed to second-degree murder), as well as complex matters in which personality data are used to address case-specific issues related to elements of a crime. Another situation in which Millon inventory results have proven useful is developing mitigation evidence for use at sentencing, including capital murder cases. The following series of cases illustrates these applications.

CASE 4.5. MITIGATING FACTORS FOR PURPOSES OF SENTENCING

John P., a 24-year-old white male, pleaded guilty to kidnapping, aggravated assault, possession of a weapon, robbery, terroristic threat, and other offenses in connection with the hijacking of a bus. Under New Jersey (where the offense occurred) law, that defendant faced a mandatory sentence because the offense involved a pistol.

The history indicates that John P. came to the attention of the mental health system early in childhood, having been referred to a clinical social worker at the age of 7 for treatment of elective mutism. The family moved out of state after 18 months of treatment. John returned to his treating social worker at age 21 because of depression and suicidal ideation, precipitated by his parents' divorce and by the death of his grandmother who had been residing with this patient at his uncle's home. Therapy was discontinued after a single session because the patient lacked insurance coverage. Two months later John consulted a psychiatrist who diagnosed him with major depression and obsessive–compulsive personality disorder. The patient was administered an MMPI by this psychiatrist which indicated possible schizophrenia and schizoid personality disorder. The patient did not return to that psychiatrist because he found him too expensive. John subsequently consulted another psychiatrist who placed him on a variety of medications on a trial basis, including Pamelor, Zoloft, Desyrel, and Prozac. John was still taking Prozac at the time of the bus hijacking. He admitted to consuming two or three beers a day and smoking marijuana daily at the time of the offense.

John reported that on the day of the hijacking, he heard voices telling him that he was going to be late for work and to "hurry up." He stated that he did not tell his psychiatrist about his auditory hallucinations, which he had been having for some time. He reported that he was afraid that he was being followed while walking in the street or driving. He stated that he had a gun in his pocket at the time of the hijacking because it had been his practice to take the weapon to work with him for protection while he walked around the city at lunchtime. He stated that as he boarded the bus on his way to work on the day of the offense, he experienced an impulse to threaten the driver with the gun and tell him to drive directly to the downtown area. He stated that when the only other passenger pulled the buzzer to get off at his stop, he pointed the gun at him and warned him to sit down. He reported that he instructed the driver to stop at a corner that was a block away from his work site and that as he left the bus he gave the driver $2, telling him, "This is for your trouble." He stated that after hiding the gun in a relative's car in the parking lot, he went to work and that he eventually became so absorbed in what he was doing that he forgot about the incident. He stated that later in the day, when he heard some of his coworkers talking about the bus hijacking, he thought to himself, "Who would do such a silly thing?" He added that as the detectives who arrested him related the details of the offense to him, his memory of the incident returned. He was placed on suicide watch at the county jail and was eventually transferred to a state psychiatric hospital forensic evaluation unit for 7 months, during which time he decompensated when he was placed on Prozac.

John's MCMI-II record was as follows: 8A 8B 2 ** 1 6B 3 6A 5 + 4 7 // C ** S * P // - ** D T * - // SS ** - *. The overall picture is that of an extremely unstable individual whose interpersonal relations are characterized by friction, fear, and oppositionalism, and who sets himself up for failure and humiliation. The elevations on Scales 2 (Avoidant), S (Schizotypal), and SS (Thought Disorder) indicate a schizophrenic personality structure in which reality-oriented thought processes are invaded by irrational, infantile, unrealistic modes of thinking that result in gross impairments of adaptation. The bus hijacking to which John pleaded guilty illustrates several features of a psychotic break with reality. First, he reported experiencing auditory hallucinations, although he denies that the voices he was hearing commanded him to perform any particular action. John committed a completely irrational act with a high probability of detection. The act did not result in any tangible gain to him because he admitted that there would have been no negative consequences if he had arrived at work late that morning. John's poor reality testing and highly punitive superego (e.g., Scale 8B) are illustrated by the fact that he found it necessary to deposit $2 in the change box upon exiting the vehicle. From a psychological point of view, this bus hijacking was an expression of the mental turmoil of a schizophrenic whose psychosis had been precipitated into active form by the loss of his grandmother and his parent's divorce. Further, in view of his self-defeating personality tendencies, it is also likely that this act represented a wish to be apprehended and placed in a secure setting where he could receive appropriate medication and supervision.

CASE 4.6. CAPITAL MURDER: MITIGATING FACTORS IN THE PENALTY PHASE

Roger P., a 20-year-old white male, was convicted of the murder of his 2-year-old stepdaughter. An autopsy revealed that the child died as a result of multiple blunt force injuries with lacerations of the rectal and genital areas. The state sought the death penalty on the grounds that the child's death was allegedly the result of the defendant's having vaginally and anally raped her. Roger had a long history of involvement with the special education and juvenile justice systems and considerable background history was available not only for him but for other family members as well. An MMPI administered to the defendant's mother approximately 10 years prior to the present evaluation was suggestive of paranoid schizophrenia and of a prepsychotic individual who was adjusting marginally. The mother, who gave birth to Roger at the age of 14, was hospitalized in a state facility on one occasion because of depression and strange behavior. A family member described the defendant's mother as "a functioning psycho" and reported that her paramour regularly beat her and it was likely that Roger witnessed these incidents. This was confirmed by the defendant, who reported memories he dated at approximately age 5 in which he saw his father strike his mother by slapping her in the face. The defendant also stated that he remembered threatening his father with a brick and warning him not to beat his mother again. He stated that his father beat him for this act of defiance. The experience of seeing one's father physically abusing one's mother is a surprisingly common feature in childhood histories of capital murder defendants whose victims are female. Roger was classified emotionally disturbed at the age of 13 and transferred to a special school. He displayed severe behavior problems and immature bowel and bladder control that was too embarrassing for him to discuss even with a psychiatrist. Also noted in the various school and evaluation reports on this child were impulsivity, oppositionalism, attention-deficit/hyperactivity disorder, violent behavior, feelings of worthlessness, minimal insight, and suboptimal judgment. There is a history of physical abuse at age 5½, at which time the defendant was "whipped" until welts appeared on his buttocks. Roger related that his worst memory was being beaten with a switch in front of the entire class by his grandmother when he was in the sixth grade.

Roger's MCMI-II record was as follows: 5 ** 6A 4 2 * 3 1 7 8B + 6B

8A " · ' // P ** S C * // D A ** H * // PP ** · * //. The extreme elevations on Scales A (Anxiety) and D (Dysthymia) are viewed as a reaction to the subject's lengthy incarceration while awaiting trial. Elevations on these scales are not uncommon among jail inmates accused of serious offenses. It is of considerable interest that Roger's response set, as indicated by his BR score of 90 on Desirability (Scale Y), is one of attempting to create a favorable impression and might initially suggest an invalid profile. Nonetheless, there are significant elevations on several scales in this record. Thus, the overall picture clearly does not indicate malingering and is interpretable as the manifestation of specific areas of psychopathology despite the subject's marked attempts to present himself as being psychologically healthy. The importance of addressing response sets in situations in which skeptical juries have rejected the defendant's denial of the offense and are assessing his character for purposes of determining a suitable penalty cannot be overstated.

The MCMI-II indicates that this is an excessively egocentric individual who tends to be exploitative of others and who values other people only to the extent to which they meet his need of the moment. In contrast to the stereotypical antisocial personality, however, Roger's MCMI-II record indicates that he suffers from distorted thought processes that result in delusional belief systems, as indicated by the elevations on PP (Delusional Disorder), P (Paranoid), and S (Schizotypal) and, to some extent, the elevation on A (Anxiety) and C (Borderline) as well. This is an individual whose ego functioning is impaired, who is highly mistrustful of others, and who tends to project his own hostility onto others and then act upon these projections with a profound loss of differentiation between external reality-based interpersonal cues and his own inner world of poorly controlled aggressive impulses and vague thought processes. In light of this dynamic, the extreme elevation on Scale 5 (Narcissistic) is interpreted as reflecting the defensive paranoid grandiosity of this man that serves to compensate for the painfully humiliating self-perceptions of worthlessness, failure, and inadequacy, as well as the social consequences of bowel and bladder incontinence discussed in his school evaluation reports. In terms of conveying to a jury that this defendant's behavior was influenced by powerful psychological factors, it is of no small significance that his mother's MMPI, administered 10 years earlier, suggested that she herself suffered from paranoid schizophrenia.

CASE 4.7. USE OF THE MAPI IN A DURESS DEFENSE

Bill T., seen for evaluation at the age of 18, had been detained at a youth shelter and subsequently at the county jail since age 14 for the murder of a 12-year-old girl during the course of a burglary. According to Bill's statement to the police and the accounts of the victim's family, Bill had been friends with the victim's 14-year-old brother and had visited the house several times. The weekend prior to the homicide, Bill had been the family's guest at a concert.

Bill was a disorganized adolescent who displayed behavior problems at school. His social history indicates that his father disciplined him in an abusive manner and that he was alienated from his mother. Bill established a relationship with Chuck, a 21-year-old man from the neighborhood, with whom he began to spend a good deal of time. This relationship served a number of emotional needs for Bill, including self-esteem enhancement from the status of hanging out with an older man, and the emotional nurturance and opportunities for identification associated with having a father surrogate. Although both parties denied that there was ever any overt sexual component to the relationship, Chuck would take Bill to his apartment and share pornographic magazines with him while they smoked marijuana. According to Bill, it was a batch of pornographic magazines that led to the burglary during which he murdered the victim. Bill had agreed to sell some of the magazines at his school for Chuck; however, before he could distribute them, his father found them in his room and confiscated them. Bill's friend threatened him with both physical harm and the ending of their relationship unless he made good on the money for the magazines. According to Bill, when he informed Chuck that he knew where he could lay his hands on some money, Chuck pressured him to rob the house.

During the course of visits to the victim's house, Bill learned where the family kept their supply of cash and also learned their daily routine for leaving the house. He knew that the family's Rottweiler would be in the house and even though the dog knew him, he brought along a knife in case he was attacked. What he did not reckon on was that his friend's younger sister often stayed in the house for a while after the rest of the family left. When Bill encountered the victim in the house, he told her to back off and threatened her with the knife. According to his account of the murder, the victim began striking him and he fended her off with his hands until he plunged the knife into her. He reported that the rest of the incident was a blur in his memory. The autopsy disclosed that the victim had been stabbed 95 times.

At the time of the trial, delayed for a few years because of juvenile court proceedings and appeals concerning waiver of the matter to adult court, the specific referral question had nothing to do with the question of the defendant's mental state at the time of the offense. Rather, the issue was whether Bill had committed the burglary voluntarily or under duress, with the duress having been imposed by Chuck. Legally, this issue spelled the difference between felony murder, carrying a mandatory 30-year exposure, and lesser offenses; if the defense could prove that Bill was not responsible for the burglary, the homicide would not have been committed during the course of a felony. Under the relevant statute, "it is an affirmative defense that the actor engaged in the conduct charged to constitute an offense because he was coerced to do so by the use of, or a threat to use, unlawful force against his person or the person of another, which a person of reasonable firmness in his situation would have been unable to resist" (New Jersey Rev. Stat. Ann. § 2C:2-9, 1982).

Bill's MAPI record was as follows: 8 ** 6 4 * 2 + 5 " 3 7 1 // G ** B * H A + D E C F " · // SS TT ** UU WW * //. The preponderance of positive endorsements of items indicating social alienation, behavioral problems, and emotional difficulties, resulted in a DSM-III-R diagnosis of borderline personality disorder in the computerized narrative report. This was consistent with other test findings and details of Bill's case history. At this point it became necessary to go beyond the diagnostic testing and case data to understand how the circumstances of the case might have amounted to coercion that the then 14-year-old Bill T. would have been unable to resist. In addition to the threat of physical force, the situation confronting Bill contained a perhaps even more potent psychological threat relating to his borderline personality disorder.

Millon (1981) states that borderlines are scattered and poorly integrated, "responding as a child would to every passing interest or whim and shifting from one momentary course to another" (p. 349). Their lack of a stable sense of personal identity causes them to become exceedingly dependent on others, with the consequence that "they become inordinately vulnerable to separation from these external sources of support" (p. 349). Further, Millon writes that borderlines "are exceedingly fearful that others will depreciate them and cast them off" and "events that stir up these fears may precipitate extreme efforts at restitution such as idealization, self-abnegation and impulsive anger" (p. 350). Finally, "the intolerance of being abandoned and the feeling of emptiness and aloneness consequent to the borderline's failure to maintain a secure and rewarding dependency relationship, cumulate into a reservoir of anxiety, conflict, and anger. Like a safety valve, these tensions must be released either slowly or through periodic and often impulsive outbursts against others" (p. 352). Thus, the threat facing Bill of abandonment by his friend, drug associate, and father surrogate was a circumstance that attacks a specific vulnerability of the borderline. The threat of abandonment typically precipitates a psychological crisis in such patients, as well as provoking them to desperate measures in order to avert the threatened abandonment. To an abused 14-year-old who gravitated toward a permissive 21-year-old as a surrogate father, the threat of abandonment, coupled with the threat of physical harm, constituted enormous pressure, creating a desperation to avoid the threatened consequences. The ultimate legal issue of whether this constituted coercion that a person of reasonable firmness in the situation would be unable to resist is, of course, a matter for the finder of fact to decide and not the expert witness, who can only educate the jury as to the emotional factors involved.

CASE 4.8. ELEMENTS OF THE CHARGES IN A CAPITAL MURDER CASE

Karen C., a 22-year-old white female, was accused of the murder of her mother. The state sought the death penalty in this case because of events that took place after the homicide rather than any characteristic of the alleged criminal act itself. The circumstances of the case are as follows. Several months after moving out of her mother's home to live with her divorced father and stepmother in another state, the defendant returned to her mother's house carrying a pistol that she had taken from her stepmother's closet. When the mother returned to the house, she had a confrontation with the defendant that involved Karen menacing her mother with the gun. During this confrontation, a shot was fired that killed the mother. In this unusual case, the data provided by the psychological examination were not to be used to address the defendant's mental state at the time of the offense or to develop mitigating factors for the penalty phase; rather, they were to be used to help establish motive, which would affect a particular aspect of the alleged offense.

In Karen's account of the incident to the police, she accidentally discharged the weapon as her mother was walking away, striking her in the back and killing her instantly. Upon determining that her mother was dead, she dragged her body from the hall into a spare bedroom. Karen then went through her mother's purse and removed her credit cards and car keys. Next, she telephoned her fiance and arranged to spend the following night at an expensive motel with him. She spent the next day shopping for a negligee to wear to the tryst. She drove her mother's car that day and also that evening when she picked up her fiance to take him to the motel. Karen treated him to an expensive dinner and also picked up the motel bill, charging both to her mother's credit card. The following day, Karen made another shopping trip, visited friends, and later had a supper of Chinese food with a 17-year-old male friend in her mother's bedroom. She modeled the outfits that she had bought that day for this friend, who was unaware that the defendant's mother was lying dead in the next room. The following day Karen visited more friends, drove around in her mother's car, and charged more items. Everyone who saw Karen that weekend described her as being in an upbeat mood and as not giving any indication that there was anything wrong.

The state's theory of the case is that Karen murdered her mother for the express purpose of stealing her credit cards and automobile. It is this felony murder aspect of the homicide that, in the state's view, warranted the capital murder charge. From the point of view of the forensic psychologist, this is an exceedingly complex matter, owing to the fact that it was easy for the prosecution to demonstrate that the mother's homicide was followed immediately by a shopping and spending spree using the victim's car and credit cards, a sequence that would lead to the presumption of a robbery motive for the slaying in a typical case. While it is obvious to those with a background in developmental psychology and psychopathology that matricide is invariably the result of complex causes, and is determined largely by factors originating in early childhood and infancy, juries tend to focus on the concrete and immediate: that is, "She killed her" and "She stole her car and ran up a big bill on her credit cards."

Karen presented as a very attractive young woman who, despite the fact that she was incarcerated in the county jail, had her hair done and wore a good deal of makeup. Her appearance was more that of a high school cheerleader than a capital murder defendant and she displayed a somewhat perky manner. She was quite engaging and did her best to impress the examiner positively.

Karen's MCMI-II record was as follows: 4 ** 5 * 6A 6B 8B 7 + 2 8A 1 " 3 // - ** - * // D A ** H * // - ** - * //. No modifier indices were elevated above a BR score of 71; thus the profile was considered to be valid. Turning first to Axis I, what is striking about this record is the elevations on Scales D (Dysthymia) and A (Anxiety), suggesting that Karen was suffering from depression and anxiety. As noted above in the discussion of case 4.6, elevations on these scales are not uncommon in jail inmates awaiting trial on serious charges and should be interpreted as situationally determined rather than indicative of a long-term disorder, unless there are other elements in the history to suggest preexisting conditions. The other noteworthy feature of these elevations is that they contrast markedly with the subject's behavioral presentation, which was upbeat and nonchalant. Thus, the MCMI-II record demonstrates that this young woman does not always display her feelings openly, but she is able to present herself according to her upbeat persona even when she is in circumstances that have a negative impact upon her emotional life. Furthermore, the moderate elevation of Scale H (Somatoform) suggests a tendency toward preoccupation with bodily functions in response to anxiety with a somatic expression of the anxiety.

The basic personality scales show elevations on Scales 4 (Histrionic) and 5 (Narcissistic), with Scale 4 being the prominent feature of the clinical picture. The Axis II diagnosis is histrionic personality disorder with narcissistic features. There are no clinically significant elevations on either the severe personality disorder or severe clinical syndrome scales, suggesting that this subject has an intact ego structure. This makes a temporary break with reality due to regression in functioning an unlikely explanation of the circumstances surrounding the offense.

Based on the MCMI-II results, the expert theory offered to counter the accusation that the murder was committed for the express purpose of gain was that the defendant's use of the credit cards, theft of the decedent's automobile, and her shopping/eating/sexual spree were a *reaction* to the murder. Further, this reaction to the murder was dictated by the defendant's personality organization, which determined her characteristic pattern of adaptation and her unique means of coping with the trauma of having committed matricide. The current histrionic personality disorder is the direct descendant of a much older clinical entity, hysteria (Millon, 1981). The hysterical character was connected to a variety of disorders in which a segment of the individual's experiencing ego was in some way dissociated from the content of consciousness. Included under these disorders were such conditions as conversion hysteria (or somatization disorder), fugue state, and multiple personality disorder. A more or less common thread is that the individual dissociates in order to rid consciousness of some unpleasant content. A well-recognized characteristic of histrionic personalities in our present nosological classification is that they are adept at repressing content while expressing a good deal of affect, thus relieving psychic tension through a direct discharge of affect. Furthermore, the tendency of histrionic personality-disordered patients to seek novelty and stimulation facilitates this tendency to repress content and to relieve tension by discharge of affect by a pattern of flooding oneself with stimulation that crowds out the unacceptable content and replaces it with pleasant, exciting, intensely emotional evocative experiences.

Karen's realization that her mother was lying dead in front of her, and that she was the author of the deed, was a trauma that precipitated a dissociative flight into reality in order to achieve a repression of the traumatic material. It is of considerable interest that every person with whom Karen came into contact that weekend described her as being in an upbeat mood, a feat that would have been virtually impossible for an individual without a personality disorder to accomplish. In order to defend against the traumatic content, Karen flooded herself with external stimulation. As long as she was having a good time, she was able to keep the horrible images at bay, not in the sense of entering a fugue state or developing an alter personality but through a strategy of losing herself in immediate experience. During this weekend, if anyone were to have asked Karen whether her mother was alive or dead, she certainly would have been able to respond in a reality-oriented manner. Her response to the trauma was not to lose contact with reality but to attempt to flee in a way that was consistent with her personality organization and characteristic style of adaptation. Thus, whatever the complex reasons behind the shooting of her mother, Karen certainly did not commit the act for the purpose of robbing her. The events cited by the prosecutor as proving that robbery was the purpose behind the murder are made comprehensible through this defendant's MCMI-II results.

CASE 4.9. USE OF THE MACI
FOR MITIGATION AT SENTENCING

Darlene is an 18-year-old female whose reckless driving resulted in the death of a 16-year-old male passenger. Two other adolescent passengers in the vehicle were slightly injured. Darlene was charged with one count of homicide and two counts of attempted homicide on the basis of her asking the other occupants of the vehicle moments before the crash, "What would you do right now if I tried to kill us?" One of the witnesses reported that Darlene had just had an argument with her ex-boyfriend, whom she dropped off moments before the accident and immediately before asking the passengers what they would do if she were to try to kill them. Compounding the situation among Darlene and her friends was the fact that this boyfriend had impregnated the other young woman in the car; this woman and the ex-boyfriend had been taunting the defendant about their relationship. Darlene admitted to having asked the others the question, and also that she deliberately sped up as they were approaching a narrow street. She insisted that she did not intend to kill or injure anyone, but that the accident was merely the result of her having misjudged how much room she had as they approached the street and her inability to swerve out of the way of parked cars on both sides of the street. Darlene's attorney felt that it would be counterproductive to attempt to present any type of mental health defense in this matter, given the circumstances, but that the defendant would be aided by whatever the psychological examination disclosed in the way of mitigating circumstances.

Darlene was seen approximately 1 month after the accident. She presented as a chunky, ungainly looking adolescent who wore thick glasses and had a cast on her left arm, which had been injured in the accident. Her affect was muted and her mood moderately depressed. She related appropriately to the examiner and was cooperative as a test and interview subject. Darlene related a history of emotional deprivation and exposure to traumatically aggressive scenes in which her father physically attacked her mother. This was compounded by the mother's death due to natural causes when the defendant was 10 years old. Although Darlene's father did not abuse her physically, he did not meet her emotional needs during the period following the mother's death in which he was her sole caretaker. He subsequently married a woman who viewed Darlene as a threat and harassed her. Darlene's stepmother eventually left the home when Darlene's father began to abuse the stepmother, as he had done with his first wife. Following the breakup of the second marriage, Darlene's father spent long periods away from home on gambling junkets to Las Vegas and other places, leaving Darlene to fend for herself. She spent her last 2 years of high school essentially living by herself and often had friends staying with her as a surrogate family. It was one of these friends, 16-year-old Joey, himself the product of a highly dysfunctional family, who died in the accident. Darlene related that Joey had asked her to become his legal guardian so that he could live with her permanently. She reacted to Joey's death by making a suicidal gesture while undergoing treatment in the hospital for the relatively minor injuries that she suffered.

Darlene produced the following MACI record: 9 2B 8B 2A ** 3 8A 1 * - // B ** G H * A E C // FF GG EE ** - * - //. In DSM-IV terms, this adolescent's highest scale scores correspond to dysthymia (Scales 2B and FF), early onset, borderline personality disorder (Scale 9), self-defeating personality disorder (Scale 8B), and depressive personality disorder (Scale 2B). The mitigating factors suggested by this MACI record include the fact that this young woman was suffering from a clinically significant depression, as well as a long-standing depressive pattern of adjusting to her interpersonal environment, that she tends to sabotage her good fortune and set herself up for humiliation and abuse, and that her ability to bind anxiety and tension is very seriously compromised, resulting in a vulnerability to panic attacks (Scale EE) and incapacitating states of emotional upset (Scale FF). In keeping with the referral questions of mitigation only, the clinical report focused solely on a description of this defendant's psychopathology without relating it to mental state at the time of the offense. The overall thrust of the report was to present the subject as a clinically depressed individual who remained at risk for suicidal behavior at the time of the examination. No attempt was made to interpret the events leading up to the accident in light of the subject's psychological problems or family history.

———◆———

Assessing Risk of Dangerousness

We have come a long way since the well-known pronouncement of the prosecution psychiatrist in *Barefoot v. Estelle* (1983) that without having examined the defendant he could state that there was a "one hundred percent and absolute" chance that the defendant would commit future acts of criminal violence that would constitute a continuing threat to society. The Court in that opinion cited the American Psychiatric Association amicus brief that two out of three predictions made by psychiatrists concerning long-term violence were wrong. The Court also cited the work of Monahan (1981), including his statement that the best clinical research currently in existence indicates that psychiatrists and psychologists are accurate in no more than one of three predictions of violent behavior, even among populations of individuals who are mentally ill and have committed violence in the past. The Court rejected the state's psychiatric testimony, stating quite bluntly: "Ultimately, when the Court knows full well that psychiatrist's predictions of dangerousness are specious, there can be no excuse for imposing on the defendant, on pain of his life, the heavy burden of convincing a jury of laymen of the fraud."

Jackson (1989), in a lengthy review of the literature on prediction of violent behavior, states that the accuracy of both clinical and actuarial methods has been consistently poor. Jackson also cites methodological problems and difficulties with definitions as the major factors that negatively affect this research. The review closes with a call for a more scientifically appropriate focus on the correct use of probability theory in framing research designs and applications, as well as a consideration of base rate data. Monahan and Steadman (1994) report that the staff of the MacArthur Foundation adopted Brunswik's lens model as the theoretical framework for their large-scale study of violence prediction. The lens model analyzes prediction problems from multiple perspectives involving cues, predictions, and criterion data. In brief, these perspectives are represented by the multiple correlations of subject-generated cues associated with the variable under consideration (e.g., number of prior arrests, acting out on the ward, or presence of homicidal ideation) with evaluators' predictions, multiple correlations of cues with a criterion variable (e.g., number of arrests for violent behavior postassessment), and correlations of evaluators' predictions with the criterion. Thus, the lens model is sufficiently comprehensive to permit simultaneous assessment of the accuracy of the predictions and the process by which evaluators combine cues in order to formulate their predictions. Monahan and Steadman (1984) cite research demonstrating the validity of such subject characteristics as drug abuse, age, and number of prior arrests in predicting rearrests for violent behavior subsequent to being released into the community.

Hart, Webster, and Menzies (1993), in commenting on the state of research methodology in violence prediction, stress the use of true and false positive and true and false negative rates in assessing outcomes. They recommend calculation of operating characteristics, including positive predictive power and negative predictive power, as standard procedure in all such research. Mossman (1994), in reacting to the comments of Hart et al. (1993), discusses the relationship of BR data to their recommended use of operating characteristics. It is worth noting here that the Millon inventories incorporate all these concepts through the use of scores computed according to standardization sample base rates and validity evidence presented in terms of operating characteristics.

Litwack (1993), on the other hand, points out that there are situations in which the most important assessments of dangerousness are not, and indeed cannot, be based on actuarial data. Litwack argues that the only scientifically rigorous method of obtaining such data would be to release extremely dangerous people into the community, analogous to the ideal way of conducting a predictive validity study of a psychometric test in educational selection. In this instance, however, the researcher does not admit subjects into the institution without regard to their predicted performance but rather lets them out without regard to the predictions. Litwack argues for a commonsense approach to these extreme cases.

In fact, Litwack (1994) has demonstrated how clinicians should be mindful to distinguish between an *assessment* of dangerousness, which is clinically and ethically feasible, and a *prediction* of actual violence, which is fraught with many limitations. He then recommends that clinicians follow three basic guidelines when asked to assess for dangerousness in a forensic case. First, the clinician should obtain details of the defendant's past history of violence and prior treatment response. Second, direct questioning should take place as to the defendant's history of and proclivity toward violence while avoiding one's own biases. Third, BR data should be sought as to the probability that individuals similar to the person being examined (e.g., in diagnosis or discharge status) will act violently if preventive action is not taken.

Toward this end, Rogers, Dion, and Lynett (1992) studied 250 adult subjects' rating of prototypical antisocial personality disorder criteria through factor-analytic techniques. They found that an aggressive behavior factor, which included items relating to such characteristics as violence, cruelty, and fighting with a weapon, accounted for a substantial portion of the variance. This type of research suggests an alternative approach to the assessment of violence potential in forensic contexts, namely, focusing on personality disorders and traits rather than the more commonly studied Axis I clinical syndromes. Maloney (1985) states:

> It must be stressed that major mental illnesses such as psychosis or organic brain syndrome do not tend, in and of themselves, to predispose individuals toward violent behavior. On the other hand, personality disorders (primarily Antisocial Personality Disorders) do seem to predispose an individual to such acting out. The examiner in assessing the future risk of an individual, must consider carefully data suggesting a personality disorder (e.g. from an MMPI profile). (p. 77)

Indeed, recent findings from research sponsored by the MacArthur Foundation indicates that while there are higher arrest rates among patients released from inpatient mental hospitals than for the general population, a consistent relationship between violence and a specific psychiatric diagnosis emerges primarily for substance abuse and antisocial personality disorder (Monahan, 1992).

Given the current state of research on the Millon inventories, examiners do not have to infer personality disorders from artificially constituted configurations of MMPI scales but can make such diagnoses on the basis of instruments (i.e., MCMI-II and MACI) developed specifically to focus on personality disorders, both from a social learning theoretical approach and in terms of the ultimate learned treatise, DSM-IV. Thus, even in the absence of specific BR data as to the prevalence of violent behavior within various personality disorders, as opposed to the population at large, psychologists can state that an individual whom they have diagnosed as having a certain personality disorder presents a greater than normal risk for such acting out because that diagnostic group is characterized by this trait. Although this approach lacks the statistical precision that represents the ideal in forensic assessment, it does address the commonsense problem cited by Litwack (1993, 1994) while avoiding the type of subjective absolutism that scuttled the dangerousness testimony in *Barefoot* (1983). And, given the present state of knowledge in this area, this is for all practical purposes the limit as to what forensic experts can say on the issue of an individual's potential future dangerous behavior.

Profile Evidence

In Chapter 3, we discussed the problems with profile evidence within the context of case law in which the Millon inventories were cited. Because of the importance of recognizing the limitations in such evidence and because forensic practitioners may find themselves asked to perform such an evaluation in a criminal case, we expand on our earlier comments here.

Attorneys occasionally refer a client to an expert for the purpose of demonstrating that the client does not fit the "psychological profile" of individuals who commit the particular alleged offense. Psychological test findings are sometimes presented as indicating that the defendant does or does not fit the presumed profile for a certain class of offenders, and this use of test data has provoked heated professional debate as to its scientific legitimacy as a basis for expert testimony. Among the issues raised are those of the relevance of such testimony to the ultimate issue before the trier of fact, the adequacy of the scientific evidence for offender "profiles," the legitimacy of inferring anything about an individual's guilt or innocence regarding a specific act based on profile evidence, invasion of the province of the jury, and whether the use of such evidence unduly prejudices juries by implying "scientific proof" of an individual's guilt or innocence.

A New Jersey Supreme Court decision, *New Jersey v. Cavallo* (1982), offers opinions on the issues of relevance, scientific acceptability, and jury prejudice and confusion. In this matter, the two defendants were indicted for abduction, sodomy, rape, and other offenses arising from an incident in which a married woman, who was 2 months pregnant, was abducted from a bar. The defendants asserted that the victim accompanied them willingly and that the sexual activity was consensual. In the absence of witnesses, the decision focused on the relative credibility of the defendants and the victim. Defendant Cavallo offered the testimony of a psychiatrist who was to give the opinion that Cavallo did not have the psychological traits of a rapist. The trial judge refused to allow the testimony under Rule 47 of the New Jersey Rules of Evidence, which states that character trait evidence is admissible only when the trial judge rules that a proper foundation has been laid for the testimony. In this case, the trial judge did not feel that the expert had sufficient expertise to give the proposed opinion. Further, the state of New Jersey argued that the proffered evidence was irrelevant in that testimony regarding whether Cavallo did or did not fit the characteristics of a rapist had no bearing on whether he may have committed this offense on that particular occasion. The New Jersey Supreme Court found that the proffered testimony was indeed relevant in that favorable character evidence has some tendency to create doubt as to whether the defendant committed that alleged offense. Under the evidentiary rules, the relevance of character evidence offered for the purpose of drawing inferences as to the conduct of a person on a specified occasion is assumed.

Turning to the issue of scientific adequacy, the court cited a prior decision, *State v. Hurd* (1981), that scientific evidence is admissible if the mode of analysis has "sufficient scientific basis to produce uniform and reasonably reliable results and will contribute materially to the ascertainment of the truth." The court assessed the scientific adequacy of the proffered testimony of Cavallo's expert according to whether particular mental characteristics exist peculiar to rapists and whether psychiatrists can determine whether an individual possesses these characteristics through a psychiatric examination. The court expressed serious concern over the possibility that juries would accord excessive weight to unreliable scientific testimony because the evidence is labeled "scientific" and "expert." In addition, the court wished to avoid a battle of the experts in which, if the defense were allowed to introduce this testimony, the state would locate a psychiatrist willing to give the contrary opinion, thus diverting the trial court's attention from the central issue of guilt or innocence to the issue of reliability of this type of expert evidence. The *Cavallo* court specifically stated "in so subjective a field as psychiatry, the experts are bound to differ."

The court noted that the defense did not offer any scientific treatise in support of the propositions that there are mental characteristics peculiar to rapists and that such characteristics can be reliably assessed through a psychiatric examination. Relying on precedents from other jurisdictions, the court in *Cavallo* held that it is not generally accepted that psychiatrists possess such knowledge or capabilities and that the defense therefore did not meet its burden of proof that the proffered testimony is based on reasonably reliable scientific premises.

Turning from "subjective" psychiatric opinion based on interview examinations to the results of reliable and valid psychological testing, the question is whether the scientific basis of psychometric profile evidence is sufficiently persuasive to qualify as admissible in courts of law. In considering this issue, it is useful to consider one of the most incisive comments ever offered concerning the judgment processes of psychologists who state conclusions in terms of probabilities. Wiggins (1973) states that it is common for psychologists to confuse the conditional probability of the hypothesized attribute given the data (HD) with the conditional probability of the data given the attribute (DH). In other words, many opinions, including expert opinions delivered on the witness stand that assert that there is a particular probability that the individual has a particular characteristic (e.g., schizophrenia, antisocial personality disorder, or inability to serve adequately as the caretaker of a child) given an observed diagnostic sign (e.g., poor form quality on the Rorschach, history of multiple convictions, or human figure drawn with visible genitalia), are grossly inaccurate. The inaccuracy resides in confusing the respective probabilities, for example, confusing the probability that an individual suffering from schizophrenia will produce a Rorschach record with poor form quality with the probability that an individual whose Rorschach record has poor form quality is suffering from schizophrenia.

Assuming for the sake of argument that schizophrenic Rorschach subjects produce a record with poor form quality 90% of the time, it is not appropriate simply to state without elaboration, "the subject's Rorschach record is characterized by poor form quality, which is a feature found in the Rorschach records of ninety percent of schizophrenics tested with this instrument." The average layperson, to say nothing of the average psychologist, will process this statement as indicating that there is a 90% probability that the individual is schizophrenic when in fact that inference is not in any way possible based solely on the cited percentage. The cited percentage is an example of what Wiggins refers to as P(DH), whereas the expert's implied conclusion is an example of P(HD). The jury certainly does not know that poor form quality is also observed in learning disabled subjects, the mentally retarded, depressed subjects, glib uncooperative antisocial subjects, and a host of others who are not schizophrenic (Exner, 1991). Probability evidence can be powerfully persuasive both when used appropriately and when used inappropriately; it is also a tricky "two-edged sword," as will be seen in Chapter 6. Wiggins's comment should guide experts' use of such evidence.

Cohen (1994) discusses this curious phenomenon in terms of syllogistic logic and also in terms of Bayesian logic as applied to the misinterpretation of the probability of a false positive, given the overall diagnostic accuracy of a psychological test. He also states that this error, couched in terms of the probability of the truth of the null hypothesis in a statistical test given a significant result, is common in many textbooks.

Peters and Murphy (1992) discuss cases in which profile evidence has been accepted by courts for the purpose of demonstrating that a defendant is unlikely to have committed the alleged offense. They cite the California Supreme Court opinion in *People v. Stoll* (1989) as being the leading case in this area, which they characterize as a minority view on the admissibility of profile evidence. The reader will remember from the discussion in Chapter 3 that the *Stoll* decision involved the admissibility of an expert opinion based, in part, on use of the MCMI.

Also cited by Peters and Murphy is the case of *United States v. St. Pierre* (1987) as an example of judicial recognition of the paucity of research evidence in support of profile testimony. In that case, the motion of the appellant to be evaluated for the purpose of determining whether he fit the profile of a sex offender was denied. In a related case, *In re Arrigo* (1986), a psychologist who had examined a father accused of sexually molesting his two preschool age sons concluded that the defendant suffered from poor impulse control, lacked empathy for others, employed denial, had sexual problems, and felt depressed and inferior. The psychologist testified that she had developed a profile based on her examination of 18 incest offenders, and that the accused fit this profile as someone capable of sexual abuse. The trial court held that this number of cases was an insufficient statistical basis on which to establish an adequate profile and rejected the evidence as lacking adequately established reliability. Finally, Peters and Murphy (1992) cite a dramatic instance of the fallibility of profile-based conclusions. In *State v. Shearer* (1990), the Oregon Court of Appeals ruled that a psychologist's opinion that the accused did not match a pedophile profile and did not have any serious sexual disorders was properly impeached with evidence that the psychologist had given a similar opinion in a prior case and that the defendant had later admitted to the sexual abuse.

Two other cases cited by Peters and Murphy (1992) bear on the issues of relevance and invasion of the province of the jury. In *In re Cheryl H.* (1984), a psychiatrist gave the MMPI and Tennessee Self Concept Scale to an individual accused of molesting his daughter. The expert testified that the defendant displayed the traits of passive dependency, guardedness, and defensiveness found in 85% of 200 fathers found to have sexually abused their daughters in a study by the UCLA Family Support Program. The appellate court threw out this testimony and questioned its logic as speculative. The court also found that the relevance of this evidence was so marginal as to be easily overcome by the tendency to mislead the trier of fact into fallacious reasoning. In *Pendleton v. Commonwealth* (1985), a defendant who was convicted of sexually molesting his two daughters over a period of years appealed on the grounds that psychological profile testimony had been inappropriately excluded. The appellate court, affirming the conviction, wrote that the proffered opinion as to the probability that the defendant had committed the alleged acts was improper as it constituted an opinion on the ultimate fact. The court ruled that such testimony invades the province of the jury as being a factual conclusion on the ultimate issue of guilt of innocence, which can only be decided by consideration of all the facts. Peters and Murphy (1992) cite a number of other cases demonstrating that courts feel the probative value of such evidence is outweighed by the danger of unfair prejudice, confusion of the issues, and misleading the jury, despite the fact that the evidence may meet the tests of relevance and scientific reliability.

In their review of studies of offender profiles, Murphy and Peters (1992) conclude that there is literature that establishes the consistency of sex offender profiles for the MMPI. However, they raise several questions that bear on the validity of making predictions based on these profiles. Most important, these authors ask how specific such profiles are to sex offenders. They cite studies by Quinsey, Arnold, and Pruesse (1980) and Dahlstrom, Welsh, and Dahlstrom (1972) which show that child molester "profiles" are also found in rapists, murderers, arsonists, and property offenders and, in fact, are commonly seen in general prison populations and general psychiatric populations. In other words, the use of such profiles to draw conclusions as to whether an individual is a sex offender or as to the probability that an individual committed a specific sexual offense is an egregious violation of Wiggins's caution regarding P(HD) and P(DH) confusion.

The issue of specificity raised by Murphy and Peters (1992) is of great relevance to this discussion of forensic uses of the Millon inventories because specificity is one of the operating characteristics of these inventories explicitly presented in the test manual and much of the published scientific literature on these instruments. The operating characteristics of these psychological tests have the virtue of being quantifiable as percentage probabilities when making statements about an individual's test results, thus overcoming, for certain classes of conclusions, virtually all the judicial objections presented in this section.

FIVE

Civil Applications and Issues

D epending on one's philosophical perspective or prior experiences as a participant in a lawsuit, the process of dispute resolution through civil litigation can be viewed as either a mechanism for obtaining justice or a source of irritation and disdain. It is not uncommon to hear public sentiments that reflect negative attitudes about attorneys and their clients who may be searching for large monetary awards. Regardless of the myths or reality surrounding these views, the civil suit still remains one of the major avenues for seeking legal resolution to a conflict between two or more individuals in the U.S. legal system. In fact, the range of remedies available in civil lawsuits is not limited only to judgments for money.

Disputes between private citizens, which are the major distinguishing characteristic of civil litigation, can take many forms. For instance, spouses may seek a divorce settlement, custody of a child, or some other form of legal relief. Of course, other forms of satisfaction are commonly sought in civil litigation as well, including monetary awards arising from a malpractice action or personal injury claim. Also in civil cases, individuals may often seek what the law refers to as equitable remedies. These forms of relief involve judicial rulings which must be followed by the party against whom the judgment is entered. Examples of equitable relief include temporary restraining orders, injunctions, and findings of fact or declarative judgments. Thus, as an example, a private citizen can petition an administrative law judge to rule, as a matter of law, that he or she is entitled to disability benefits.

In this chapter, the focus is on how the Millon inventories can be used in the context of various civil disputes. As Chapter 4 illustrated, the specific context in which these instruments may be used can have a direct impact on the results obtained and the interpretation of those results. For example, an individual who has claimed personal injury or disability may be motivated to malinger symptomatology in order to obtain financial gain. On the other hand, a parent who wants custody of a child or an individual claiming that a state licensing board has unfairly labeled him or her as an impaired professional has strong motivation to deny or minimize psychopathology.

Given the interactive effects between a psychometric instrument's properties and the context in which it is used, this chapter focuses on the use of the MCMI and MACI in cases involving questions of civil and administrative law. The specific topics to be addressed include (1) disability determination, (2) personal injury, (3) liability issues in assessing suicide and sexual abuse victims, (4) child custody evaluations, (5) screening of corrections and police officer candidates, and (6) assessment of impaired licensed professionals. Again, these particular areas represent a broad range of applications for these instruments, but they do not represent the complete range of potential uses. These topics were selected based on the amount of attention given to each in the literature, as well as the relative importance of these issues in forensic practice. In addition, some sections from the previous chapter on criminal applications have direct implications for civil matters as well. For instance, the section on malingering and deception in Chapter 4 can be referred to when these issues are of concern in evaluations of an individual in a civil matter. As in Chapter 4, selected case examples are also included to illustrate some of the issues and principles discussed.

DISABILITY DETERMINATION

The assessment of patients with physical or medical problems is an important facet of cases in which disability is claimed. A significant amount of attention must be given to the interplay between both personality characteristics and emotional difficulties and the etiology, psychological consequences, and treatment of physical illnesses and conditions. Whereas clinicians working in this area might utilize the Millon Behavioral Health Inventory (MBHI; Millon, Green, & Meagher, 1982b), many have instead chosen to apply the MCMI. The reasons for such an application of the MCMI appear to be due to the larger research database on the MCMI relative to the MBHI (e.g., Blaney, Millon, Morgan, Eisdorfer, & Szapocznik, 1990; Briner, Risey, Guth, & Norris, 1990; Herron, Turner, & Weiner, 1986; Jay, Grove, & Grove, 1987; Malec,

Romsaas, Messing, Cummings, & Trump, 1990), the fact that clinical assessment of psychological disorders in medical patients is often directed toward determining whether a mental health referral is necessary, and the MCMI's adherence to DSM classification.

Clinical experiences and observations reveal that a common MCMI profile occurs in populations in which physical conditions are present; the so-called spike-H profile. When Scale H (Somatoform) is elevated above a BR score of 74 and all other clinical scales fall below this level, the configuration could be referred to as a spike-H. This clinical codetype is very similar to the well-known "conversion V" on the MMPI/MMPI-2, the shape is just inverted. Clinical experiences have generally shown that if the MCMI and MMPI or MMPI-2 are given together, a spike-H will usually occur if an MMPI 1–3/3–1 codetype is present. The person complains of vague somatic problems that often include fatigue, weakness, dizziness, and sleep difficulties. Low scores on other clinical scales indicative of distress, such as A (Anxiety), D (Dysthymia), N (Bipolar: Manic), R (Posttraumatic stress), SS (Thought Disorder), CC (Major Depression), and PP (Psychotic Delusion), point to the denial of any psychological concerns. Symptoms of physical illness are emphasized to obtain secondary gain. Any psychological difficulties are manifest in the form of physical problems or symptoms. A large degree of denial and repression is usually found, with either Scale 4 (Histrionic) or Scale 7 (Obsessive–Compulsive) on the basic personality scales elevated, reflecting a style in which the person has strong dependency needs that are extremely difficult to acknowledge or recognize. Interpersonal relationships tend to be either superficial and lacking in depth, if Scale 4 is elevated, or emotionally distant, if Scale 7 is elevated. Strong feelings of anger and hostility may also be present but difficult to express. These individuals keep a fairly tight control on these feelings and they are not prone to acting out aggressively. In most instances, they are rigid in their thinking and often try to impress others with their conventional and moralistic ideas. As with the MMPI 1–3/3–1 codetype, these individuals are not good candidates for psychotherapy because they are not psychologically minded and reject any interpretations suggestive of a psychological component to their physical problems. Whether this style reflects a genuine reaction to actual disability or reveals a somatization disturbance will usually be revealed by a thorough history, complete with medical records.

An example of these issues is provided in case 4.3 in Chapter 4. The case is from an evaluation of a woman referred by her attorney to determine whether she was malingering or whether she was disabled and therefore unable to work.

PERSONAL INJURY

A tort, or "civil wrong," in personal injury and liability law is defined by four basic elements: a duty owed by one party to another, a violation of that duty, compensable damages suffered by the injured party, and a proximate cause linking the damages to the violation of the duty. The first of these elements — duty — refers to the responsibility of the defendant in a civil case to behave in such a way as to refrain from causing injury to others. Examples of defendants' duties include keeping walkways free of snow, driving a motor vehicle in a safe manner, and, for psychotherapists, refraining from sexual exploitation of patients. Examples of violations of a duty include allowing snow to remain for several days on a walkway, thus causing a hazardous condition, operating a motor vehicle in a reckless manner, and, for a psychotherapist, having sexual contact with a current or recently terminated patient. Compensable damages refer to those injuries or losses caused by the defendant's tortious behavior for which the plaintiff seeks to be made whole. Finally, proximate cause refers to the causal factor linking the defendant's violation of duty to the damages sustained by the defendant.

In personal injury cases, psychologists are rarely called upon to render opinions as to duty or violation of duty. One exception to this limitation occurs in cases of a clinician's violation of professional or ethical standards, such as instances of sexual exploitation of patients by psychotherapists. In these types of cases, the plaintiff's expert may be asked to discuss the duty of a therapist to provide competent treatment and how certain misconduct constitutes a violation of that duty.

One commonly recognized function of the psychology expert is assessment of the plaintiff's mental condition in connection with the question of compensable damages. Apart from the effects of head trauma, which are more appropriately left to neuropsychologists to determine, the general issues that arise in this type of evaluation include depression, somatic preoccupations, posttraumatic stress disorder, and, of course, malingering.

In many cases the question of compensable damages, insofar as it figures into the expert's testimony, is secondary to that of proximate cause. Consider, for example, an individual who is involved in a motor vehicle collision, sustains physical injuries, and subsequently presents with a severe emotional disorder. In evaluating the plaintiff's emotional disorder, the expert may assess it as an extremely pathological condition with a poor prognosis that will result in more or less constant suffering and incapacitation for the rest of the client's productive years. Even so, the plaintiff is not entitled to any compensation from the defendant unless it can be demonstrated that the collision was the proximate cause of the disorder or that the disorder interacted in some fashion with the physical injuries caused by the collision to compound the effects of those injuries. The proximate cause is sometimes defined as the "near cause," or as "the straw that broke the camel's back." So important is the issue of causation in cases involving psychological disorders that the psychologist is often referred to as the causation expert.

In rendering opinions as to causation, experts sometimes overlook the fact that a preexisting emotional disorder or personality disorder may make the plaintiff more susceptible to certain pathological effects of physical injuries or psychic trauma, even though the accident or other event did not cause the emotional disorder per se. This doctrine is known in tort law as the fragile vessel theory or, alternatively, as the egg-shell skull theory. In the language of legal precedent, "the defendant must take the plaintiff as he [*sic*] finds him [*sic*]" (*Watson v. Rinderknecht*, 1901). In other words, if the defendant's negligently shooting off fireworks results in startling an individual with a heart condition, precipitating a heart attack, the defendant cannot claim to be responsible for nothing more than the psychic pain and annoyance that the startling loud noise would cause in a normal person on the grounds that a person in normal health would not have suffered a heart attack as a result of the defendant's negligent actions.

Thus, it is important to document any preexisting mental conditions in plaintiffs as these may make such an individual less resilient when exposed to traumatic events or injuries. Barton (1985) reports on the case of *Ngai v. United States* (1979), in which a 39-year-old tenured teacher with an 11-year history of schizophrenia contracted Guillani–Barre syndrome (GBS) as a result of a swine flu vaccination. The plaintiff suffered minimal neurological deficits as a result of the vaccination but contended that these deficits nevertheless precipitated a serious psychological reaction, which caused her schizophrenic condition to deteriorate. The government claimed that any deterioration of the plaintiff's condition was unrelated to the GBS but was a natural progression of the preexisting psychotic disorder. The judge ruled that Mrs. Ngai indeed suffered minimal neurological deficits as a result of the vaccination and that she also suffered psychological consequences as a result of not being able to perform her job duties as a result of the neurological damage. The judge further stated that the plaintiff's schizophrenic condition probably combined with her neurological and psychological deficits to interfere with her ability to hold her job. Barton writes, "Without finding an exacerbation of the plaintiff's schizophrenia, the judge declared that the plaintiff's preexisting condition tenuous enough that when the psychological reaction was added to her other problems, the combination was sufficient to reduce her work performance below its previously adequate level" (p. 45).

In rendering opinions as to causation of mental injuries, it is particularly important to avoid such statements as "The client's schizophrenic symptoms are now in evidence once more after a three year period of remission; however, the traumatic injury caused by the defendant played only a minor role in the recurrence of the symptoms, as this client has been suffering from schizophrenia, chronic undifferentiated Type, for many years." A "fragile vessel" will not shatter unless it receives a tap, albeit a light one.

In personal injury cases it is particularly important to list DSM-IV diagnoses for any psychological condition found in examinees. The fondness of the legal system for reducing the complexities of human experience to discrete categories requires this of expert witnesses who testify regarding compensable damages. Often the witness is compelled on cross-examination to provide a specific rationale for diagnosing a client with some disorder, especially when there are insufficient observational data or distorted observational data through biased reporting of fact witnesses. For example, one witness might testify, "Our company's investigator found that the plaintiff is not socially isolated at all; she has been spotted leaving her house in the company of other adults many times in the last six months." It may simply be that the client's relatives are concerned about her social isolation and persuade her to leave the house with them, under protest. In such a case, if avoidant personality disorder, for example, is among the client's preexisting conditions complicating her recovery from the injuries caused by the negligent actions of the defendant, it is important for the witness to be able to adduce some scientific data to justify the diagnosis. It is here that the operating characteristics of a test are of value, as well as the fact that the basic metric of the Millon inventories, the BR score, is framed in such a way as to take into account population base rates, thus increasing diagnostic accuracy over other methods.

Although it is difficult to explain this concept to lay jurors, it is well worth the attempt. An appropriately simple presentation of BR concepts employing such language as "What are the chances that the patient has . . . " and "Once the score reaches this level, the patient resembles those standardization sample cases whose treating clinicians say that they have the disorder" will do a great deal to counter any argument that the witness is being arbitrary in assigning or withholding a particular diagnostic label based on a specific cutoff score.

Finally, it is vital to address the issue of malingering in personal injury cases. Discussion of the Validity and other modifier indices should be presented on direct examination so that the witness has control over the presentation. It should be remembered that recent research shows that the Desirability (Y) and Debasement (Z) scales are not unidirectional, as is asserted in the MCMI-II manual, but that both high and low scores on these two scales are interpretable in regard to the examinees response set. Unusually low Desirability suggests an attempt to present an unfavorable impression on the test and unusually low Debasement suggests an attempt to present a socially desirable facade. However, because of the nature of the BR score on the Millon inventories, specific cutoff levels on the low end of these scales are difficult to derive. Thus, when basing testimony on quantitative data, the cutoffs discussed in Chapter 4 and presented in Table 4.2 are the most useful indicators of malingering, response sets, and other attempts at impression management.

CASE 5.1. SOMATIC PREOCCUPATION IN A CLIENT ACCUSED OF MALINGERING

June, 55-year-old female, is a divorced health care professional who had been out on disability for 3 years at the time of her examination. Originally disabled because of severe carpal tunnel syndrome, she sustained mild head injuries in two automobile accidents subsequent to leaving her job. After the first accident she developed chronic migraine headaches, various physical complaints, memory problems, and dizzy spells accompanied by a clouding of consciousness. She reported seizure-like episodes in which she suffered involuntary jerking of the shoulders, "flashing lights," partial blindness, and impaired speech. She presented at her local hospital emergency room on three occasions upon suffering these episodes and each time extensive neurological testing failed to disclose organic injury or other abnormality. Her most recent episode occurred while she was driving home from an appointment with her treating psychiatrist. She suffered an ophthalmic migraine while driving and fear of another seizure or syncope. June pulled the vehicle off the road for a half hour during which she was in a confused state. Emergency room medical testing was negative for any organic condition that might have produced this constellation of symptoms.

June had been living alone since her last adult child moved out of her home 5 years prior to the examination. Although she had something of a support network among neighbors, she did not have any close friends. Her children were in constant contact with her by telephone but did not visit her frequently. Physically she is an attractive, engaging woman with no obvious handicaps. She comes across as somewhat lonely and needy, expressing a sense of hurt that she is misunderstood by the insurance company physicians, who do not believe that she has any organic problems.

June's MCMI-III record was as follows: - ** 4 * 7 5 + 2B " 3 1 6A 8B 2A 8A 6B // - ** - * // - ** - * // - ** - * //. Although not noted in the summarized record because of reporting conventions for the clinical syndrome scales, the subject's score on Scale H (Somatoform) was 69. Further, Scale X (Disclosure) was 26, Scale Y (Desirability) was 65, and Scale Z (Debasement) was 56.

First, it is noted that this is clearly not a record in which the subject is making a conscious attempt to present herself in a pathological light. Her Disclosure score of 26 indicates that she is being guarded in her responding rather than admitting to a variety of psychological symptoms that she does not in fact have. Her Desirability score of 65 indicates that she is attempting to portray herself in a positive light, and her Debasement score of 56 also rules out any suspicion of malingering.

The Axis II section of the June's MCMI-III record is remarkable for histrionic personality traits. This is a woman who is adept at engaging others by presenting herself as being in distress. Her repeated visits to emergency rooms appear to be, to some degree, an acting out of this pattern, as her mild neurological symptoms provide a plausible and objective basis for her distress, thus making her deserving of the help and attention of others. Histrionic personality disorder patients are also frequently focused excessively on bodily symptoms, reacting in an exaggerated fashion to discomforts that others would simply try to ignore.

Although not high enough to register in the numerical score summary, June's Scale H (Somatoform) score of 69 suggests a preoccupation with somatic concerns. This is a score level that falls somewhat below the classical spike-H pattern noted in case 4.3 and the score configuration does not suggest that this client's symptoms are solely the result of somatic conversion of anxiety.

Viewing her symptoms in conjunction with her history of two head traumas, June's life circumstances as a middle-aged divorcee living alone, and the results of other psychometric testing, the overall picture is that of an individual who is probably suffering from postconcussional disorder (which was also her treating psychiatrist's diagnosis of her) and who is quick to seek the assistance of others by portraying herself as incapacitated. The chief therapeutic task is to encourage this client to cope with her symptoms without excessive anxiety or dependence on others. In terms of causality issues, the patient's current problems are clearly the result of her head injuries, with her recovery complicated by her preexisting histrionic personality traits. Whereas a less dependent individual (it will be recalled that histrionic personality disorder is the active variant of Millon's dependent dimension) would have achieved a fuller recovery, the head trauma precipitated a series of events resulting in this particular patient's current psychological distress and exacerbation of her dependence on others and is therefore the proximate cause. Precisely *which* head trauma out of the two accidents was responsible is a question that is well beyond the scope of this examination, but one that is for the trier of fact to determine.

CASE 5.2. SUICIDAL IDEATION IN A WRONGFUL TERMINATION ACTION

Aaron, a 50-year-old married, African American male, sued his former employer after being terminated when the company was bought out by another company. There is a prior history of litigation against the company as a result of a hand injury that Aaron sustained after having been employed there for 2 years. On that occasion, his hand became caught in a machine while he was feeding material into it, causing severe injuries requiring the amputation of three fingers and a loss of part of the palm on his nondominant left hand. He was awarded 100% disability for that hand injury. He sued the company and also the manufacturer of the equipment causing the injury and settled both cases prior to trial. He returned to work at the company 9 months later, performing the same job. The corporate takeover took place when Aaron had been employed there for 21 years. Subsequent to being let go, Aaron learned that he would be replaced by a white employee who lacked many of the client's qualifications and experience in several facets of plant operation and was capable of supervising only one of the plant's departments, whereas he was capable of running any operation within the plant.

Aaron, who had not had any psychological treatment at the time of his severe hand injury, complained of depression, sleeplessness, excessive nervousness, marital problems, and suicidal ideation attributable to his termination, which he alleged was racially discriminatory. He had not consulted a mental health professional for treatment of these conditions, although his attorney sent him for an evaluation by a psychiatrist, who felt that Aaron had been "traumatized" by the termination and that he was suicidal and severely depressed. A subsequent psychological report, also requested by plaintiff's attorney, echoed these findings, including a paragraph that was virtually identical to a paragraph in the psychiatric report. The specific referral questions raised by the defense counsel, who had requested that the plaintiff submit to the present examination, were whether he was at risk for suicidal acting out and whether he had sustained any psychological damage beyond the ordinary suffering associated with being terminated from long-term employment.

Dyer (1991) differentiates among various levels of adverse reactions to events. At the pathological end of the continuum there is trauma proper, defined as an event of such emotional intensity that the individual's psychological coping mechanisms are overwhelmed. A truly traumatic event produces actual physiological changes in the brain's arousal mechanisms and can produce posttraumatic stress disorder (PTSD), with typical oscillation between symptoms reflecting hyperarousal and numbing (James, 1994).

Lower down on the continuum there is the phenomenon of adjustment disorder, which is a pathological reaction to a distressing event or set of circumstances that is beyond the normally expected reaction. The adjustment disorder can manifest in depressed mood, anxiety, behavioral problems, or some combination of these symptoms, but it lacks the specific posttraumatic arousal/numbing constellation of symptoms associated with PTSD. By definition, an adjustment disorder is, at most, of 6 months' duration.

At the mild end of the continuum lie the normal pain and suffering phenomena that are the expectable consequences in normals following an upsetting event or set of life circumstances. For example, one might be driven to distraction by the itching and inconvenience of a leg cast after suffering a serious fracture in a "trip, slip, and fall" case. Although acknowledging the seriousness of such a situation and the individual's degree of annoyance, frustration, and general emotional upset, this can hardly be called a trauma or even an adjustment disorder. It is a normally expectable reaction that should not be psychologized or medicalized by giving it a label it does not warrant. Dyer (1991) proposes the adoption of the Yiddish word *tsouris* as a lay-diagnostic term that accurately depicts this sort of normal pain and suffering, and he discourages the inappropriate application of the term "trauma," including such concoctions as "posttraumatic anxiety neurosis" that appear from time to time in forensic psychiatric and psychological reports.

Aaron relayed during his examination that subsequent to being terminated, he began his own home repair business on a part-time basis. He did telephone solicitation to develop a customer base and also had advertising flyers printed up, which he distributed around his town. He reported that the business did not generate enough money to pay all the family's bills and that this led to a great deal of arguing between him and his wife, who was forced to go to work to take up the slack financially. When questioned about the depression and suicidal idea-tion, Aaron reported that he felt nervous and depressed, primarily about money. He stated that he thought about shooting himself but reported that he did not possess a gun. He commented that he would be "too scared" to shoot himself and added, "I thought maybe I could eat myself to death," and mentioned that actually he had gained a good deal of weight since being terminated from the company. He stated that he did not seek treatment for the depression but just read the Bi-ble a great deal and talked to his mother. He stated, "I don't think I'm a really suicidal person. It's just when things go bad you have thoughts like that." Extensive questioning did not disclose the presence of symp-toms of PTSD. Aaron displayed a normal range of affect during the session and exerted effort on the various tests of the battery.

His MCMI-II record was as follows: · ** · * 3 7 + 1 2 8B 6B 5 " 8A 6A 4 " // · ** · * // · ** D A * // · ** · * //. The BR score for Disclosure (X) was 20, Desirability (Y) 50, and Debasement (Z) 52.

As with the preceding case, this client was being somewhat guard-ed in his responding to the test items, as reflected in his low BR score on Scale X. Scales Y and Z indicate no tendency to skew the results in either a pathological or unrealistically positive direction. Although Aaron did not wish to reveal much about himself in taking the MCMI-II, he clearly was not malingering.

Turning to the Axis I section of the record, his subjective com-plaints of nervousness and depression are corroborated by the eleva-tions on Scales D (Dysthymia) and A (Anxiety). Although not high enough to be included in the summary scoring notation, there is also an elevation on Scale H (BR = 72). This appears to be a result of Aaron's endorsement of items dealing with sleeplessness. It is also to be recalled that he does objectively have a good deal to be concerned about in the somatic area, given his severe hand injury for which he received medi-cal, but not psychological, treatment. It is also important to note that there are no elevations on any of the severe clinical syndrome scales, des-pite the fact that the prior psychological and psychiatric reports depicted him as being one step away from either a mental hospital or a morgue.

The Axis II section of the record sheds some light on the dynam-ics behind this man's dysthymia and anxiety. The elevations on Scales 3 (Dependent) and 7 (Compulsive) suggest a mildly dependent individu-al who looks to others to take care of his needs in exchange for his being a helpful, cooperative subordinate who follows the rules. Indeed, his adaptation appears to have been just that, as indicated by his lengthy term of employment at a company to which he gave 21 years and most of one hand. In such cases, the company often comes to be relied on as a benevolent parent, which would be consistent with Aaron's turning to his mother for advice and comfort rather than consulting a therapist for his depression after being terminated. The act of letting this African American worker go after so many years of loyal service, combined with the act of replacing him with a less qualified white worker, was an insult and rejection on two levels. Beyond the objective level of perceived injustice and racial discrimination, the company had broken its contract with this dependent, conforming man and that abandonment meant that he had lost the acceptance and approval of a somewhat personified and idealized corporate entity that had been an important source of reinforcement for him.

The report to the defense attorney concluded that Aaron was indeed suffering from dysthymia and symptoms of anxiety and that his termination was the main precipitant. The depression was not incapacitating, as the client was able to start his own business and promote it. Had he been less dependent and overly conforming in his interpersonal adaptation style, it is likely that he would not have developed the depressive symptoms. It was further concluded that this client was not suicidal and that he had never been in any danger of self-harming behavior, despite the allegations of plaintiff's experts. Finally, the subject clearly had not been "traumatized" by the termination but had indeed experienced significant financial and marital adversity as a result of being let go.

LIABILITY ISSUES
IN TEST INTERPRETATION

All mental health practitioners recognize the fact that they may be held responsible if their professional conduct fails to meet a certain level of care. In fact, malpractice insurance is a necessity for anyone holding themselves out to others as a service provider. Because the use of such psychological tests as the MCMI and MACI is an essential part of the procedures employed by many professionals, it follows that a duty of care and responsible practice must be followed when using these instruments. The following sections outline some specific issues and concerns that need to be recognized by those who utilize the Millon inventories. By attending to these issues, the practitioner may avoid potential problems that may lead to professional liability. In particular, the following sections discuss specific problems in assessing suicide risk and child abuse.

Suicide Assessment

The assessment of suicide risk is always a difficult task for any clinician because of the complex array of factors involved. Some of the problems interfering with an effective suicide assessment include determining whether the patient is a short-term versus long-term risk, predicting changes in life stressors, and the interaction between family dynamics, severe psychopathology, and suicidal behavior. Although no psychometric instrument can replace a thorough clinical interview and history, some helpful information can be derived from the MCMI and MACI. This information can then be used in other aspects of the overall assessment.

It is important to recognize that the prediction of eventual suicide is not a task at which clinicians are particularly effective. Furthermore, suicide risk cannot be characterized according to a particular diagnostic category (Hawton, 1987; Hendin, 1986). A number of methodological problems have contributed to the lack of research support for psychometrically based indicators of suicide risk. These include inappropriately combining suicide attempters with patients exhibiting only suicidal ideation and the long period that frequently elapses between the time of test completion and eventual suicide.

Despite the lack of strong evidence for the predictive utility of the MCMI (Joffe & Regan, 1989; McCann & Gergelis, 1990; McCann & Suess, 1988) and the lack of research on the MACI generally, the patient responses to individual items and the resulting profile can guide further assessment. The first task in examining test results should include a review of specific items designed to assess suicidal thoughts and feelings directly. On the MCMI-II, four items ask directly about suicide and are presented in Table 5.1. The MCMI-III has two items that ask directly about suicide and are also outlined in Table 5.1. On the MACI, six items involve direct assessment of suicidal feelings and behaviors; these are provided in Table 5.2. It is important for all users of these instruments to routinely check the patient's responses to these items for each and every administration of the test. Even if computer-generated interpretive reports are used, in which the items are scored and reported if endorsed, the clinician should examine these items before sending the answer sheet to NCS for scoring.

The reasons for this practice are both practical and legally relevant. First, although clinicians frequently ask about suicidal ideation or intent in a clinical interview, the test questions may be phrased in such a way as to elicit different aspects of suicidal thought that might not be covered in an interview. For example, recent ideation and chronic thought are differentiated by MACI questions 107 and 156.

TABLE 5.1. MCMI Items with Suicide Content

MCMI-II

  59. I have given serious thought recently to doing away with myself. (True)

  79. Serious thoughts of suicide have occurred to me for many years. (True)

 115. Sometimes I feel like I must do something to hurt myself or someone else. (True)

 136. In the last few years, I have felt so guilty that I may do something terrible to myself. (True)

MCMI-III

 154. I have tried to commit suicide. (True)

 171. I have given serious thought recently to doing away with myself. (True)

Note. Items are from the *Manual for the Millon Clinical Multiaxial Inventory—II* and the *Millon Clinical Multiaxial Inventory–III Manual,* by Theodore Millon, 1987 and 1994, Minneapolis, MN: National Computer Systems. Copyright 1987 and 1994 by Theodore Millon. Reprinted by permission.

Thus, the patient's responses can be used as a stimulus for further exploration of suicidal thoughts and feelings in subsequent interviews. Second, some patients may be unwilling or unable to communicate their thoughts or feelings adequately in an interview, due to such factors as vague or confused thought processes, unelaborative speech, or evasiveness. Consequently, some patients may be capable of expressing their feelings about suicide more effectively through responses to these questions, whereas others may be willing to express themselves only in a noninterpersonal situation such as taking a self-report test. Finally, clinicians frequently rely on a profile interpretation and avoid examining specific items. If a patient was successful in suicide and the clinician addressed lethality adequately in the interview yet failed to examine the items in Tables 5.1 and 5.2, the clinician would be caught in a

TABLE 5.2. MACI Items with Suicide Content

  16. I think everyone would be better off if I were dead. (True)

  54. I sometimes get so upset that I want to hurt myself seriously. (True)

  88. Killing myself may be the easiest way of solving my problems. (True)

 107. More and more often I have thought of ending my life. (True)

 123. I have tried to commit suicide in the past. (True)

 156. I've given thought to how and when I might commit suicide. (True)

Note. Items are from the *Millon Adolescent Clinical Inventory Manual,* by Theodore Millon, 1993, Minneapolis, MN: National Computer Systems. Copyright 1993 by Theodore Millon. Reprinted by permission.

difficult position if, during subsequent civil litigation, an opposing attorney encountered a positive response to one or more of the items. Users of the tests can avoid such a situation by routinely screening face-valid items, discussing any noteworthy responses with the patient, conducting any additional questioning as appropriate, and integrating these findings into the overall evaluation of lethality.

In addition, research on suicide and the MCMI reveals that specific profiles may be suggestive of suicidal ideation or intent which can be explored in more detail through interviewing and history taking (Joffe & Regan, 1989; McCann & Gergelis, 1990; McCann & Suess, 1988). Configurations on the basic personality scales, which involve Scales 2A (Avoidant), 8A (Passive–Aggressive), and 8B (Self-Defeating), or a codetype consisting of Scales 1 (Schizoid), 2A (Avoidant), 3 (Dependent), 8A (Passive–Aggressive), and/or 8B (Self-Defeating), may reflect increased feelings of suicide. Likewise, when Scale C (Borderline) is elevated above a BR of 75, suicidal ideation may be present. In addition, profile patterns that suggest strong self-deprecatory thoughts or feelings, as indicated by Scales Z (Debasement), D (Dysthymia), R (Posttraumatic Stress), or CC (Major Depression), may point to heightened feelings of hopelessness and suicidal rumination. These profile configurations can be used to explore issues of lethality in more depth; however, they are by no means the only ones that occur in patients with suicidal symptomatology. A variety of codetypes may be found in patients for whom suicide is an issue. Nevertheless, there is no specific item, scale elevation, or profile codetype that has been shown to be predictive of a future suicide attempt or completed suicide.

Assessment of Child Sexual Abuse Victims

It comes as no surprise to anyone that professionals are placed in the position of being required by state law to make a report to state authorities in cases in which the sexual abuse of a child is suspected (Melton et al., 1987). Although there are documented cases in which mental health professionals have been unsuccessfully sued for making such reports (see Chapter 3 for one such example), courts have taken a liberal view of the actions of professionals in making such reports and have held on public policy grounds that professionals should not be dissuaded from making reports. Moreover, child abuse reporting laws waive any confidentiality or privilege that might otherwise prevent a professional from making a report (Guyer & Ash, 1985). Therefore, a professional who acts in good faith in making a report will not be held liable.

It is rare to see a court decision in which a clinician has been sued for failure to report an incident of abuse, though county agencies and

TABLE 5.3. MACI Items with Child Abuse Content

14. I feel pretty shy telling people about how I was abused as a child. (True)
55. I don't think I was sexually molested when I was a young child. (False)
72. I hate to think about some of the ways I was abused as a child. (True)
129. I'm ashamed of some terrible things adults did to me when I was young. (True)
137. People did things to me sexually when I was too young to understand. (True)

Note. Items are from the *Millon Adolescent Clinical Inventory Manual,* by Theodore Millon, 1993, Minneapolis, MN: National Computer Systems. Copyright 1993 by Theodore Millon. Reprinted by permission.

other child advocacy services have been the defendant in litigation for failing to take appropriate action in tragic instances in which a child was harmed or killed by an abusive parent or guardian. Though individuals who use the Millon inventories may find some solace in these trends, the legally relevant issue still remains of face-valid items dealing with abuse on the MACI. Table 5.3 lists five items on the MACI that ask directly about sexual and physical abuse in adolescents. As with the suicide items, the clinician would be wise to examine the responses to these items in Table 5.3 for each administration of the test, prior to sending the answer sheet for scoring. Some teenagers may deny ongoing abuse in an interview for such reasons as embarrassment, defensiveness, or denial. However, they may be disposed to admitting to such issues in a less threatening manner, as in responses to questions on an impersonal questionnaire.

This procedure can be of particular importance for professionals working in agencies that may come under investigation later should a child be injured or the abuse alleged be ignored. If records document no abuse but one or more of the MACI abuse items are endorsed, such evidence may be difficult to explain in court. Therefore, examination of responses to these individual items and exploration of any noteworthy responses on subsequent interviews would constitute sound forensic and clinical practice and may be able to provide even greater protection to an abused child.

CHILD CUSTODY EVALUATION

As in several other areas of forensic practice, the psychologist who conducts child custody evaluations is faced with the difficult task of responding to legal questions with information derived from clinical data. Clearly, a detailed discussion of the components that comprise an adequate child custody evaluation is beyond the scope of this chapter. Nevertheless, most scholars of child custody evaluations recognize the potential use of psychological tests in assisting with the complex decisions that must be made in an adequate evaluation (Blau, 1984). Personality instruments such as the MCMI-II can provide the psychologist with valuable information on the parents' personality traits and any possible clinical symptomatology that may impact on the nature of the particular environment they might provide for the child. Likewise, the MACI may be used in evaluating psychological concerns and disturbances in adolescents who may also be involved in the evaluation process.

Although some have questioned the use of the MCMI-II in child custody evaluations because it was developed as a measure of psychopathology, not intended for normal subjects (Ackerman, 1995), this instrument provides important information in these matters. In evaluations in which the nature of the parent–child relationship is to be assessed, the Millon inventories provide information on potential clinical symptoms and personality disturbances that can impact adversely on this relationship. Couples undergoing marital therapy for treatment of relationship difficulties are customarily seen in outpatient settings and by private practitioners. The MCMI-II and MCMI-III normative samples contain a significant number of individuals from these settings, so couples with relationship conflicts are represented in the normative sample. Moreover, because child custody is a highly conflicted situation in which some form of personality disturbances or psychopathology is suspected or presumed, the Millon inventories provide a useful measure of psychopathology that must be considered in making child custody determinations. Therefore, we strongly advocate the use of the MCMI-II in child custody evaluations. This particular use of the instrument is endorsed by Dr. Millon, whose caution against its use with normals refers to applications as a self-exploration tool and in personnel selection (Theodore Millon, personal communication, October 1993).

The important factor to remember when using the MCMI in child custody evaluations is that no single personality trait or group of characteristics ensures that one will be a good or poor custodial parent (Musetto, 1985). As such, because one parent may have a 2A–8A or 5–6A personality codetype, he or she is not necessarily a more or less desirable parent. MCMI results need to be placed in the context of a comprehensive child custody evaluation, one in which direct observations can be made of parent–child interactions such that inferences about one's personality style can be applied to the assessment of both the strengths and the deficits in parenting potential. To take direction from Halon (1990), the child custody evaluation must be comprehensive, with a focus, and with specific questions that must be answered. It would be incorrect to assume that specific MCMI codes or scale elevations are reflective of parenting skills. Nevertheless, the MCMI can add to the evaluation by assessing basic personality styles of parents, screening for areas of psychopathology that may have an impact on the quality of the environment a particular parent might provide, and assessing response styles and levels of overall disclosure in the evaluation process. Given the degree of conflict that is often generated in heated custody disputes, parents tend to put their best foot forward. Thus, MCMI profiles will frequently show evidence of low disclosure and high levels of desirability.

The following case example illustrates many of these issues in defining the focus of an evaluation as well as in using the MCMI-II to assess specific questions.

CASE 5.3. CHILD CUSTODY EVALUATION

Ms. B., a 37-year-old white female, was referred by her attorney for evaluation to assess her suitability as a parent for her 6-year-old son. The legal situation of this case was such that Ms. B.'s husband was seeking sole custody of the child because, as he claimed in his court petition, he felt his wife was emotionally unstable, physically cruel, and severely alcoholic. Ms. B.'s attorney sought an independent psychological evaluation specifically to address her emotional stability, to determine whether she had a problem with alcohol, and to assess her suitability as a parent. Because Ms. B. and her attorney both requested strict discretion and confidentiality, the son was unavailable for evaluation, either alone or with his mother, because it was feared that he might make known to his father the fact that an evaluation was being conducted. Thus, the attorney and Ms. B. were notified prior to beginning the evaluation that because of the inability to assess the parent–child relationship directly, the question of her suitability as a parent could not be addressed. The focus of this evaluation would have to be limited to her emotional stability and alcohol use. Both Ms. B. and her attorney were agreeable to this stipulation.

A revealing history was taken that suggested significant impairment in most of her relationships. She had a history of conduct problems during adolescence, including oppositional behavior and running away from home on more than one occasion. Ms. B. was in her second marriage and both marriages were characterized by severe conflict which surrounded her resentment over spouses limiting her activities outside the home, such as socializing with friends and working. Frequent emotional outbursts, including physical fights with her siblings, extramarital affairs, and periods of several days when she would leave home in an angry tirade characterized the relationships with her family. There was also a history of heavy alcohol use, which included several blackouts, family and marital conflict over her drinking, hiding liquor bottles around the family home, and a driving while intoxicated (DWI) arrest. Ms. B. had a strained relationship with the children from her first marriage and a poor relationship with her mother and siblings; she viewed them as "deceptive" and "out for themselves." She was involved in a lengthy incestuous relationship with her natural father during adolescence but addressed this topic with indifference and denial, stating she had viewed it then as a "natural" part of a father–daughter relationship. However, she also recognized that there were things she had "blocked out." There was no history of psychiatric treatment in the past, and except for her DWI, she had never been in legal trouble. Her medical history was unremarkable and there was no other drug use aside from alcohol.

On interview, Ms. B. was well dressed and neatly attired. She was sociable, friendly, yet superficial and displayed euthymic mood and affect. She minimized her husband's accusations and felt that the reports made by family members were "exaggerations." Despite the fact that she provided her history openly, she minimized the nature of her lifelong problems and blamed family members for her misfortunes.

The MCMI-II profile for this woman yielded a personality code of 5 ** 4 6B * 6A 8A + 7 2A 1 " 8B 3 // · ** · * // and a clinical syndrome code that yielded no elevations above a BR score of 60: · ** · * // · ** · * //. With respect to her level of disclosure, Ms. B. was not willing to acknowledge problem areas. As is common in child custody evaluations, Ms. B. underreported the degree of psychopathology she experienced, hoping to create an impression that she did not experience severe problems. This test finding is consonant with her demeanor on interview, as well as her motivation to disprove the accusations made by her husband. Still, her personality profile was elevated in a 5–4 codetype which is consistent with her history. She tends to be superficial and gregarious in her interactions with others. A noted proclivity for acting impulsively and an inability to delay gratification is characteristic of this codetype, which was consistent with her erratic behavior. Because of a pattern of brief and fleeting infatuation with social friends and activities, there is a lack of predictability and dependability in her actions. Moreover, there is little regard for the consequences of her behavior, leading to a pattern of irresponsibility, disrupted family relationships, and broken promises. Reports from her husband and teenage children confirm these findings inferred from the MCMI-II personality profile.

Noticeably absent was an elevation on Scale B (Alcohol Dependence); no face-valid items dealing directly with alcohol use were endorsed. The history and interview, however, confirmed a diagnosis of alcohol dependence. This discrepancy in findings between the MCMI-II and interview is due primarily to Ms. B.'s attempt to minimize the severity of her alcohol problem. Moreover, she did not view alcohol use as a difficulty at the time of the evaluation because she had managed to abstain from use for 6 weeks prior to the evaluation and thus viewed the problem as "under control." Upon further questioning, it was learned that one of her husband's conditions for possible reconciliation was that she enter treatment for her drinking problem. Ms. B., in an attempt to "prove" that she did not have a drinking problem and would not be coerced into following his demands, had refrained from alcohol use. As such, her denial of problem areas and resistance to having external limits placed on her actions fit with her personality pattern revealed by the MCMI-II. Diagnostically, Ms. B. met criteria for alcohol dependence and a histrionic personality disorder.

PARENTAL FITNESS ASSESSMENTS

State child protective services are major consumers of psychological services and are often court mandated to arrange evaluations of their clients. The most frequently requested type of examination is a parental fitness assessment in which the main referral question is whether the individual is psychologically fit to serve as the primary caretaker of a child. Related issues are what sort of rehabilitative services the client requires, the client's prognosis for benefiting from such services, and what visitation schedule, if any, is appropriate given the client's psychological condition. The three primary areas of danger to the child that must be assessed include physical abuse, sexual abuse, and neglect. A salient issue in many cases involving special needs children is the capacity of the birth parent to provide adequate cognitive or language stimulation in cases of intellectually/neurologically impaired children or to respond in an empathic, competent manner to the child's defiant or negativistic behaviors in cases in which the child's problems involve acting out.

It is important to differentiate parental fitness examinations from divorce/custody assessments. In the latter case the parties typically, but not invariably, are able to parent their children well enough to avoid child protective services involvement. Referral questions in parental fitness examinations are of a qualitatively different sort. In cases involving parental fitness, the referral itself is occasioned by some egregious failure of the parent to provide adequate care for a child and there is nearly always a serious psychopathological condition present in the clinical picture.

The current explosion of drugs in every sector of society has produced many cases of parents neglecting their children because they are too impaired chemically to discharge their responsibilities satisfactorily. There are also many cases of parents referred for fitness evaluations because they gave birth to a drug-addicted child, often prematurely as well. Curiously, in many inner-city areas where drugs are endemic, this pattern has become accepted as the norm. As one drug-addicted mother of four remarked with a degree of pride during an assessment, "This baby was born with drugs in his system, yes, but he wasn't like my other three. All of them were born addicted to drugs. He wasn't born addicted." Care should be taken when employing the MCMI-II in parental fitness assessments that subjects are literate enough to complete the instrument.

CASE 5.4. IMPULSIVE ABANDONMENT OF THE CHILD

Ruth, a 32-year-old female, has 2 years of college credit from a southern university. She left school after suffering what she described as a nervous breakdown and was in and out of hospitals over the next 5 years. She attributed the initial breakdown to having smoked marijuana laced with PCP. She was diagnosed with schizophrenia and bipolar disorder and was on Prolixin and Cogentin for a year. She experienced periodic depressions since that time. She admitted to having an alcohol problem and stated, "I don't know if I drink because I'm miserable or if I'm miserable because I drink." She admitted to consuming usually between one and 2 liters of rum in two days and to daily drinking. At the time of the examination she was living alone and working as a bartender. When questioned about drugs, Ruth replied, "No, not really. I have done it and if it's there I do. I don't look for it. I don't buy."

Ruth came to the attention of state child protective authorities as the result of an incident in which she brought her 19-month-old daughter to the house of the child's biological father and dumped her on the porch, leaving her unattended while no one was home. She blamed the child protective services and "the system" for forcing her to abandon the child, stating that she was not receiving sufficient attention and support from the girl's biological father.

Ruth's MCMI-II record was as follows: 4 5 6A 8A ** 6B 8B * 2 3 + 1 " 7 " // C ** - * // - ** T A B D * // - ** - * //. The record is remarkable for elevations on scales measuring narcissism, histrionic tendency, passive–aggressive traits, and antisocial traits. These findings provide a clear explanation of the client's behavior involving her daughter. First, there is a decidedly self-dramatizing aspect to the act, communicating a level of frustration so profound that Ruth, unable to cope with being neglected and taken for granted by her paramour, thrusts the child upon him and storms off. Second, her narcissistic disregard for her daughter's safety is reflected in her high scores on Scales 5 (Narcissistic), 6A (Antisocial), and 6B (Aggressive/Sadistic). Further, this behavior, constituting gross disregard for the infant's physical safety, is consistent with a borderline level of personality organization, as reflected in her high score on Scale C (Borderline).

The clinical syndrome scale scores also provide a telling picture of Ruth's psychopathology. The high scores on Scales B (Alcohol Dependence) and T (Drug Dependence) point up the significance of drug and alcohol problems in the clinical picture. These scores, combined with the elevation on Scale D (Dysthymia), suggest a depressed alcoholic who cannot decide whether she drinks because she is miserable or whether she is miserable because she drinks.

As would be expected from the nature of the subject's behavior toward her child and the dismal MCMI-II results, her clinical condition was assessed as very poor and it was recommended that she undergo detoxification, substance abuse rehabilitation, and psychotherapy, as well as having a psychiatric consultation for medication, before even being considered for a return of custody of the child. Her prognosis was assessed as poor.

CASE 5.5. SEVERE PHYSICAL ABUSE OF A 5-YEAR-OLD

Neal is a 26-year-old father of a 5-year-old who had been in his custody by court order for approximately 1 year. He won custody of the boy after a bitter and protracted court battle during which his former girlfriend alleged that he had physically abused her on numerous occasions. Neal burst into the offices of the local child protective services unannounced one day and demanded that they take his son off his hands, as the boy's behavior had become intolerable. When informed that the state could not take custody of a child unless there had been documented abuse or neglect, Neal insisted that they take the child from him, adding that he felt that he was going to abuse him if he did not get some respite. The supervisor determined that the boy was at risk and placed him in a foster home. Upon being placed, the child described in detail a series of beatings that his father had inflicted on him as a routine form of discipline. A medical examination confirmed that this child had welts and scars on his body consistent with his account of routine severe beatings. Neal was referred for a psychological examination in order to determine his service needs and whether there was any realistic possibility that the child protective services could work toward reuniting him with his son.

Neal presented as an intense, angry, confrontational individual who asserted that the scheduled time was not sufficient for the examiner to understand him and that the examiner should just let a tape recorder run while he spoke and carefully review it over the weekend rather than attempt to take written notes. Neal related that his father did not want him to grow up to be a drug addict or robber and therefore beat him with extension cords, slippers, and other objects. He had a litany of complaints against his former girlfriend, who had sued him in court over a number of years for child support. He admitted to having inflicted some of the scars on his son but accused his former girlfriend of having inflicted the rest while the child resided with her. He commented, "If I didn't care about him I wouldn't spank him so that he doesn't grow up and rape your daughter or shoot you or carjack you and blow you away." He also asserted that this sort of punishment would discourage the child from growing up to be a drunk driver and killing the examiner's wife as she and the examiner were coming out of that restaurant to which they like to go on weekends. He then launched into an elaborate, vivid, and emotionally charged account of his son throwing a cat against a wall and being punished for it by being made to sit in a chair. Although Neal began to narrate this as though it had actually occurred, he admitted in response to a question that it was merely a hypothetical illustration of how he imparted concepts of proper behavior to the child.

Neal's MCMI-III record was as follows: - ** 2B 8A 2A 6B 5 8B * 1 6A + 7 4 " 3 " // - ** P * // A ** R * // - ** - * //. This subject evidently feels a good deal of anxiety much of the time, consistent with his history of physical abuse at the hands of his father. This could also account for the elevation on the Scale R (Posttraumatic Stress Disorder) of the MCMI-III. However, it is also likely that his high Scale R score is the result of his responding positively to scale items referring to "a terrible thing that happened to me" in terms of his belief that he was being traumatized by his former girlfriend, who was harassing him with legal action in connection with custody, visitation, and child support matters. In light of the subject's disorganized behavior, it is clear that in spite of the intended purpose of the father's beatings, Neal had little capacity to experience anxiety as a signal of unacceptable impulses or as a means of regulating his behavior, but that he suffered from chronic nervous tension that actually impelled him to action.

The elevations on the P (Paranoid), 8A (Passive–Aggressive), 5 (Narcissistic), and 6B (Aggressive) personality disorder scales capture the clinical picture of this individual quite well. He tends to project his own unacceptable impulses onto the child, whom he then treats in an aggressive, sadistic manner. The subject's peculiar fantasy about his son's killing the cat was a good example of the phenomenon of projective identification in which the subject projects his own aggressive impulses onto another and then experiences an empathic understanding of the other person's projected, rageful state. The unfortunate consequence of this dynamic between Neal and his son was that it did not matter whether the boy actually did something or whether the father projected it onto him; Neal *knew* that it was necessary to beat his son savagely to curb those impulses either way.

The report characterized Neal as suffering from a moderately severe mental disorder and as alternating between depressive tendencies and a suspicious, confrontational, aggressive stance toward others. It was noted that this individual was alternately moody, irritable, demanding, and antagonistic and that he tends to orchestrate grandiose dramas in which he is persecuted, wronged, and slighted, necessitating some form of aggressive retaliation. Neal's perspective on the world is an extremely infantile one and he is oblivious to the needs and feelings of others. He is insecure, tense, anxious, and explosive. He displays defects in reality testing and impulse control. The report listed a negative prognosis for sufficient positive change through psychotherapy to enable this man to parent a child appropriately. It was recommended that Neal not be considered as a viable candidate for custody of his son and that the state abandon its efforts to work with this man toward reunification.

CASE 5.6. CAPACITY TO PROVIDE ADEQUATE PARENTING

Ellen is a 34-year-old woman whose children have been removed from her home on several occasions because of neglect. These events were associated with a lifestyle that included homelessness, drug abuse, and repeated incarcerations. This subject was residing with her father at the time of the examination. She satisfactorily completed a drug rehabilitation program, and for several months had been living an organized lifestyle that included successful biweekly visits with the children. The caseworker from child protective services noted that this client appeared to be rather dependent on her father and that it was his close supervision that seemed to be keeping her together. Ellen petitioned the court for return of the children on the basis that her stabilization clearly indicated that she was ready to parent them appropriately.

Ellen's MCMI-II record contained BR scores exceeding 100 on the 8B (Self-Defeating), C (Borderline), 8A (Passive–Aggressive), 2A (Avoidant), and 3 (Dependent) personality disorder scales. It is also noted that her BR score on the Debasement scale was 90, whereas Desirability was only 63. This is quite unusual in a parental fitness assessment record as it is highly typical to attempt to project a maximally positive impression, which would result in a high Desirability score and low Debasement. The subject also had BR scores above 75 on Scales D (Dysthymia) and A (Anxiety).

First, we note that Ellen suffers from psychic distress in the form of mild anxiety and depression. She is in adequate contact with reality most of the time; however, her highest BR score scale, Borderline, indicates that she tends to regress to transient disorganized mental states in which her reality testing suffers. She presents as a socially inept individual who is uncomfortable around others and who avoids social situations unless she can fortify herself with heroin or cocaine. She tends to set herself up for situations that result in humiliation, exploitation, or punishment. She is irritable, negativistic, and oppositional in response to efforts to correct her behavior. Lacking autonomy and mature boundaries, for which the negativism appears to be an infantile substitute, Ellen seeks out competent partners on whom she develops an intense dependence. Invariably she ends up exploited, abused, and rejected by these figures. Given her borderline level of ego organization, these rejections lead to brief psychotic regressions, as they are a typical trigger for individuals with borderline personality disorder to "fall apart" psychologically. In the past, heroin and cocaine have provided buffers against such experiences, with the tensionless, nirvana-like state associated with heroin intoxication replicating for this emotionally needy client the peaceful, dozing state of early infancy.

The report advised intensive individual psychotherapy for Ellen. The child protective service agency was advised to seek out responsible relatives with whom to place the children on a long-term basis while Ellen was recovering. Her superficially good adjustment while residing with her father was attributable in large measure to the father's supervision and support, as the caseworker had suspected. Given her low level of ego organization, resistant attitude, self-defeating tendencies, and long history of reliance on drugs to dull her psychic suffering, the prognosis for this client was listed as guarded.

EVALUATION OF LAW ENFORCEMENT CANDIDATES

The use of psychological tests to screen for various forms of psychopathology is not limited strictly to inpatient and outpatient mental health settings. Professionals working in various applied settings typically rely on psychological test data as one part of an overall evaluation process for such things as the screening of job applicants. Use of the MCMI for the screening of psychopathology in preemployment evaluations is a "gray area" that requires one to have some expertise in modifying interpretive strategies. That is, the practitioner who ventures into this area must not overinterpret MCMI profiles. There is little research on the use of versions of the MCMI for the screening of corrections and police officer candidates. Nevertheless, there are some rational grounds at least for considering the use of the instrument for such a purpose. The following issues are discussed in light of the introductory caution that more research is necessary to determine the MCMI's utility and applicability and that the MCMI-II is not a job test that will provide information on how well an examinee will perform as a law enforcement officer because no specific job skills are evaluated by the test. Other instruments such as the Inwald Personality Inventory (Inwald, Knatz, & Shusman, 1983) provide measures of more job-related skills. The MCMI-II should be restricted to use as a screening measure for clinical symptomatology (e.g., substance abuse) or for evaluation of known psychopathology that has been learned from the interview, history, or records.

As noted earlier in Chapter 1, the MCMI was designed to aid in identifying and diagnosing psychopathology in clinical populations. Particular BR score cutoffs are utilized to determine the presence of a syndrome if a BR score exceeds 74 or the prominence of a disorder if the BR score exceeds 84. In many settings in which psychological evaluation takes place, questions often arise as to whether there is evidence of psychopathology in individual cases. The hiring of employees for such so-called high risk positions as police and corrections officers often involves psychological assessments aimed at screening out those candidates who have emotional disturbances that might interfere with effective job performance. As noted by Lowman (1989), psychopathology per se does not preclude a candidate from being hired; however, such factors as substance abuse, thought disorder, personality disturbances, and depression or anxiety may have an impact on the safety of the employee as well as on those who are served by the employee. In this capacity, the MCMI-II may be helpful in screening for evidence of psychopathology. The following case example illustrates some of these principles.

CASE 5.7. EVALUATION OF A POLICE OFFICER CANDIDATE

Mr. B. a 28-year-old white male, is married and has a high school education. He was referred for a psychological evaluation to assess his overall emotional stability and his suitability to enter training as a police officer for a local law enforcement agency.

The history reveals a fairly stable pattern of relationships. Mr. B. maintains regular contact with his family and described an unremarkable childhood. He attended public schools up until the eleventh grade, when he voluntarily left school to enlist in the Air Force. Mr. B. passed his high school equivalency diploma examination and completed 4 years as a security police officer in the military. He was promoted regularly and received an honorable discharge. He worked regularly as a security guard after his release from the Air Force. He had no history of substance abuse, arrests, or medical problems. He reported himself to be happily married for 4 years and he had one child. He had no history of psychiatric difficulties.

In addition to an extensive interview and a battery of psychological tests, Mr. B. was administered the MCMI-II. Results yielded a valid profile with no scales elevated above a BR score of 74. The validity scales revealed Mr. B. to be nondisclosing (common in preemployment screenings) and he did not demonstrate any tendencies toward social desirability or complaining response styles. On MCMI-II personality scales, the following code was obtained: - ** - * 3 4 + 6A 5 7 " 1 8B 6B 2A 8A '' // - ** - * //. The clinical scales were likewise low and revealed no evidence of psychopathology: - ** - * // - ** - * //. Overall, the MCMI-II, as one portion of the entire assessment, suggests the absence of psychopathology. It could be argued, however, that the low disclosure level represents an evasiveness on the part of this candidate to being open about problematic areas. On the other hand, such a response style may also reflect either the absence of any concerns or an adaptive response set to the employment screening process (i.e., people motivated to obtain a specific job want to make a reasonably positive impression and are capable of doing so). A common response set in job screening settings is the social desirability style in which candidates underreport psychopathology and attempt to highlight positive personal attributes (Lowman, 1989). In many job screening evaluations, MCMI-II profiles generally reveal social desirability response sets through elevations on

Scales Y (Desirability), 7 (Obsessive–Compulsive), and, to a lesser extent, 3 (Dependent) and 5 (Narcissistic). In the case of Mr. B., information obtained in other testing and through clinical interview was consistent with the MCMI-II results. The examination yielded no evidence of obvious or subtle psychopathology and it was recommended, based strictly from a psychological perspective, that he be accepted for police officer training.

USE OF THE MCMI-II WITH IMPAIRED PROFESSIONALS

Professions and licensed trades are regulated by boards that have a unique mix of legislative, executive, and judicial powers. Whether constituted under the aegis of the state's education department, as is the New York State Psychology Board, or under the state consumer protection division, as is the New Jersey Psychology Board, regulatory boards are charged with developing and enforcing regulations governing the licensed profession or trade, conducting such licensure tasks as examination of candidates and renewal of licenses, and similar tasks to ensure that the public receives high-quality services delivered in an ethical manner by licensees. Increasingly in psychology and other professions as well, the business of regulatory boards is taken up with complaints of unethical behavior by licensees. The prevalence of certain classes of offenses is, to some extent, determined by the types of professional activities normally conducted by licensees in particular disciplines. In psychology, for example, with frequent intimate dyadic interaction between practitioners and clients, complaints of sexual behavior constitute a significant percentage of the allegations brought to the board. In dentistry, where practitioners typically have access to a variety of controlled substances, drug abuse complaints, which are comparatively rare in psychology, are frequent

Professional boards are mandated to investigate all consumer complaints of substance. This process may be restricted to directing the licensee to provide a written response to the complaint and then taking some mild corrective action in the case of minor offenses. In New Jersey, for example, regulations provide for an initial evaluation of the complaint by the professional board and sending notice of the outcome of this initial consideration to the complainant. The letter advises the complainant that he or she has the right to request an appearance before the board. If the charges are of a more serious nature, the board conducts an investigative inquiry in which some or all of the parties are summoned before a committee of the board to give testimony under oath. An investigative inquiry may result in the board taking no action, a formal expression of disapproval regarding the licensee's conduct, and agreement among the parties and the board that may include restoration of money or property to the complainant, rehabilitation for the licensee, or more serious sanctions.

The most lenient class of sanctions available to professional boards is a letter of reprimand that is placed in the licensee's permanent file. Other possible sanctions include suspension of prescription privileges, requirement for supervised practice, psychotherapy, drug rehabilitation, or suspension or revocation of the individual's license to practice. The licensee may be assessed fines and investigative costs, which may run to tens of thousands of dollars.

Most matters are resolved by means of a consent order, which is negotiated between the board and the licensee or counsel. The licensee is free to reject the proposed order, at which point the board may constitute itself as a quasi-judicial body and conduct a formal hearing on the matter based either on its own decision to proceed in this manner or on a request by the licensee for a formal hearing. Alternatively, the board may refer the case to an administrative law judge. In either case, the board may employ expert witnesses to give testimony about characteristics of the licensee or the alleged incompetent or unethical behavior. Psychologists are often called upon to provide expert assessment and/or testimony in disciplinary actions before various professional boards.

Whether testimony is given before a judge of administrative law or before the board itself sitting as a judicial body, the process is the same as testifying in a trial court. Experts are expected to give opinions based on professional judgment, scientific findings, well-accepted theory, and clinical observations. In the case of a board hearing, the procedure is less formal than a court of law and rules of evidence are not as strictly followed. However, there is considerable administrative law precedent in many states that guarantees due process to licensees accused of unethical behavior. In New Jersey, for example, administrative due process requires agencies, at a minimum, to provide parties with adequate notice, a chance to examine opposing evidence, and the opportunity to present evidence and argument in response before imposing substantial sanctions (Becker, 1994). It is of interest, however, that in New Jersey, the standard of evidence for formal hearings held by professional boards is, as of this writing, "preponderance of the evidence rather than "beyond a reasonable doubt," or even "clear and convincing evidence."

Typical referral questions on which psychologists are asked to deliver opinions include assessment of the overall psychological functioning of the licensee; whether the licensee's continuing practice would constitute a danger to the public; whether the individual suffers from any personality disorder, clinical syndrome, or addiction that would impair his or her capacity to practice the profession; and what interventions would be necessary to effect an adequate rehabilitation of the licensee. Experts retained by professional and occupational boards are also occasionally asked to address referral questions that are specific to the facts of a given case, such as an evaluation of the respondent's version of events in light of the circumstances. Although these referrals can have elements in common with cases in the criminal justice system, where the expert's testimony will be employed at the time of trial, they more typically resemble sentencing hearing referral where the prospects for rehabilitation and specific needs for services are at issue. The MCMI-II has been found in practice to be quite useful in assessments of distressed or impaired professionals. The following cases provide examples of how test results have been useful in addressing a variety of referral issues.

CASE 5.8. A DEPRESSED DENTIST WITH SUBSTANCE ABUSE

Dr. A., a 39-year-old male, was referred to a state board of dentistry after he was arrested during the course of a traffic stop when he was found to be in possession of cocaine and Vicodin, a semisynthetic narcotic analgesic, which is similar to codeine and dispensed by prescription. He received probation for this offense. The dental board's investigator also reported that Dr. A. had been hospitalized for a suicide attempt and received treatment for depression. Dr. A. was subsequently ordered by the board to enter the Impaired Dentists Program. His first urine sample, administered through that program, was positive for marijuana. He minimized this as casual social use of the drug, not connected with issues of recovery. Dr. A. sold his dental practice while he was hospitalized for depression and was not practicing as a dentist during his first evaluation. He was, however, teaching operative dentistry at a major university three times a week.

Dr. A. reported that his father, a hard-driving entrepreneur who was ill with cancer, had coerced him into becoming a "doctor." After Dr. A. failed to win acceptance to medical school, his father pressured him to go into dentistry, telling him that he wanted to see him graduate as a doctor before the father died of cancer. Despite his strong preference for other types of work, Dr. A. acceded to his father's demands, and became a dental doctor. He reported that he found the day-to-day office practice of dentistry extremely boring, citing this as a factor that contributed to his depression.

Dr. A. reported that he began to use cocaine when his mother also developed cancer 5 years before his arrest. His use of the drug progressed from 1 gram per week to 5 grams per week when his father "emotionally abandoned" him subsequent to his mother's death. Dr. A.'s suicide attempt, which consisted of sitting in the garage with the car engine running, was precipitated by an upsetting telephone conversation with his father. The suicidal behavior was interrupted by the client's wife and brother-in-law, who convinced him to turn off the engine.

Dr. A.'s diagnosis at the facility where he was treated was "moderate depression." He received cognitive therapy and was not feeling either depressed or suicidal at the time of the evaluation. His first MCMI-II was as follows: 5 ** 2 * 8B 3 4 6A 6B 8A 7 + 1 " - // - ** - * // D ** - * // - ** - * //. Consistent with the two major scale elevations, the diagnoses of the narrative report were dysthymia and narcissistic personality disorder. Millon (1981) notes that dysthymic disorder is the most common Axis I condition encountered in patients with narcissistic personality disorder. This is a common consequence of life circumstances that deflate the individual's grandiose self-image. At that point, the patient's imperious, self-absorbed style of adaptation to interpersonal reality breaks down, producing the depression. Further, clinical experience shows that narcissism is closely connected with abuse of "hard" drugs such as cocaine, which is apparently an agent that helps the individual shore up a failing narcissistic grandiosity.

Another factor in this case is the subject's dissatisfaction with his professional activities. Kilburg, Nathan, and Thoreson (1986) discuss the sources of stress affecting professionals to the point of causing occupational and personal impairment. They cite boredom and a sense of staleness as particularly damaging to professionals' emotional health. "If the person cannot adjust, a sense of chronic dissatisfaction can arise, which in some people can lead to serious depression — even thoughts of suicide" (p. 24). A compounding factor in the case of Dr. A. is his narcissistic personality disorder, which led to a sense that he was above the mundane responsibilities of patient care in a suburban dental practice.

The recommended interventions in this case included mandatory psychotherapy to address characterological and recovery issues, revocation of drug prescription privileges, and restriction of dental practice to work under the direct supervision of another licensed dentist who would be responsible for restricting the subject's access to dental medications and monitoring the quality of his patient care.

The board referred Dr. A. for a reassessment 2 years later in connection with his application for a relaxation of the restrictions on his dental license. He had been in individual psychotherapy during the interim with a psychologist specializing in substance abuse issues and he had made good progress in his program of recovery. The only exception was the subject's failure to report for a urinalysis because he was on vacation.

The subject was more spontaneous and displayed a much more positive and lively affect than when seen previously. He reported that he was now employed full-time as an associate professor at the dental school where he had been a part-time clinical instructor. He related that he was continuing in psychotherapy and that he also attends Alcoholics Anonymous (AA) and Narcotics Anonymous (NA) meetings. He employed a good deal of 12-Step language in discussing his program of recovery. He stated that as part of a community service agreement, he was also providing dental services to county jail inmates. He said that he found working with the jail inmates particularly challenging because of their extremely poor dental health. The impression was that he had at last found a challenge befitting his superior talents. He reported that he did not wish to return to the private practice of dentistry and that he was merely seeking a suspension of the requirement for weekly urinalysis, reducing the frequency to 10 samples per year, and elimination of the requirement that he submit a letter to the dental board every time he uses a prescribed medication with analgesic or sedating effects.

Dr. A.'s second MCMI-II record was as follows: 5 7 ** 6B 4 * 6A 8B 8A + 1 3 2 " - // - ** - * // - ** T B * // - ** - * //. The subject's depression has lifted and he no longer registers a clinical elevation on Scale D (Dysthymia). He is more open and honest about his substance abuse problems as a result of his involvement in AA, as reflected in the elevations on Scales T (Drug Dependence) and B (Alcohol Dependence). Although the subject still shows a considerable elevation on Scale 5 (Narcissistic), he made the impression of being less narcissistic and self-absorbed on this second occasion and his Scale 5 score was significantly lower. His aggression, instead of being internalized in the form of depression, was now discharged outward, as indicated by the significant elevation on Scale 6B (Aggressive/Sadistic). The elevation on Scale 7 (Compulsive) is interpreted as a reflection of Dr. A.'s defensiveness in responding to the MCMI-II, suggesting improved ego functioning. It should be noted that clinical experience reveals the most common profile for dentists undergoing this type of evaluation to be a 7–3 or 3–7 pattern. Although the MCMI-II manual interprets this as a somatizing pattern, it appears in this population as a socially desirable, defensive response set.

Based on the MCMI-II and other findings, it was recommended that Dr. A. continue in AA at a mandatory frequency of twice weekly, that he continue in psychotherapy, that the urinalysis frequency be reduced from weekly to monthly, but with random analyses rather than regularly scheduled ones, and that he continue to be required to report all use of prescription analgesics or sedatives to the board. With respect to practice restrictions, it was recommended that the subject not be given any prescribing privileges but that he be allowed to engage in unsupervised practice as long as he has no access to controlled and dangerous substances in the workplace.

CASE 5.9. A DENTIST ACCUSED OF STATUTORY RAPE OF A PATIENT

Dr. B., a 40-year-old male, was referred by a state dental board in connection with disciplinary proceedings against him arising from an alleged sexual assault of a 20-year-old female patient in his dental office. According to the referral letter prepared by the deputy attorney general representing the board of dentistry, the victim visited Dr. B.'s office for a routine dental cleaning at the end of the workday when the licensee's staff had left for the day. The theory of the dental board's investigator was that the patient had been given a knockout preparation by the subject under the pretext of administration of a routine sedative, as the victim was found to have traces of alcohol and chloral hydrate in her system. The combination of these two substances is popularly known as a Mickey Finn. The dental board was particularly concerned that this fact indicated a possibility that the sexual assault was premeditated, as a popular brand of chloral hydrate for use in dentistry does not contain any alcohol and the victim did not report having consumed alcohol on the day of the incident.

The issue of premeditation was, in fact, one of the specific referral questions in this matter. Other questions raised by the board included whether Dr. B. had a chronic sexual problem that would present a danger to patients, what safeguards, if any, should be instituted if the subject were permitted to continue in practice, and what form of psychological or other treatment would be appropriate for this licensee.

Dr. B. presented as a mildly obese individual who was talkative and friendly during the examination. He appeared to be greatly invested in having the examiner like him. He made many extraneous comments during the course of the preliminary interview that appeared to have the purpose of making the interaction seem more casual and less clinical. He related that he was suffering from sexual problems that had their origin in his wife's refusal to have sex with him unless he wore a condom. He stated that prior to his wife's insistence on condoms, they had been using coitus interruptus as their sole form of birth control. He complained that when his wife refused to have unprotected sex with him, he became impotent and their relationship "went down the tubes." He described his wife in idealizing terms, citing her many artistic and practical talents. He related a fantasy of retiring to the Caribbean with his wife on a boat on which she was the captain and he was the cook. At the same time, Dr. B. complained about his wife's refusal to have children with him during the 14 years of their marriage.

Dr. B.'s explanation of the sexual assault of his patient was that it was the result of pent-up anger toward his wife. When questioned specifically about the sedation procedures that he had employed prior to treating this patient, he responded that he was not at liberty to discuss that issue on the advice of his attorney. He did state that the victim "liked the gas" and that he gave her nitrous oxide to prepare her for the routine cleaning. He reported that while he was administering the nitrous oxide, the victim told him that he looked like the actor Don Johnson of the television show *Miami Vice* and that she then took off the nasal hood and "grabbed" him. He related that he responded to this by kissing her and helping her to get undressed. He stated that he then picked her up and carried her to another room where they masturbated each other. He denied any sexual penetration of the victim, adding, "I tried like heck to get an erection and there was no way on earth." He reported that his attorney had scolded him for admitting that he carried the victim to another area of the office, as this made it appear that the victim was completely helpless. It is noted that the victim's statement to the police indicated that her last clear memory, prior to the sexual assault, was of being in the dental chair and that she woke up in a daze in another area of the office without her clothing on and in the embrace of Dr. B. In regard to his admission that he had carried the victim to the other part of the office rather than having her walk there, Dr. B. stated, "Believe it or not, I thought it was romantic."

Although Dr. B. insisted that the sexual activity was consensual, he stated that he felt badly for the victim and wished to make some sort of restitution to her. He reported that the victim filed a civil suit against him and that his dental practice had suffered to such an extent because of this incident that he felt he would be forced to sell the practice and go to work as a salaried employee for another practitioner. He cried as he discussed his legal and financial problems arising from the sexual assault and did appear to feel some degree of remorse in spite of his assertion that it was consensual sex and not statutory rape.

Dr. B.'s MCMI-II record was as follows: 3 2 8B ** 7 1 * 8A + 4 6A 6B 5 " · // · ** · * // · ** · * // · ** · * //. Essentially, the subject is a dependent personality disorder with prominent avoidant and self-defeating personality traits. This is a passive, inadequate, fearful individual whose aggression is expressed in masochistic ways, including setting himself up for humiliation and disgrace, as with the offense that resulted in criminal charges and professional ruin for him. It is characteristic of such an individual that he committed the sexual assault by first rendering the victim helpless through the administration of sedating medication rather than by employing direct threats or coercion.

The report to the dental board, based on the MCMI-II and other testing and clinical observations, including an interview with the subject's treating therapist, states that the sexual assault was the result of an isolated regression in ego functioning precipitated by the subject's marital crisis. The issue of premeditation could not be addressed directly with Dr. B. as he had been advised by counsel to refrain from discussing the issue of what substances he had administered to the victim. The subject was assessed as having a negligible risk of future sexual assaults because of his remorse and regret, positive response to psychotherapy, stern and punitive conscience, and enormous suffering in connection with the financial and legal consequences of his behavior. It was recommended that Dr. B. continue in at least weekly psychotherapy with his present therapist, who had specific expertise in treating sexual offenders, and that if the subject were allowed to continue to practice dentistry, he be required as a condition of his license to have another staff member present in the office at all times while interacting with patients.

CASE 5.10. A DENTIST WITH POLYSUBSTANCE ABUSE

Dr. W., a 40-year-old male, was referred by a state dental board in connection with his application for reinstatement of his license to practice dentistry. He had surrendered his dental license according to the terms of a consent order signed approximately 1 year prior to the examination. Dr. W. came to the attention of the board as a result of an incident in which a police officer observed him staggering out of the building where his office was located and then collapsing to the ground. The police transported Dr. W. to a hospital emergency room and found codeine and Valium in his pocket. Dr. W. failed all the behavioral sobriety tests administered by the police but left the hospital against medical advice before a scheduled blood sample could be taken. The dental board's investigation disclosed that Dr. W. had been self-medicating with controlled substances for a condition that had initially been diagnosed as multiple sclerosis. The diagnosis was later revised to vitamin B-12 deficiency. He had a prior history of nitrous oxide abuse, which aggravated his vitamin deficiency. He was charged with possession of a controlled dangerous substance and admitted into a pretrial intervention program with treatment for substance abuse.

The specific referral questions included whether Dr. W. had a current substance abuse problem and whether he had any personality disorder or other psychological problem that would affect his ability to practice dentistry. If there were any findings indicating that his license should not be reinstated, additional referral questions would include any restrictions that should be placed on his license and whether he required psychotherapy, substance abuse counseling, or other interventions.

Dr. W. presented as soft spoken and controlled. He appeared to be defending against a depression, although he managed to remain focused and alert throughout the session. He admitted to self-medicating with nitrous oxide and codeine when he received the initial diagnosis of multiple sclerosis. When asked whether he had been under the influence of controlled substances at the time of his collapse in the street, he replied that he believed that a blood screening was done at the hospital and that the results were negative. As noted above, a screening had been ordered but not completed because he left the hospital without authorization.

The subject, whose father was a dentist, described his choice of dentistry in a rather flat, unenthusiastic manner, suggesting ambivalence regarding his career choice. He reported that he had lived with a woman who constantly raided his supply of controlled substances and that prior to his arrest he had friends who smoked marijuana with him. He reported that his father used to prescribe Nembutal, a barbiturate sedative and hypnotic, for his mother "not for any dental purpose." He admitted further that he had previously used nitrous oxide recreationally with a female dental assistant. When questioned as to why he had ordered thousands of Valium, Librium, aspirin with codeine, and other controlled dangerous substances from a pharmaceutical wholesaler, he replied that it was because his girlfriend often stole medications from him. He stated that his personal use of these medications amounted to no more than 10 to 18 pills per month to relieve the pain of his medical condition. He added that if he had been consuming all the medications himself, he would have experienced withdrawal symptoms, which he denied.

Dr. W.'s MCMI-II record was as follows: 8A 6B ** 8B * 4 5 3 6A 1 2 + 7 " - // - ** - * // T ** - * // - ** / * //. The MCMI-II Axis I diagnosis is psychoactive substance abuse NOS and on Axis II it is passive–aggressive personality disorder. The MCMI-II narrative report describes Dr. W.'s drug use in the context of his personality disorder: "Edgy, irritable, and hostile, he may use drugs not only to aid him in unwinding his conflicts, in moderating his tensions, and in permitting him a measure of narcissistic indulgence, but also to serve as a statement of resentful independence from the constraints of social convention and expectation." Thus for this individual, who was deeply resentful of having to follow in the footsteps of his father by entering the profession of dentistry, drug abuse was more than simply a means of self-medication for his medical symptoms. Rather, it represented a passive–aggressive rebellion and statement of resentment stemming from deep-seated characterological issues and had little to do with any medical crisis.

The report to the dental board stressed that the subject lacked self-insight and appeared to have profited little from his psychotherapy. His fabrication of negative blood test results when questioned about his sobriety at the time of his arrest underscored his denial and evasiveness regarding his drug abuse, as did blaming his girlfriend's theft of his medications for his ordering thousands of units of controlled and dangerous substances (CDS) from a pharmaceutical supply house. Recommendations included continuing psychotherapy, continued involvement in AA and random urine testing, and denial of CDS prescription privileges. If the subject were to be reinstated as a practicing dentist, his license should be restricted to supervised practice with another licensed dentist monitoring his clinical and interpersonal effectiveness.

CASE 5.11. SUBSTANCE ABUSE AND PSYCHOSIS IN A DENTIST

Dr. S., a 45-year-old male, was referred by a state dental board in connection with his petition for renewal of his dental license. His license to practice dentistry in another state had been suspended on an emergency basis because of "drug dependence and mental illness." He voluntarily surrendered his license and relocated. After gaining licensure in the state in which the dental board referred him for a psychological examination, he failed to renew that license when he paid with a check that was returned for lack of funds and then left the state without notifying the dental board. The referral questions in this matter included whether the subject suffered from mental illness, substance abuse, or other problems that would constitute a danger to the public if he were to be reinstated as a practicing dentist.

Dr. S. related that he was the third of six children in his family of origin and that his mother died when he was 7 years old. His father attempted to raise the children singlehandedly and the subject was forced to begin working at the age of 7½ years in order to help pay his elementary school tuition. In 1965 he married a woman with whom he had gone to high school. That marriage broke up because of Dr. S.'s affair with another woman. He stated that he had problems with nitrous oxide in the early 1970s and he had fractured his skull while working in his dental office in 1974. He was comatose for 10 days as a result of that injury and underwent brain surgery for removal of a blood clot. He reported that he lost a year of work and he was also hospitalized at a drug rehabilitation facility during that period.

When questioned about his license suspension in the other state, Dr. S. reported that he had been working at a franchised dental clinic at the time. He said that he discovered a problem with the call buzzer system in the office and that the apparatus was emitting low-voltage electricity that affected the sensations that his patients were experiencing while under nitrous oxide. He stated that he experimented on himself to determine whether he would experience unpleasant sensations while under nitrous oxide when he activated the call box. He related, "When I took those squawk boxes down I couldn't feel it. All I did was sit there and get high." He stated that the other dentists associated with him in the practice did not believe his story about the low-voltage electricity interacting with the gas and forced him to leave the practice. He reported that he had a "whole history of experiences" with nitrous oxide where he suffered from "weird experiences" and that he would then use more of the gas "to figure out what was going on." Dr. S. further reported that he had a problem with his hands trembling while practicing as a dentist at another location and that he employed nitrous oxide to calm himself. He reported that he underwent treatment at a sanitorium in yet another state at which time he was diagnosed as alcoholic in addition to his nitrous oxide dependency.

Dr. S.'s MCMI-II record was as follows: 2 ** 8B * 1 6A 7 6B + 4 8A 5 3 " - // - ** - * // - ** D B * // - ** - * //. The MCMI-II diagnosis on Axis I is dysthymia and alcohol abuse and on Axis II it is avoidant personality disorder and prominent self-defeating and schizoid personality traits. Millon (1981) indicates that avoidant personality disorders occasionally decompensate into psychotic states that characterize schizophrenia, as the cognitive disorganization of that disorder represents an extension of the avoidants' characteristic protective maneuver of interfering with their cognitive clarity in order to dilute the impact of painful feelings and recollections. It was the examiner's clinical impression that Dr. S. had a psychotic level of personality organization, as his Rorschach record indicated some looseness of thought processes and his account of his nitrous oxide experimentation to investigate the "squawk box" electrical emissions also suggested thought disorder combined with a tenuous hold on reality. Further, Dr. S.'s repeated loss of his dental license through negligence and drug involvement is consistent with his prominent self-defeating personality traits, as diagnosed by the MCMI-II.

Dr. S. was assessed as having a poor prognosis for significant positive change through therapy or counseling. He was described in the report to the dental board as a potential danger to the public if he were to be reinstated as a practicing dentist. Moreover, in light of his severe manifold problems, even partial reinstatement with restrictions on his access to anesthetics would not provide adequate protection. The recommendation was that the dental board deny Dr. S.'s petition for reinstatement.

CASE 5.12. SUBSTANCE ABUSE IN FRONT OF OFFICE STAFF

Dr. J., a 27-year-old female, was referred by a state dental board in connection with a complaint from her employer to the effect that she had been observed by other staff members using nitrous oxide during office hours and in between appointments with patients. The board's investigative report states that one of the dental assistants in the office observed Dr. J. inhaling nitrous oxide in an operatory for about 10 minutes at 11 o'clock in the morning. Dr. J. was in between seeing patients at that time. This happened on multiple occasions and during one occurrence Dr. J. told the assistant that she was going into the back room "to party with the nitrous." This behavior was also observed by one of the dental hygienists in the office. A third staff member, also a dental assistant with L.P.N. certification, reported that she encountered the subject in one of the operatories when she was about to close the office. Dr. J. was inhaling the nitrous oxide for a half hour. The assistant observed Dr. J. about to fall off the chair and pulled her back onto it. She reported that when she asked Dr. J. if she was all right, the licensee's eyes were glassy and her speech was slurred. The subject inhaled oxygen for a few minutes and appeared to recover. The assistant also reported that Dr. J. confided in her that she had inhaled the nitrous oxide to the point of becoming ill and throwing up. Dr. J. also admitted to this assistant that she had been "high" on nitrous oxide while administering an injection to a patient. Further, the assistant reported that Dr. J. had offered to write her a prescription for Phenergan with codeine, telling her that it was "good stuff." In addition to the allegation of nitrous oxide abuse, the subject was discovered to have written a prescription for Phenergan with codeine for her sister. This cough medication is never prescribed in connection with any legitimate dental use.

When interviewed by the board's investigator and the deputy attorney general representing the board, Dr. J. admitted to having inhaled nitrous oxide in the office on three occasions. She stated that on two of these occasions she used the gas to relax herself while she scaled her teeth. She stated that the first time she had inhaled nitrous oxide it had been at the suggestion of the assistant who had reported that she nearly fell out of the chair. Dr. J. insisted that she and this dental assistant were passing the nosepiece back and forth to inhale the gas. She denied being a drug or alcohol abuser and denied ever having worked on a patient while under the influence of nitrous oxide. The dental assistant, when interviewed subsequently, stated that Dr. J.'s claims that she had urged her to inhale the gas and that she had passed the nosepiece back and forth with her were lies and false accusations. The dentist in charge of the practice was informed of Dr. J.'s accusations against this assistant; he stated to the investigator that this assistant had been in his employ for 10 years and that he considered her to be absolutely trustworthy. He stated that he had never observed any of his employees using nitrous oxide and that he had never received any information that any of his employees had used the gas, with the exception of Dr. J., whom he discharged as soon as he verified the allegation that she had been observed engaging in this activity.

Dr. J. submitted a report from her treating psychiatrist, whom she began to see after being discharged by her employer. She was evidently capable of persuading this psychiatrist that she was blameless and that she had been unjustly accused by jealous staff members, as he wrote her a glowingly optimistic recommendation declaring her fit for the practice of dentistry. It is of interest that Dr. J. was also licensed in a neighboring state. Her difficulties with the dental board did not affect her out-of-state practice and she continued to work as a part-time employee in another dental office both during the investigation of her case and after the close of the investigation when the dental board in the first state suspended her license to practice there.

Dr. J. presented as an attractive, poised, stylishly dressed young woman who related appropriately to the examiner. Dr. J. gave an account of her use of dental gas that was consistent with her statement to the investigator — that with the exception of the one recreational use suggested by the dental assistant, she had only used gas to scale her teeth on two occasions. She stated that she was completely restored to sobriety after inhaling some oxygen and denied having worked on patients while under the influence of nitrous oxide. She categorically de-nied ever having given the appearance of being impaired while work-ing on patients and offered as proof of this the suggestion that had she looked impaired, the patients would have complained about her. She denied any interpersonal problems with other staff members in the practice and was unable to offer any explanation as to why they should all falsely accuse her of abusing the nitrous oxide, except that perhaps the L.P.N. dental assistant did this in order to cover up her own drug activity. Dr. J. denied any experimentation with recreational drugs such as marijuana and stated that she had an alcoholic drink only on rare occasions.

Dr. J.'s MCMI-II record was as follows: · ** 4 7 * 3 5 + 6A 6B " 2 1 8A 8B // · ** · * // · ** · * // · ** · * //. Additionally, the modifier indices were as follows: Scale X (Disclosure) = 15, Scale Y (Desirabili-ty) = 85, and Scale Z (Debasement) = 0. The MCMI-II narrative report notes that this is a rather defensive record. The report lists no diagno-sis on Axis I and a histrionic personality disorder and obsessive–com-pulsive personality disorder with prominent dependent traits on Axis II. The report to the dental board describes the subject as immature and lacking in personal autonomy. It is interesting to note that despite evidence of substance abuse, Scale T (Drug Dependence) was not elevat-ed in Dr. J.'s record. The subject uses denial and minimization to an extreme degree. She tends to be shallow and ingratiating, displaying a rigid conformity and compliance, except when disinhibited by the effects of nitrous oxide and, quite possibly, other substances. The den-tal board was advised that this licensee was a danger to patients and would continue to be so until she acquired the maturity and self-direction necessary to handle the professional responsibility of a prac-tice that entails the administration of drugs that have a potential for abuse. It was recommended that Dr. J.'s prescription privileges be sus-pended, that she be restricted to supervised practice only, that she be required to have psychotherapy specifically focusing on substance abuse issues, and that any future employers be informed of her problem and be required to indicate to the board that she is either forbidden to use dental gas or that her use of this agent must be closely supervised by another staff member.

CASE 5.13. ABUSE OF PRESCRIPTION MEDICATION BY A DENTIST

Dr. Z., a 60-year-old male, was referred by a state dental board for an examination in connection with an investigation of his practice. The board received a complaint from the state Medicaid director to the effect that several Medicaid patients had observed this dentist sleeping in his office, on some occasions even falling asleep while working on patients in the dental chair. The board's investigators found that the subject's office was deplorably dirty and there were dozens of dental implements, many of them rusty, scattered all over a countertop. Rather than sterilizing his dental instruments in an autoclave, Dr. Z. employed a cold sterilization solution. The investigators reported that the instrument trays were dusty and contained debris. Dental mirrors and explorers were present in the cold sterilizing solution, which was cloudy and also contained debris. A second operatory contained a filthy sink and was cluttered, dirty, and dust laden. There was an empty 1-gallon bottle of wine in the room and in a small cabinet in that room there were two cocaine pipes that contained water and a black film at the end of the straw attached to the bottle. The subject at first stated that the cocaine pipes belonged to his son, who was a crack addict, and then stated that they belonged to his former dental assistant. He reported that this assistant and her two brothers had been living with him at his late mother's apartment until the assistant was arrested for violation of her probation. He admitted that he had fallen asleep at the office during work hours and attributed this to his taking Halcion, a hypnotic and sedative. He was unable to explain to the investigators why he had been taking this medication.

The specific referral questions included whether the subject had a substance abuse problem and whether he presented any characterological or emotional disorder that would constitute a danger to the public. Dr. Z.'s examination was preceded by two failed appointments. On the first occasion, when the examiner contacted Dr. Z. after the scheduled appointment time, he stated that he had been trying to get in touch with the examiner to inform him that he did not have the fee. On the second occasion, the examiner telephoned slightly after the scheduled time and was told by someone at that number that Dr. Z. had gone through a red light because of faulty brakes and was directed by the police to pull his car off the road and to refrain from driving it. Earlier in the day, the examiner had received an answering machine message from Dr. Z. to the effect that he might be a little late because his car had no brakes and he had to drive very slowly.

During the course of the examination, Dr. Z. admitted that he had fallen asleep while taking Halcion. He stated that the pills belonged to his ex-wife and that he had been taking them "just to relax." He stated that on another occasion he had fallen asleep with a bite of sandwich in his mouth. He also admitted to having a crack dealer come to his house to supply him with a quantity of the drug to give to his ad-

dicted teenage son. He stated that he feared that his son would be arrested and sodomized in jail if he allowed him to go for a ride in a
stolen car to purchase the crack. He complained that his former dental assistant took advantage of him and stole things from his home while
she was living with him. He stated that this assistant also brought two
of her brothers to live with him and that the brothers also stole from
him. He remarked, "It's like anybody I ever helped turned around and
buried me." Dr. Z. related that his mother, whom he described as "a
modern, up-to-date woman" who had been a dancer, had died a few
years earlier. It was the examiner's impression that the subject had not
worked through this loss, which apparently coincided with the onset
of at least some of his current interpersonal and substance abuse
problems.

Dr. Z.'s MCMI-II record was a follows: - ** 3 * 1 7 2 + 4 8B 5 6B
" 8A 6A // - ** - * // - ** - * // - ** - * //. The MCMI-II diagnosis of dependent personality disorder with schizoid features adequately describes
the subject's overall style of adaptation, except that clinically he also
appears to have prominent self-defeating traits. It should be noted that
neither Scale T (Drug Dependence) nor Scale B (Alcohol Dependence)
appears as an elevation in this record. As Craig (1993a) points out, Scale
T is useful when the individual is willing to admit to some extent that
he or she suffers from a drug problem, but that this scale has a high
false negative rate due to its inability to pick up addicts who are in
denial regarding their addiction. Scale B has good positive predictive
power and it appeared that, in spite of the presence of liquor and wine
bottles in his office, the subject was not alcoholic but rather drug dependent.

The report to the dental board characterized Dr. Z. as emotionally immature and dependent with idiosyncratic and unrealistic thought
processes. He was assessed as having a clear substance abuse problem,
as evidenced by his use of a hypnotic/sedative agent to alleviate anxiety while working on patients during office hours. Millon's (1981) theory views personality disorders as the individual's adaptation to
interpersonal reality to maintain psychic equilibrium. According to the
theory, Axis I symptoms represent a failure of the patient's adaptation
strategy in which the psychic system becomes overwhelmed by environmental stressors leading to such clinical symptoms as depression, anxiety, psychotic regressions, and so forth. Clinically, it appeared that Dr.
Z.'s compliant, infantile dependency no longer protected him after the
death of his mother and, to some extent, the earlier loss of his wife
through divorce. He had been extremely dependent on both of these
women and was consequently left without a psychic anchor. It is telling that Dr. Z. attempted to relieve his anxiety by taking medications

that had belonged to his ex-wife and that he attempted to reestablish a relationship of naively trusting dependence with a new figure, whom he brought to live with him in his deceased mother's apartment. Recommendations to the dental board included referral to the Impaired Dentists Program, individual psychotherapy, and random urine monitoring. The dental board was advised to allow Dr. Z. to resume practice only after the above interventions had been put in place and the treating practitioners felt that he had become drug free and had worked through his denial, dependence, and pathological grief reaction to recent object losses.

Although this series of cases on impaired professionals includes only dentists, these cases illustrate several important considerations that generalize to evaluations of any impaired professional. It cannot be stressed enough that a key part of the evaluation is accessing the licensing board's investigative report which outlines facts leading to the professional's being called before the board in the first place. Also, a comprehensive psychosocial history, clinical interview, and mental status examination are also necessary components to the evaluation. Often, information from the licensee's history can shed light on the potential reasons for unethical, unprofessional, or illegal behavior on the part of the impaired professional (e.g., being "pushed or forced" into a profession by a parent). The MCMI-II can provide highly valuable and useful psychodiagnostic information that can place the problematic behavior within the context of the professional's personality structure, which in turn can lead to appropriate and individualized recommendations.

SIX

Psychometric Issues in Court

The psychometric properties of a test are of primary importance when evaluating its accuracy and utility. Indeed, the reliability (often conceptualized as the consistency and stability of a test by psychologists) and the validity (conceptualized as the accuracy of a test in measuring what it is supposed to measure) are of primary importance when constructing a psychological instrument. One issue concerning psychometric principles that causes great confusion for attorneys, judges, and jurors is the inherent differences in how law and psychology define the terms "reliability" and "validity."

Psychologists take the term "reliability" to mean the repeatability and consistency of a measure; thus, reliability goes to the issue of whether a test instrument will, assuming no intervening factors, yield the same result over time if it is designed to measure an enduring psychological trait as opposed to a transitory state. Also, reliability deals with whether the finite set of test questions on a single test form provides an accurate estimation of the individual's standing on the trait being measured. It is not the subject's performance of the particular set of test items in which we are interested but, rather, the subject's standing on the underlying trait measured by the test. The scale's degree of accuracy in estimating this parameter based on its sample of test items is assessed through correlational methods that measure the internal consistency of the scale's content. On the other hand, lawyers often interpret reliability to mean the trustworthiness of a witness (cf. *Black's Law Dictionary*, 1990); the legal concept of reliability thus is similar to the way validity, or truthfulness, is conceptualized in psychology.

For a psychologist, test validity refers to whether a test "measures what it claims to measure." Various forms of validity (e.g., face, content, criterion, and construct) are evaluated to establish that a test does or does not measure what it purports to measure. Again, lawyers view validity differently, referring instead to "legal sufficiency," or "having legal strength or force . . . incapable of being overthrown or set aside" (*Black's Law Dictionary*, 1990, p. 1550). From a legal point of view, validity appears to suggest the stability (i.e., reliability) of a legal decision or standard.

Despite the confusion that appears at first glance, introduction of psychometric issues into court proceedings is facilitated once all parties understand how terms are being applied. Our discussion of reliability and validity refers to these terms in their traditional manner in psychological science, as psychometric properties of a test. This chapter discusses psychometric issues relating to the Millon inventories with an emphasis on their implications for expert testimony. Initially the discussion addresses basic questions of reliability and validity, including the internal structural validity of the inventories as disclosed through factor analysis. The focus then turns to a comparative study of the precision of measurement of the MCMI-II in comparison to the MMPI-2, including some gross inconsistencies involving the latter instrument. The chapter closes with a consideration of the operating characteristics of the MCMI-II, noting the advantages and pitfalls of testifying in regard to this type of validity evidence.

PSYCHOMETRIC PROPERTIES OF THE MCMI-II

Reliability

Internal consistency statistics for the individual scales of the MCMI-II are reported in terms of Kuder–Richardson (K-R) 20 coefficients in the test manual (Millon, 1987, p. 129). For the basic personality disorder scales, the median K-R 20 reliability is .88, with the values ranging from .86 to .93. Thus, all the basic personality disorder scales exceed the .80 criterion cited by Heilbrun (1992). Reliability coefficients for the three severe personality disorder scales are all .90 and above. For the basic clinical scales, the K-R 20 coefficients range from .84 to .95, with a median of .87. Values for the three severe clinical scales range from .84 to .90. Thus, all the MCMI-II scales meet or exceed the .80 criterion.

It is noted that all internal consistency statistics for the MCMI-II are computed using the K-R 20 instead of Cronbach's coefficient alpha. Although both statistics yield the average of all possible split-half reliabilities for the test, coefficient alpha is the more general statistic with regard to scoring format. The K-R 20 coefficient is a special case of coefficient alpha for dichotomously scored scales and is therefore inappropriate for the MCMI-II, which employs a 0–3 weighted scoring system based on the polythetic theoretical model underlying the development of the instrument. However, given that the results of weighted and unweighted scoring of MCMI-II scores are essentially the same (Retzlaff, Sheehan, & Lorr, 1990), the use of K-R 20, rather than the more appropriate Cronbach's alpha measure, is likely to have had no more than a negligible effect on the results.

Stability coefficients for the MCMI-II scales are also presented in the test manual (Millon, 1987, p. 126). A study of nonclinical subjects, retested at 3- to 5-week intervals yielded stability coefficients for the basic personality disorder scales ranging from .80 to .89, with a median value of .85. The values for the severe personality disorder scales range from .79 to .89. For basic clinical syndromes the values range from .78 to .88, with a median of .80. For the three severe clinical syndrome scales, the values range from .78 to .91.

Stability coefficients for samples of psychiatric outpatients and inpatients are somewhat lower. For a sample of 47 inpatients tested at intake and discharge, the values for the basic personality disorder scales range from .59 to .75 (median .73) and the severe personality disorder scales range from .49 to .64. Stability coefficients for the clinical syndromes in this group are somewhat lower, ranging from .43 to .66 with a median of .57. Millon (1987) comments that the difference in stability between the personality disorder and clinical syndrome scales is to be expected on the basis of theory, as clinical states and syndromes (for treatment of which the subjects were presumably hospitalized) should be less stable than personality disorders, which represent enduring patterns of adaptation. Also to be taken into account in the evaluation of these findings is the fact that retest occurred at discharge, at which point subjects should have demonstrated sufficient positive change to warrant their release into the community.

Given the popularity of two-scale configuration analysis, it is instructive to consider the stability of 2-point MCMI-II codes in addition to the individual scales. A study of this type for the sample that provided the individual scale stability data discussed above is presented in the MCMI-II manual (Millon, 1987, p. 127). Forty-five percent of the sample had the same first and second highest scales, either in the same (25.8%) or in reverse (19.1%) order. Given the constraints of less than perfect reliability of two scales and the use of psychiatric samples tested at various phases of the treatment process, including admission and discharge retesting, the 45% figure is quite respectable.

Factorial Structure

Choca et al. (1992) review the factor-analytic literature on the MCMI-II, including the study of 769 cases from the normative sample reported in the test manual. In that study, an eight-factor solution yielded a general maladjustment factor accounting for 31% of the variance, an acting-out/self-indulgent factor accounting for 29% of the variance, an anxious/depressed/somatizing factor accounting for 13% of the variance, and other factors reasonably consistent with the theoretical underpinnings of the instrument. Choca et al. (1992) conclude that scale-based factorial studies of the MCMI have generally produced factors interpretable in terms of the classic triad of affective, paranoid, and schizophrenic disorders; psychoanalytic theorist Karen Horney's schema of moving toward, against, and away from others; and Millon's detached, dependent, and independent polarities.

McCann (1991) examined the factorial structure of the MCMI-II and the convergent and discriminant validity of the MCMI-II against corresponding scales of the MMPI. His factor analysis of the MCMI-II employing only prototypical items, with the overlapping items removed, found some support for Millon's theoretical dimensions of detached, dependent, independent, and ambivalent personality styles. In addition, the active–passive polarity as discussed in Millon's theory appeared in the analysis as positive and negative loadings on the same factor for the Dependent and Histrionic scales, respectively, and positive and negative loadings on a single factor for the Passive–Aggressive and Obsessive–Compulsive scales, respectively. The Narcissistic, Paranoid, and Antisocial scales all loaded positively on the same factor, although according to the active–passive structure of the theory, Antisocial and Narcissistic scales should have had opposite loadings, as antisocial personality disorder is classified as active–independent and narcissistic personality is passive–independent. Similarly, both components of the detached dimension, Schizoid (passive) and Avoidant (active), loaded positively on the same factor, along with Schizotypal, supporting the detached dimension concept but without the active–passive distinction. Interestingly, the discordant dimension did not break out as a separate factor. This may be due to the fact that the discordant scales, Aggressive/Sadistic (6B) and Self-Defeating (8B), were not part of Millon's original theoretical formulation (Millon, 1981) but were added when the corresponding personality disorders were introduced in DSM-III-R as disorders requiring further study. Those disorders were not retained in DSM-IV but remain as part of the basic personality disorders section of MCMI-III.

Strack, Lorr, Campbell, and Lamnin (1992) performed a factorial study of both the 13 personality disorder and the nine clinical syndrome scales of the MCMI-II. Subjects were 253 male inpatients and outpatients. Their factor analysis of BR scores on the personality disorder scales produced a four-factor solution that accounted for 83.5% of the common variance. This solution provided support for Millon's original typology of detached, dependent, independent, and ambivalent styles. The first factor had high loadings for Narcissistic, Aggressive/Sadistic, and Paranoid and a moderate loading for Antisocial, with Narcissistic and Antisocial constituting the independent group of disorders and Paranoid as a pathological extension of that group. The second factor included high loadings for Schizoid, Avoidant, and Schizotypal, all of which make up the detached group, with Schizotypal representing the more severe pathological extension. Histrionic, the conceptual opposite of the detached disorders, loaded negatively on that factor. Obsessive–Compulsive and Passive–Aggressive, the two ambivalent scales, loaded in opposite directions on the third factor, which also included high loadings for Borderline and Self-Defeating. The fourth factor was defined by a high loading on Dependent and also contained a moderate loading for Self-Defeating, and a somewhat weaker loading for Histrionic, the last being the active variant of the dependent group. It is of interest that, as with the McCann (1991) study, discordant did not break out as a separate factor, although the original Millon (1981) fourfold scheme of dependent, independent, detached, and ambivalent held up well.

Of interest to forensic practitioners is the fact that studies have also shown a meaningful factor structure on the MCMI among offender populations. McCormack, Barnett, and Wallbrown (1989) found four stable factors in a sample of jail inmates. The factors found by these researchers include social isolation, impulsivity, anxious ambivalence, and paranoid psychoticism. Ownby, Wallbrown, Carmin, and Barnett (1989) found five factors in a sample of correctional inmates. These factors were social withdrawal, affective disruption, anxious attachment, exploitative interpersonal attitudes, and active/passive orientation. These studies reveal a common factor structure among criminal offender populations that closely corresponds with the underlying theoretical dimensions upon which the MCMI is based.

Validity

The MCMI-II manual presents the results of a large validity study of the instrument that employed clinicians' diagnoses of two samples of patients as the criterion. Diagnoses of personality disorders were formulated on the basis of excerpts from a draft of DSM-III-R criteria in the first study and on the basis of Millon Personality Diagnostic Checklist (MPDC) results in the second. Although this latter procedure ensured greater reliability of criterion scores as opposed to diagnoses without benefit of a psychometric checklist, the fact that the content of the MPDC and MCMI-II are so closely linked introduces some degree of inflation of the relationship simply as an artifact of this similarity. It is stressed, however, that the clinicians' diagnostic ratings were independent of the clients' MCMI-II scores and that there was no direct criterion contamination in either of the two studies.

In the first study, which employed the MCMI-II's normative sample of 825 patients, clinicians saw their patients for one or two sessions only. They were instructed to fill in only one diagnosis each for Axis I and Axis II. In the second study, which is actually two distinct studies with the results presented together in the test manual, diagnostic judgments were made on the basis of extensive clinical data—either an examination employing instruments other than the MCMI-II or at least six sessions of therapy. As noted above, the clinicians in this study used the MPDC, which encompassed criteria from both the DSM-III-R and from Millon's theory of personality, which also provided the basis for the MCMI-II. These raters were not limited to a single diagnosis on each of the two axes but were allowed to list three, of which only the first two were included in the data analysis. The first study in this group was conducted on 236 therapy patients. The second study had a sample size of 467, and rating clinicians were all either Millon's present or his former colleagues, doctoral students, or attendees at full-day MCMI workshops. The test manual lists median BR scores for the entire instrument for subsamples of cases diagnosed as having each disorder on the basis of clinicians' ratings. Separate statistics are presented for the large normative sample and for the combined results of the smaller sample studies that had more reliable criterion data and greater rater knowledge of each subject. Data for the subsamples are compared with the means on each variable for the entire normative sample in the graphical presentation of these data.

PSYCHOMETRIC PROPERTIES OF THE MCMI-III

As stated earlier, we recommend the MCMI-II for most forensic applications instead of the MCMI-III because of the limited validity data on the latter instrument at this time. The reliability, factor-analytic, and validity data are reviewed to provide a summary of the MCMI-III's current status.

Reliability

The number of items making up each MCMI-III scale is in most cases 50% less than the number of items making up the MCMI-II scales for corresponding constructs. This reduction in scale length has had some mild effects on internal consistency of the individual scales. Cronbach's alpha coefficients for the clinical personality scales range from a low of .66 on Scale 7 (Compulsive) to a high of .89 on Scales 2A (Avoidant) and 2B (Depressive), with a median of .81 (Millon, 1994a, p. 31). The severe personality scales have internal consistency coefficients ranging from .84 to .85 and the clinical and severe syndrome scales range from .71 on Scale N (Bipolar: Manic) to a high of .90 on Scale CC (Major Depression) and a median of .86. The modifier indices have alpha levels of .86 on Scale Y (Desirability) and .95 on Scale Z (Debasement). Overall, the shortening of MCMI-III scales has resulted in a slight decrease in internal consistency as compared to the MCMI-II. Still, 20 out of 26 scales for which internal consistency coefficients could be calculated meet or exceed the .80 cutoff suggested for forensic application by Heilbrun (1992).

Stability coefficients were calculated as test–retest correlations in a sample of 87 individuals over varying intervals ranging from 5 to 14 days (Millon, 1994a). All MCMI-III scales show good to excellent stability, with coefficient values ranging from .82 on Scale PP (Delusional Disorder) to .96 on Scale H (Somatoform). Each MCMI-III scale exceeds the .80 criterion.

Factorial Structure

There are no factor-analytic studies currently available on the MCMI-III. Unfortunately, there are also no such data presented in the manual (Millon, 1994a). Thus, the underlying structural organization of the scales and their correspondence to the underlying theoretical dimensions in Millon's theory are presently unknown.

Validity

One unique aspect of the MCMI-III is its reliance on DSM-IV criteria in generating items for the test. In this regard, the MCMI-III has excellent content validity against DSM-IV as outlined in Appendix A of the manual (Millon, 1994a). At this time, however, systematic research results on criterion-related validity are not available. Current efforts are underway to gather validity data on the MCMI-III scales through an extensive clinical research program (Theodore Millon, personal communication, March 1995).

PSYCHOMETRIC PROPERTIES OF THE MACI

Reliability

The MACI manual presents internal consistency data for the 12 personality pattern scales and the 15 expressed concern and clinical syndrome scales for the development sample of 579 cases (Millon, 1993). For the personality pattern scales, these values range from .74 for Scale 3 (Submissive) to .90 for Scale 8B (Self-Demeaning). The median value is a respectable .84. Coefficient alpha statistics for the modifier indices and clinical syndrome and expressed concern scales range from .73 for Scale Y (Desirability) and Scale D (Sexual Discomfort) to .91 for Scale B (Self-Devaluation), with a median value of .79. Additional internal consistency statistics were computed for a cross-validation sample of 333 cases. These results are quite close to those for the development sample.

Stability coefficients were computed for a subsample of 47 cases from the cross-validation group tested from 3 to 7 days apart. These values range from .57 for Scale E (Peer Insecurity) to .92 for Scale 9 (Borderline Tendency), with a median retest correlation of .82. In all, most of the MACI scales meet or exceed the .80 standard outlined for forensic psychological testing in Heilbrun (1992).

Factorial Structure

Dyer (1985), in a review of the MACI's predecessor, the Millon Adolescent Personality Inventory, notes that the test manual presents a factor analysis based on the administration of the test to 569 males and 569 females. The analysis resulted in four orthogonal factors accounting for greater than 75% of the variance, providing useful information as to the underlying structure of the instrument. Unfortunately, whereas the MACI manual lists scale intercorrelations for all clinical syndrome, expressed concern, and personality pattern scales, there is no factor analysis presented in the MACI manual and no such studies that could be located in the subsequent literature on the test.

Validity

Validity results for the MACI are given in the form of criterion-related validity studies employing clinicians' ratings and scores on other personality measures as the criteria (Millon, 1993). In the first study employing clinicians' ratings, the sample consisted of 74 males and 65 females. Clinicians were asked to rate which of the test personality characteristics (excluding Scales 2B and 9) most closely approximated their impression of the client and also which scale was second closest.

Similar judgments were made for the clinical syndromes and expressed concerns. For the 10 personality pattern scales that were rated, the correlations range from .08 to .27, with a median value of .18. Correlations for the expressed concerns scales range from .00 to .43, with a median value of .14. Correlations for the clinical syndrome scales ranged from .09 to .37, with a median value of .27. Results for a cross-validation study of 127 males and 67 females were somewhat higher. Despite the rather low concordance between the MACI scales and clinician ratings, these findings are consistent with typical findings that self-report instruments tend to show low correspondence with clinician ratings (Widiger & Frances, 1987).

Data comparing MACI scores with scores on other psychometric instruments are briefly summarized in the text of the manual and presented in tabular form in an appendix (Millon, 1993, pp. 108–112). Comparison measures include the Beck Depression Scale, Beck Hopelessness Scale, Beck Anxiety Inventory, Eating Disorder Inventory-2, and Problem Oriented Screening Inventory for Teenagers. Scores on the Drive for Thinness and Body Dissatisfaction scales of the Eating Disorder Inventory-2 correlated .75 and .88, respectively, with Scale AA (Eating Dysfunctions) of the MACI. Scores on Scales FF (Depressive Affect) and GG (Suicidal Tendency) of the MACI correlated .59 and .67, respectively, with Beck Depression Inventory scores and .59 and .65, respectively, with Beck Hopelessness Scale scores. These scores are in the expected direction and indicate that Scales FF and GG of the MACI are tapping the same types of pathology as are the Beck instruments. However, Scale EE (Anxious Feelings) of the MACI correlated only .10 with the Beck Anxiety Inventory, although MACI Scales AA (Eating Dysfunctions), A (Identity Diffusion), and B (Self-Devaluation) all correlated in the .40s with the Beck Anxiety Inventory. MACI Scales CC (Delinquent Predisposition), F (Social Insensitivity), G (Family Discord), and BB (Substance-Abuse Proneness) showed moderately high relationships with the corresponding scales on the Problem Oriented Screening Inventory for Teenagers. Taken in aggregate, the patterns of correlations with other instruments provide a moderate degree of support for the construct validity of several MACI scales.

PRECISION OF THE MCMI-II COMPARED TO THE MMPI-2

Recall Heilbrun (1992) recommends a reliability figure of .80 as a minimum standard for psychological assessment instruments that provide a basis for expert testimony. Referring to clinical rather than forensic applications of psychological test, Cicchetti (1994) writes:

When the size of the coefficient alpha or other measure of internal consistency is below .70, the level of clinical significance is unacceptable; when it is between .70 and .79, the level of clinical significance is fair; when it is between .80 and .89, the level of clinical significance is good; and when it is .90 and above, the level of clinical significance is excellent. (p. 286)

As noted above, all the personality disorder and clinical syndrome scales of the MCMI-II meet or exceed the .80 criterion for internal consistency, and nearly all the scales meet or exceed the standard for test–retest stability. The MMPI-2 manual notes that the reliabilities for the basic scales of that instrument are slightly lower (Butcher, Dahlstrom, Graham, Tellegen, & Kaemmer, 1989). The section of the MMPI-2 manual headed "Reliability of the Basic Scales" states, "Data on the test–retest reliability and internal consistency of the basic scales are provided in Appendix D. These values range from .67 to .92 for a sample of 82 men, and from .58 to .91 for a sample of 11 women" (p. 31). Table D-1 of the MMPI-2 manual (Butcher et al., 1989, p. 88) lists retest data for samples of 82 males and 111 females with values within the ranges indicated in the text. However, the table represents retest data only and does not mention internal consistency. For such data on the basic and supplementary scales we shift to Tables D-7 and D-8 of the MMPI-2 manual (Butcher et al., 1989, p. 91). In those tables we find that, for samples of males ranging from 1,056 to 1,127 and for samples of females from 1,342 to 1,442, the internal consistency coefficients are dramatically different. For example, for a sample of 1,097 males the coefficient alpha for MMPI-2 Scale 6 (Paranoia) is .34. Though listed in the MMPI-2 manual as .3366, we shall follow the convention of rounding to two decimal places in order to avoid giving a spurious impression of scientific precision. For a sample of 1,407 females, the internal consistency coefficient for MMPI-2 Scale 6 is .39. In the same table, we find that for samples of 1,095 males and 1,378 females, the coefficient alpha values for MMPI-2 Scale 3 (Conversion Hysteria) are .58 and .56, respectively. Turning to Table D-8 in the MMPI-2 manual (Butcher et al., 1989, p. 91), which lists internal consistency values for the supplementary scales, we find that for a sample of 1,098 males, the coefficient alpha for Scale O-H (Overcontrolled Hostility) is .34. Noting that for reliability statistics the value represents a direct indication of true score versus error variance (unlike a Pearson product-moment correlation between two separate variables that reflects the square root of the shared variance), we find that fully two thirds of the variance of Scales 6 and O-H is error variance. Furthermore, for a sample of 1,402 females the coefficient alpha for Scale O-H is an astounding .24, indicating that fully three fourths of the variance is error variance and only one fourth is true score variance. None of these surprising findings are given any attention whatsoever in the text of the MMPI-2 manual.

In his presentation of standards for forensic use of test, Heilbrun (1992) states that "the use of less reliable tests [less than .80] would require explicit justification by the psychologist" (p. 265). Focusing for the moment only on the 13 validity and basic clinical scales of the MMPI-2 that are commonly relied on, only 3 of the 13 scales for males and only 4 of the 13 for females have alpha coefficients that meet the .80 standard (Butcher et al., 1989, p. 91). For clinical personality scales in which three quarters, or even two thirds, of the variance is error variance, the only plausible justification that an expert could offer when confronted on the stand with the above results would be having relied on the text of the manual, rather than the tabled values in the appendix, to determine the adequacy of the instrument's precision of measurement.

Whether by oversight or otherwise, this omission is extraordinarily misleading. For decades one of the most frequently heard criticisms of the MMPI has been that it lacks adequate reliability. That is certainly a central issue in assessing the value of the first revision of the instrument, which had been used in its original 1940's form for nearly half a century. In such a case, one would think that the authors, and certainly the manual editor, would be scrupulously careful about the presentation of reliability data for the revision.

In light of the MMPI-2 findings discussed above, it is useful to explore some theoretical issues as to the importance of stability versus internal consistency in evaluating the psychometric precision of an instrument. Stability should not be confused with internal consistency; stability refers to the ability of the test to measure a trait consistently over time, and this statistic is used as a gauge of whether the construct measured by the instrument is a long-term trait or a transient state. There are instances in which it is not desirable for a scale to have high stability, as for instance when the construct being assessed is one that will be expected to change frequently according to environmental conditions. Test items such as "Recently I have gone all to pieces" would not be expected to yield high stability coefficients because what is being measured is obviously whether the subject is undergoing a reaction to some specific environmental stressor. However, items such as "Whenever I have a problem with family, friends, or money I go all to pieces" are intended to measure a more enduring trait and therefore would be expected to be stable over time. The most common error regarding assessment of a test's precision of measurement is to regard stability as being a sufficient condition rather than merely a necessary one when enduring traits are the constructs being assessed.

Heilbrun (1992) makes this error in posing standards for forensic use of psychological tests. He states that for measuring trait variables with objective tests, the .80 criterion "would refer primarily to test-retest reliability" (p. 265). Internal consistency is the necessary, and in the case of measurement of transient emotional states the sufficient, condition for establishing precision of measurement.

It may be helpful in understanding the distinction to recall that a psychological test is merely an estimate of true score on the basis of a fallible one-time observation. This is stated forcefully by Van der Linden (1994), who views psychological tests as being merely standardized experiments and warns against treating them as though they were yardsticks. In a discussion of the limitations of psychological measurement, using as an example an IQ test, he writes:

> The truth about IQ tests is that, notwithstanding our daily parlance, they are not measurement instruments at all in the same sense as physics has its thermometers, balances, and stopwatches! In fact, they are just standardized experiments used to collect such qualitative data as responses to problems formulated in test items. (p. 12)

We tend to lose sight of this fact when we interpret small differences among personality test scale scores as though we indeed were reading a psychic thermometer rather than merely drawing inferences based on a one-time sample of subjects' verbal behavior.

One theorist who stresses the importance of stability over internal consistency is Cicchetti (1994). He states:

> ... one noted statistician held the ... view that coefficient alpha is to be preferred over both test–retest and interexaminer reliability. Specifically, Nunnally ... noted that "if coefficient alpha is low for a test, a relatively high correlation between retests should not be taken as an indication of high reliability." (p. 286)

Cicchetti questions the validity of this argument, pointing out that items with low or high ceilings can produce identical scores if divided in an odd–even basis but will intercorrelate zero as a matter of mathematical necessity. He further argues:

> Alternatively, there is the cogent argument that very high levels of internal consistency merely inform that items hang together well at a particular point in time. That is to say, the same level of internal consistency for the same subjects some weeks later may be based on completely different responses (e.g., between odd and even items) remains the same at each testing, coefficient alpha will be high, but test–retest reliability will be low. (p. 286)

When one considers the likelihood of the hypothetical situation posed by Cicchetti (1994) — that individuals will maintain the same ordering of responses on odd–even items while giving "completely different responses to the same test items at two different times" — the argument is unconvincing. If subjects vary their responses, they are guided by their current affective or clinical state in interaction with the content of specific test items and clearly not by whether the test item is odd or even, at least when responding to personality scale items. Further, Cicchetti's argument that items with very high or very low ceilings will intercorrelate zero, even though they hang together in terms of content, does not apply to personality scales, where most items are selected to have some degree of pull but at the same time not too much.

A more cogent argument is that advanced by Nunnally (1967). Nunnally points out that stability, although a necessary condition for reliability, is not a sufficient condition. He states that it is possible for a psychometric scale to have very high test–retest reliability with zero internal consistency if subjects simply respond that same way on both occasions. This is a much more likely outcome than subjects giving completely different responses across situations while maintaining the same order with respect to odd–even items. In the case of personality measures, it may simply be a matter of subjects remembering what they said the first time.

Cattell (1967) rejects the notion that stability can be considered a form of reliability at all. He states:

> A fourth coefficient which is frequently classified with reliability coefficients, but does not actually belong there, or, indeed, with the true test consistency coefficients at all is the stability coefficient. Measured simply as the correlation between a test and itself, readministered (same administrator and scorer) after an appreciable time interval, it may be called the uncorrected stability coefficient. (p. 63)

The importance of internal consistency is further illustrated by the concepts of true score and error variance on which classical test theory measures of reliability are based. A psychological test is a one-time, fallible estimate of a subject's true standing on the variable of interest. Measures of internal consistency estimate the true score (defined as the average of administrations of an infinite number of parallel forms of the instrument) by constructing parallel forms within the test through various combinations of splits. In theory, the test estimates the individual's standing on the variable that the instrument purports to measure. Under the domain-sampling theory, the variable of interest may be assessed via test items drawn from a particular content domain. For example, paranoid personality disorder may be assessed by means of items tapping suspiciousness, grandiosity, hostility, defensiveness, and other traits associated with this type of personality organization. Dependent personality disorder may be assessed by test items belonging to a different content domain that has little, if any, overlap with the paranoid content domain. Accurate assessment depends on taking an adequate sample of content from the specific domain in constructing the scale. Some redundancy of content is necessary in order to control for factors such as idiosyncratic processing of the item content. Consider, for example the following two test items:

A. You can never be sure what other people are thinking about you.
B. Those who pretend to be your friend can secretly be your enemy.

Hypothetically we would expect an individual high in paranoia to endorse both of these items positively because of their similar content. However, it is entirely possible for a paranoid subject to respond false to the first item by processing the content in the following manner: "False. You can *always* be sure that other people despise you and seek to do you in!" Item B, although it has essentially the same content as a distrust indicator, would elicit a positive endorsement because its wording does not trigger the distorted cognition that item A does. Thus, in order to achieve a reasonably adequate assessment, the content of the scale must be such as to ask the question in a number of different ways via items that are closely related in content, as a result of sampling from a *single* domain.

Consider the case of scales developed through empirical keying techniques without regard to content homogeneity. The selection of scale items solely on the basis of their correlation with membership in a particular diagnostic group runs the risk of yielding a scale that comprises items from several different content domains, most likely including *some* from the domain corresponding to the variable of interest. Thus, in terms of the target variable, a scale emerges that has some valid variance and a good deal of error variance. This situation is comparable to receiving a shortwave radio transmission under adverse atmospheric conditions. Try as one may to adjust the antenna and the various dial settings on the receiver, the transmission comes through as little signal and a great deal of noise. Some of the target program content comes through, but it is frequently obscured by static. The bottom line is that in a fallible, one-time estimate of a subject's standing on a particular trait, it is desirable to have as much "signal" and as little "noise" as possible determining the scale score.

One counter to the criticism of low internal consistency of MMPI-2 scales that is circulating in various workshops is that the item inter-correlations change according to the subject group. For example, the argument runs, although MMPI-2 Scale 6 (Paranoid) items have a low intercorrelation in the standardization sample at large, they *are* highly intercorrelated in subsamples of paranoid subjects. Thus, the internal consistency statistics for the entire standardization sample have no bearing on the measurement of someone who is truly paranoid. Of course, the argument that the items are "highly intercorrelated" in a paranoid sample does not refer to an actual statistical demonstration. It refers to the clinical theory that these attributes co-occur with greater frequency in paranoid subjects than in others. From the perspective of empirical reality, as opposed to theory, we would *necessarily* expect a *lower* intercorrelation of these items in a sample of paranoid subjects than in the standardization sample as a whole, assuming that the scale has even minimal validity. This is because by employing a subsample of individuals who score somewhat higher on the variable in question, we are restricting the variance of scores on that particular scale. Correlation means shared variance, that is, those who score high on one variable score high on the other *and* those who score low on one variable socre low on the other. In the case of split-half reliability, those who score high on one half of the scale score high on the other half and those who score low on one half score low on the other half. Removing the low scorers ensures a lower correlation: Attenuated variance means attenuated covariance, clinical theory notwithstanding. And, we might add, in terms of forensic applications, it is the reality of empirical research findings and the mathematical necessity of psychometric theory that are persuasive to judges and juries when properly presented, not speculative (albeit logically cohesive) clinical theory. The "rational validity" school associated with clinical theory is now merely a quaint vestige of the era in which the authority of the "doctor" was accepted unquestioningly.

UNDERSTANDING AND TESTIFYING ABOUT OPERATING CHARACTERISTICS

In addition to the graphical presentation of data for the clinicians' rating studies, the MCMI-II and MCMI-III manual present the criterion-related validity data in terms of operating characteristic tables (Millon, 1987, 1994a). The operating characteristics of psychological tests have been receiving increasing attention in recent years as an alternative method of assessing test validity and utility. Operating characteristics, originally deriving from the field of medical diagnosis (Cicchetti, 1994), expand on the notions of true and false positives and true and false negatives taught for the last several decades in graduate psychology programs. Table 6.1 defines the operating characteristics of a measure in terms of the familiar twofold contingency table.

Colloquially, we may conceive of the operating characteristics as answering a series of questions as to the probabilities of certain events. These questions represent a framework for communicating somewhat abstract validity and utility concepts to a judge and jury in simple, straightforward language without having to resort to additions and divisions of true and false positives and negatives:

Sensitivity. What are the chances that a subject who has *X* disorder will be picked up by the test and identified as having the disorder?

Specificity. What are the chances that a subject who does not have *X* disorder will be categorized by the test as not having the disorder?

Positive predictive power. What are the chances that a subject who is diagnosed by the test as having *X* disorder actually has it?

Negative predictive power. What are the chances that a subject who is categorized by the test as not having *X* disorder is actually free of the disorder?

Overall hit rate or diagnostic power. What are the chances of a subject being accurately diagnosed on the test? ("Test" here refers to any individual scale and not to the multiscale instrument as a whole.)

It should be noted that sensitivity and positive predictive power, although both based on percentages of the true positive cases, are very

TABLE 6.1. Classification Efficiency Terminology

Above Millon scale cutting lines	Clinician DSM-IV diagnosis	
	Positive	Negative
Positive	True positives (A)	False negatives (B)
Negative	False negatives (C)	True negatives (D)
Total	Total positives (A + C) +	Total negatives (B + D) = N

Note. Prevalence or base rate = (A + C)/N; sensitivity or true positive rate = A/(A + C); specificity or true negative rate = D/(B + D); positive predictive power = A/(A + B); negative predictive power = D/(C + D); overall diagnostic power or proportion correctly classified = (A + D)/N. Taken from the *Manual for the Millon Clinical Multiaxial Inventory–II*, by Theodore Millon, 1987, Minneapolis, MN: National Computer Systems. Copyright 1987 by Theodore Millon. Reprinted by permission.

different questions. It is positive predictive power that is usually considered the bottom line for clinicians, as it provides an answer to the question: "If I diagnose the subject as having X disorder on the basis of the measure with known operating characteristics (apart from any other diagnostic criteria that I might use), what are the chances that I am right?" Sensitivity provides an answer to the question: "If the subject has X disorder, what are the chances that I will detect it?" Again, this refers to diagnoses based on the single measure, apart from any other diagnostic criteria available to the clinician.

In terms of forensic work, the payoff matrix is usually structured with a heavier negative payoff for opinions relating to positive predictive power, where the witness is affirmatively stating that the subject has a disorder, than for sensitivity, which relates to the witness's capacity to detect a disorder that is present. This is because it is typically the expert's affirmative opinions that are attacked on cross-examination rather than conditions that the expert did not find (though this latter area can also be a subject of attack on some cross-examinations).

The operating characteristics presented in the MCMI-II manual (Millon, 1987) for the 703 patients included in the two more sophisticated validation studies described above are impressive. In a study of the basic and severe personality disorder scales, with a criterion of primary and secondary diagnoses by clinicians matched against MCMI-II score on the particular scale ranked either first or second, the positive predictive power ranged from 58% (self-defeating personality disorder) to 80% (antisocial personality disorder). In a study of Axis I clinical syndromes for the same group using a BR cutoff score of 75 as indicating the presence of a disorder, MCMI-II scales were compared with clinicians' ratings. Positive predictive power ranged from 50% for thought disorder to 92% for alcohol dependence.

The above results are impressive, especially when considered in light of the prevalence data. It is noted that in the studies just described, lower positive predictive power is associated with lower prevalence. This is not only an important consideration in interpreting the operating characteristics for clinical purposes but also one that is vitally important for experts who are cross-examined on such data in court. As is often pointed out in workshops on forensic psychology, the rigid format of court testimony, as opposed to the less structured scholarly and scientific debate with which psychologists are more familiar, creates pitfalls for expert witnesses. Jurors and many judges are naive as to the complexities of personality theory, psychological measurement, and diagnosis and are therefore learning about these concepts during the course of the expert's testimony. The expert is not allowed to respond freely to distortions of the testimony that may be introduced on cross-examination, and sharp attorneys can capitalize on this fact to create the appearance that the expert's conclusions are ridiculous, even though they may be thoroughly acceptable and valid scientifically.

Consider the following scenario. An expert testifies that a client has a diagnosis of schizoid personality disorder based partially on the expert's own observations and partially on the MCMI-II. The cross-examining attorney shows the expert a copy of the test manual and after eliciting the statement that the expert considers this to be an authoritative document containing technical information about the test, has the expert turn to Table 3-15 (Millon, 1987, p. 174). This table lists operating characteristics for a second study of personality disorders in which comparisons were limited to the first personality disorder listed by treating clinicians rather than the first or second as was the case with the study discussed earlier. In that table, compiled under much more stringent criteria, the prevalence (i.e., base rate) for schizoid personality disorder is 4% and the positive predictive power of MCMI-II Scale 1 (Schizoid) is 38%. After perhaps eliciting an admission from the expert that current federal standards for scientific evidence, as per *Daubert v. Merrell Dow Pharmaceuticals* (1993), discussed in Chapter 2, requires assessment of the true and false positive rates for diagnostic procedures, the attorney asks the expert to explain what a false positive is. The attorney then asks the witness to tell the jury what the false positive rate is for schizoid personality disorder as measured by Scale 1 according to Table 3-15 in the MCMI-II manual (Millon, 1987, p. 174). The expert concedes that the false positive rate is 62% (i.e., 1 minus the positive predictive power, or $1 - .38$). The following exchange ensues:

Q: Then, doctor, are you saying that more than half of the individuals diagnosed as having schizoid personality disorder by the test actually do not have this disorder according to the results of the study?

A: Yes.

Q: Doesn't that mean that I would do better by flipping a coin?

A: Ummmm . . .

Q: I mean, doctor, I don't have a Ph.D. in psychology, but I think that if I flipped a coin I would get about fifty percent false positives. Now, isn't fifty percent better than sixty-two percent false positives?

A: Ummm . . .

Q: Thank you, doctor, I don't have any more questions.

A: But . . . but . . .

J: There has been no question put to you doctor. Please do not say anything.

Thus, it appears to the jury that the expert's diagnostic procedure yields classification results that are inferior to those obtained by chance. The expert has allowed the cross-examining attorney to frame the problem for the jury in an incorrect manner, leading the jury to think that the procedure misclassifies 62% of all subjects, in which case the proverbial fair coin would clearly be better.

What has escaped the expert's notice is that the attorney is equating the subsample diagnosed by the criterion ratings as having schizoid personality disorder with the entire sample of the study. In other words, the attorney's questions refer to the 4% of subjects with schizoid personality disorder as though they constituted the entire sample of 703, instead of being only the 28 subjects (4% of 703) who were found by their treating clinicians to have the disorder. Thus, in response to the attorney's question, "Doesn't that mean that I would do better by flipping a coin," the witness should have stated, "Emphatically not. Flipping a coin would yield a false positive rate of ninety-six percent and a true positive rate of four percent. We do nearly ten times better than chance in our true positive rate using the MCMI-II Schizoid Personality Disorder scale." This is because the true and false positives are computed on a group already preselected for the presence of the disorder. If we were to employ a coin-flip method on the entire sample, half the subjects would be classified as having schizoid personality disorder and half would not. Given a prevalence rate of 4%, and assuming a fair coin, this procedure would place 14 of the 28 subjects with the disorder in the positive group (352 subjects, which is half of 703 rounded up) and 14 in the negative group (352 subjects). Thus, we would have a true positive rate of 4% (14/352) and 96% false positives (338/352), not 50% and 50% as the attorney's cleverly framed questions imply. Perhaps this is what the witness was attempting to convey after the cross-examination had concluded and at the point when the judge prohibited any further comments, absent any new questions posed by counsel.

It is useful for experts to point out in such a situation, on direct examination if possible, that the disorder in question has quite a low prevalence rate and that this factor, by itself, tends to lower the positive predictive power. It is also important to point out that 97% of subjects whom the test classifies as not having the disorder, in fact, do not have it (negative predictive power) and that 98% of subjects who do not, in fact, have the disorder are not classified by the test as having it (specificity). Testifying about operating characteristics can be extremely persuasive if one is aware of the pitfalls and damaging to credibility if one does not recognize such traps.

SEVEN

Preparation of Testimony

There are many mental health professionals who actively avoid any clinical work that may result in a courtroom appearance. Even when a treatment case or clinical evaluation unexpectedly becomes part of a legal dispute (e.g., old treatment records are subpoenaed in a divorce proceeding), many practitioners will do practically anything to avoid testifying. Any trial attorney who has requested records or reports from a practitioner has encountered such responses as "I'm too busy right now," or "I can send you the record, but I don't want to testify." Informal discussions with colleagues in the mental health field may reveal a genuine interest in many cases that arise in the legal system, but the possibility of having to go to court to testify is enough to dissuade many professionals from taking part in forensic work.

The purpose of this chapter is to provide general guidelines for preparing and offering testimony in a court of law. As with any other area of practice, the clinician who knows how rules and procedures in a legal context operate, who is prepared, and who has experience will feel much more comfortable in the role of an expert witness, although even experienced forensic experts become somewhat anxious when having to testify. Although many of the principles and guidelines in this chapter are general and can be applied to any component of forensic evaluation, the focus is on the Millon inventories. Those who are seeking a more detailed discussion of the nuances of expert testimony in general can consult other sources (Blau, 1984; Brodsky, 1991; Ewing, 1985b; Shapiro, 1984, 1991).

There are many settings in which an expert may be called upon to testify at a deposition, where the major task is to discover facts and issues that may be relevant and thus raised at trial. Although a deposition is different from testimony provided at trial, there are still important considerations when being deposed as an expert witness. Thus, the material in this chapter will be applicable to depositions as well. In addition, the expert witness may provide testimony at an administrative hearing before an administrative law judge, in a family court hearing, or in open court at a civil or criminal trial. Regardless of the setting, practitioners are advised to prepare themselves according to the principles discussed in this chapter.

At the trial level, expert witnesses will find that their testimony is viewed differently by each of the opposing attorneys, the judge presiding over the case, or the jury hearing evidence. The general structure of testimony consists of the following sequence: When a particular side in a legal dispute wants to prove a fact or support an argument at trial, evidence is presented, often in the form of witnesses called to provide testimony. The purpose of direct testimony is to allow the witness to "tell a story," as Mauet (1988) has framed it. Direct examination essentially introduces facts, expert opinion, sequences of events, and other information to be weighed by the trier of fact (i.e., judge or jury). Following direct testimony, the opposing attorney is permitted an opportunity to question and challenge the witness on any issues raised during direct examination. In some instances following this process, called cross-examination, the attorney who originally called the witness can then conduct what is referred to as redirect examination. The purpose of redirect is to explain or develop issues raised during cross-examination. The judge will limit such redirect testimony only to those matters raised during cross-examination. In rare instances, the witness may be re-cross-examined about issues raised during redirect examination. Generally, the longer an expert testifies on direct and cross-examination, the greater the likelihood that redirect and re-cross-examination will take place. However, a judge will frequently limit the degree of such follow-up questioning to avoid wasting valuable court time, to prevent harassment of witnesses, and to make sure that jurors do not become confused.

It is important to understand this general framework for testimony because it explains why the expert is treated in a particular manner while testifying. For instance, the questions asked and the attorney's demeanor denote a respect for the witness during direct examination because the expert is assumed to be supportive of the attorney's case. Cross-examination, on the other hand, may initially appear respectful, perhaps to lull the expert into a premature sense that his or her testimony will be over soon. Before long, however, the questions turn challenging, persistent, and complex and the attorney's tone becomes hostile, belittling, or perhaps abusive. One must understand that the job of an effective cross-examiner is to discredit the witness in order to gain support for his or her case. Even on redirect examination, the attorney who was once seen as a friendly and respectful ally, may be terse and will challenge any concessions made by the expert during cross-examination if his or her original case was weakened. Thus, redirect is meant to repair any damage that may have been done to the case via cross-examination.

As unsettling as the process sounds, providing testimony can be an intellectually challenging and professionally rewarding experience. By supporting one's opinion with scientifically established principles in court, one can effect change and influence legal outcomes that can improve the quality of life for some or the administration of justice in society as a whole. Also, greater respect for one's profession by lay observers can be particularly rewarding as a professional when testimony is offered in an objective, clear, and reasonable manner and when others find one's work interesting, thorough, and valued. For example, it can be quite gratifying for the expert to be approached after trial by the opposing attorney who was so hostile and attacking on cross-examination with the following compliment: "I think you handled yourself well at trial and I thought you were objective, rational in your thinking, and you made sense. I have another case that I might be able to use you on. Can I have your card?"

This chapter is meant to help those practitioners who utilize the Millon inventories as part of their forensic evaluation prepare for courtroom appearances. In particular, some general guidelines for preparing testimony are addressed, followed by issues that may arise when one is being qualified as an expert through voir dire. The chapter then discusses specific techniques and strategies for providing direct testimony and for handling attacks and challenges on cross-examination.

GENERAL PRINCIPLES FOR PREPARING TESTIMONY

The key to providing coherent, relevant, and sound testimony as an expert witness is to adequately prepare well in advance (Hess, 1987). As with any setting in which the professional is expected to teach or to instruct others, adequate preparation is the surest way to get the audience, in this case the trier of fact, to understand the message. Several opportunities during a psychologist's training provide good experience for how one can go about preparing. The challenge of sitting in defense of a thesis or dissertation, presenting papers at professional meetings and symposia, serving as a professor or instructor in academic settings, or presenting workshops or educational programs to other professionals are all ways in which the expert learns from experience that preparation is the key to effective presentation.

When providing testimony in court, some professionals may approach the task with uncertainty and trepidation. However, there are several ways to prepare for testifying both as an expert in general and with respect to the Millon inventories specifically. In general, one good method for preparing as an expert witness is to "learn the ropes"; here, consulting books and treatises on how to testify can be invaluable. Some volumes that are particularly useful for learning the role of an expert and the way in which to conduct one's self appropriately include Blau (1984), Brodsky (1991), Melton et al. (1987), Ewing (1985a), Shapiro (1984, 1991), and Weiner and Hess (1987). Audiotapes are another resource to help in preparing for the role of an expert (Ewing, 1985b). It is also necessary to know how an attorney is likely to prepare for cross-examination; thus familiarity with Ziskin and Faust's (1988) volume *Coping with Psychiatric and Psychological Testimony* will be of great assistance. This is particularly true when preparing to testify on Millon inventory results because this three-volume set has a section devoted to a critique of the Millon inventories which is designed to help attorneys formulate a cross-examination. Particular methods for dealing with such attacks are discussed later in the chapter.

Another method for preparing to testify is to observe other mental health professionals in the role of expert witness. This can be achieved in a number of ways: Develop a relationship with an attorney who can notify you when expert testimony is to be provided in a particular case. Also, with recent advances in telecommunication, television cameras allowed in courtrooms, and *Court TV* in particular, you can be exposed to the type of expert testimony that is effective and that which is not by watching television. Consulting with colleagues who have testified and attending continuing education workshops are also useful methods in preparing to testify as an expert. As Brodsky (1991) has commented, expert witnesses should come to feel less like an alien in the courtroom; by being present often in a courtroom, one develops a sense of "place identity" (p. 50), as if the courtroom is a place where he or she belongs.

There are several ways to prepare for those court appearances in which the Millon inventories will be a significant portion of the testimony. The first step is to become familiar with the basics of scoring, administration, construction procedures, normative samples, and psychometric issues related to reliability, validity, and operating characteristics. This can generally be achieved by a thorough reading of the test manuals and Chapter 6 of this volume. Those who are unsure of their skills in utilizing the Millon inventories can also prepare for foren-

sic use by attending continuing education workshops on these instruments. NCS's Professional Assessment Division, the publisher of the
Millon inventories, sponsors several national workshops each year. Of
course, supervised experience and consultation with colleagues is
another avenue for achieving expertise with the instruments. Finally,
reading texts on the Millon inventories (e.g., Choca et al., 1992; Craig,
1993a, 1993b) is valuable for organizing material to support conclusions made in a forensic report and on direct and cross-examination.

Once the expert has a familiarity and expertise with the instruments, there are some general guidelines to follow in preparing testimony for a particular case. These guidelines are presented here in
the form of 10 principles that are relevant to preparing forensic evaluations. Although they do not represent an exhaustive list, they are the
ones we feel are the most important or helpful. They have been derived from material found in Ewing (1985b) and Mauet (1988) and therefore represent perspectives from both a forensic psychologist and a trial
lawyer.

*Principle #1: Begin preparation for testifying even before starting the evalu-
ation.* Expert witnesses may be asked about any issues that are related
even remotely, to the opinions they give. To qualify as an expert, the
professional must give relevant education, training, and experience that
make him or her in possession of information that is not available to
the trier of fact. On direct examination, the expert must list the techniques and procedures used in arriving at an opinion; cross-
examination can attack qualifications and may be used to uncover biases
that can influence the expert's opinion.

Thus, preparation for such testimony should begin before actually taking the case. The expert should make sure that he or she is qualified to perform the evaluation; that he or she is trained to give certain
tests, such as the Millon inventories, and, once the decision to take the
case has been made, what procedures will need to be carried out. When
testifying this approach makes it easier to outline the procedures used
in the evaluation.

Also, the expert should examine personal biases prior to conducting a forensic evaluation. If, for example, the psychologist approaches
a child sexual abuse evaluation with the belief that children always tell
the truth about such matters and can never be mistaken or influenced
by others in their reports, such a bias might be revealed on cross-
examination. The professional should either reevaluate his or her beliefs in light of established research findings and clinical observations
or should decline to accept the case.

One can never begin preparing for testimony too soon; the assumption should never be made that testimony will not be required—anything is possible and the forensic psychologist should expect his or her work to be examined in court.

Principle #2: Make sure the Millon inventory being used is appropriate for the person being evaluated. A psychologist once approached one of the authors (J. T. M.) at a Millon inventory workshop with the MCMI-II profile of a 16-year-old boy who was being evaluated for his potential to commit violence after he had made homicidal threats against another person. The profile was marginally valid, as this boy's level of disclosure was extremely high, and numerous scales across the entire profile were highly elevated. The profile was indicative of a severely impaired, confused, and possibly psychotic individual. At first glance, one could say that this administration was inappropriate because the boy was too young to be given the MCMI-II and should have been administered either the MAPI or MACI. There were some sound reasons why the psychologist chose the MCMI-II over these other tests. For one, the MACI was unavailable commercially at the time of the evaluation and the MAPI was felt to lack any scales that measured psychopathological symptoms that were of primary importance, such as the presence of thought disturbance, severe personality disruption, and depression. The boy had some attentional difficulties that made use of the lengthier MMPI impractical. Also, the boy had been out of school for over a year, had no reading difficulties, was functioning autonomously at a job, lived on his own, and was self-supporting; in many ways, he was functioning socially as an adult. The psychologist appropriately interpreted this youth's MCMI-II with great caution, seeing his numerous elevations as a reflection of the tremendous psychological turmoil he was experiencing; the person against whom he had made homicidal threats was an older man who had sexually abused the boy over a period of several years. The MCMI-II profile was interpreted as a "cry for help," as the teenager had few resources to express himself adequately to others.

For clinical purposes, this administration of the MCMI-II was useful to the psychologist and could be justified on some grounds; from a forensic standpoint, however, there would be numerous problems. To testify as to why such an administration of the MCMI-II was performed, the potential for a nightmarish attack on cross-examination is great. Therefore, it is good practice to make sure that the person being administered a particular Millon inventory in a forensic case is similar to those individuals who make up the normative sample as described in the manual.

Principle #3: Be able to support interpretive statements made from Millon inventory test results. There are two keys to being able to support test interpretations. The first is to be familiar with the research and clinical literature on the Millon inventories. This material can be accessed through interpretive guides such as those written by Choca et al. (1992) and Craig (1993a, 1993b), as well as articles that are published in peer-reviewed journals. The second manner in which interpretive statements can be supported is to keep the Millon inventory results in proper perspective and not to extend them beyond their intended purposes. For example, in an evaluation of mental state at the time of offense, MCMI-II results indicating delusional thought content and disturbed thought processes do not mean that the defendant was therefore insane at the time of the offense. They merely suggest that the defendant shows signs of psychosis, but the psychologist must now determine what relationship these symptoms bear to the defendant's mental state at the time of the offense. Likewise, an MCMI-II profile indicative of borderline personality disorder does not mean that the individual's instability, moodiness, and angry outbursts render him or her an unfit parent in a child custody evaluation. The clinician must evaluate the impact these findings have on the parent–child relationship and the individual's role as a parent.

Therefore, Millon inventory interpretation should be firmly grounded in the characteristics actually measured by a particular scale or configuration and should not be extended into areas in which little support exists for their validity.

Principle #4: Know the legal issues involved. Part of the challenge to keeping Millon inventory results in their proper perspective is to know the legal definitions and issues involved in a case. If the psychologist is asked to evaluate the defendant's competence to stand trial, for example, the legal definition of this concept should be looked up.

To illustrate this principle, consider the definition of a defendant's inability to proceed for trial, which in New York State, for example, represents the legal principle of competence to stand trial. The statute defines incompetence as "a defendant who as a result of mental disease or defect lacks capacity to understand the proceedings against him or to assist in his own defense" (New York Criminal Procedure Law §730.10). A careful reading of this statute reveals that psychological testing will have little bearing on such issues as the defendant's capacity to understand the legal proceedings and to assist his or her attorney with the defense.

Of course, testing with the Millon inventories can assist in making a diagnosis of mental illness or with assessing for potential malingering, but such issues have a peripheral level of importance. Knowing the legal issues involved in a particular case can be invaluable. An opposing attorney on cross-examination may ask the expert to define such legal concepts as "murder," "insanity," "best interests of the child," and so forth. As Ewing (1985b) suggests, those mental health professionals who have minimal familiarity with legal issues can easily access the information in a law library at most state and federal courthouses. Another option is to request a copy of the relevant statutes and cases from the attorney with whom the psychologist is working and who will be calling the expert as a witness. Even the judge presiding over a case can provide relevant legal materials if the expert has been appointed by the court to perform an evaluation.

Principle #5: Know the facts of the case. Numerous experts in the field of forensic psychology have recommended that the psychologist should be familiar with all factual elements in a case (Blau, 1984; Ewing, 1985b; Shapiro, 1984, 1991). Therefore, adequate preparation for testimony should include reading all relevant documents regarding a case, including police reports, court papers, witness statements, and any other pertinent materials. Again, this standard of practice not only prepares the expert for testifying in general but can also assist with placing psychological test results in their proper perspective in the overall evaluation.

Principle #6: Keep detailed notes. Attorneys can become quite specific and perhaps even picky in their questioning about the procedures used by a mental health expert. Keeping detailed notes about the content of interviews, telephone conversations, and other evaluation strategies is a key element to being prepared for testifying. The professional's notes provide a useful reference to refresh his or her memory and they enhance the perception among observers in court that the professional took great care and was actively involved in the evaluation process. In addition, detailed documentation about other issues can be useful, and sometimes necessary, in providing testimony. For example, a detailed record of the date the MCMI or MACI was given, the time taken by the defendant or litigant to complete the test, the conditions under which the test was administered, and other details can be extremely helpful. Some attorneys may question the validity of results on psychological tests that were administered, under conditions that may have fostered fatigue (e.g., giving the MACI to a teenager after 4 hours of interviewing and intellectual testing), or where the defendant's responses may have been contaminated by outside influences (e.g., an adult taking the MCMI-II in the recreation room of an inpatient hospital unit). Documentation of the circumstances surrounding test administration can be useful in meeting such challenges.

Principle #7: Always review your deposition or grand jury testimony before testifying. Those who are unfamiliar with legal procedures may relax after they provide testimony at a deposition or grand jury hearing because they feel "the worst is over." However, such procedures are merely fact-finding tools that are used prior to trial. Though the atmosphere for deposing a witness may appear less formal, often taking place in an attorney's office without a judge presiding, the deposition is still sworn testimony and it can be used to impeach an expert's testimony at trial. Blau (1984) has made the point that *experts should never waive the signing of their deposition.* Signing the deposition permits an expert to review his or her testimony, correct any mistakes in transcription (e.g., misspelled test name or scale), and receive a copy of the testimony. By reviewing this material prior to testifying, the practitioner can prepare his or her testimony in accordance with the content of the deposition. This practice avoids the likelihood that the expert will testify to a fact, procedure, or opinion that directly conflicts with the testimony provided in the deposition, thus decreasing the chances of impeaching direct testimony at trial.

Principle #8: Take responsibility for preparation; don't allow the attorney calling you as a witness to prepare your testimony. A colleague once participated in a widely publicized murder trial in which a man claimed insanity after he killed a young girl. The psychologist was asked to conduct a narrowly tailored evaluation with a specific question whether or not the defendant had any present symptoms or past history of psychosis. The psychologist prepared in advance of trial several pages of questions and answers for the district attorney who called him as a witness to use on direct testimony. The attorney adhered in large measure to the material prepared by the psychologist, except for a few questions that dealt with issues that were thought to be potentially confusing to a jury and irrelevant to the major points raised in the psychologist's report.

As it turned out, the defense attorney's cross-examination was limited to issues that the psychologist had anticipated. Although he had little prior forensic experience, the psychologist reported that his testimony went smoothly, and on reflection, the process was not nearly as dreadful as he had anticipated. The court regarded his testimony highly and a detailed letter from the district attorney to the psychologist after trial praised the detailed preparation that had been done on the direct testimony.

Any expert is wise to use a similar approach to preparation of testimony. A well-established principle in forensic practice is that the expert understands his or her area of expertise better than anyone else in the court; that is what makes him or her an expert witness. Therefore, the expert is in the best position to prepare relevant topics, issues, and areas for development during direct testimony. A cue book, in which copies of relevant diagnostic criteria from DSM-IV, tables and data from test manuals, research summaries, and other reference material is available, can be quite useful in preparing for trial (Blau, 1984). Active preparation by the expert can enhance his or her confidence in and comfort about testifying.

Principle #9: Critique your own work. Because the expert witness is in a position to know what issues and concepts are important to formulating a conceptualization in a case, he or she is also in a position to anticipate areas in which the opinion might be attacked on cross-examination. Anticipating questions that may challenge one's training, experience with a particular test, thoroughness, reasoning, or personal biases can be invaluable. A mock cross-examination by the attorney calling the expert or by a respected colleague can be useful in preparing for cross-examination. By anticipating where they are susceptible to attack, expert witnesses increase their chances of coming across as composed, confident, and nonargumentative.

Principle #10: Keep it simple. Too often, test interpretation and psychological evaluation reports become filled with professional jargon and confusing technical language. It is important to remember that interpretive statements for individual tests, technical material in test manuals, and diagnostic criteria can be confusing to someone who is not well acquainted with the behavioral sciences. Testifying that a defendant or litigant's "internalized structural cohesiveness can be compromised by severe decompensation" might be meaningful to the expert, but it may be nothing but a confusing mess to a judge or juror. Instead, testimony, reports, and conclusions or opinions should be kept as simple as possible while still communicating what it is that the expert is trying to say. Thus, jurors will more likely understand what the expert means when he or she says that "the defendant's ability to think clearly and rationally, to handle overwhelming emotions, and distinguish what is real from what is fantasy is impaired when stressors exceed the defendant's ability to cope effectively." Simplicity makes for more effective teaching and, thus, more understandable expert testimony.

QUALIFYING THE EXPERT WITNESS

The process by which expert witnesses are examined as to their credentials is known in many jurisdictions as voir dire. In general, the attorney presenting the expert's testimony will request that the witness give a summary of his or her professional training and experience in order to demonstrate for the court that the expert possesses a level of expertise in the particular area beyond that of the average juror and is therefore able to render scientific or professional opinions. In some cases, especially when the expert has testified before a particular judge on many occasions, the opposing counsel will stipulate to the witness's credentials as presented in the curriculum vitae. However, in cases in which the witness is relatively unfamiliar to the judge, or in cases in which there is a jury, the opposing attorney will often challenge the expert's competence to give an opinion on the specifics of the case. In other instances, the opposing counsel may delve into the details of what may appear to be impressive credentials with the objective of creating the impression that the expert is exaggerating his or her professional accomplishments.

Experts should be attuned to a number of issues when presenting credentials on the stand. First, when listing professional distinctions that sound impressive and are intended to have the effect of enhancing credibility, avoid those that do not actually have much substance to them. For example, members of the American Orthopsychiatric Association have the option of applying for Fellow status. Although Fellow of the American Orthopsychiatric Association sounds more impressive than Member, the only qualification for Fellow status is having been a member for 5 years and paying a higher annual membership fee. Thus, if the expert emphasizes being a Fellow of a particular organization before the jury without disclosing that it is not an honor based on any particular accomplishment, the opposing counsel is likely to effect a damaging attack by eliciting this fact and then characterizing it in unflattering terms. For example, the cross-examining attorney may ask, "So you don't have to do anything but hang around the organization for five years and pay more money in order to be able to bill yourself as a 'Fellow,' do you Doctor?" On the other hand, professional distinctions such as Diplomate status, conferred by the American Board of Professional Psychology (ABPP), should be included in the expert's initial presentation of credentials. If the witness's Diplomate status is questioned, the witness has the opportunity to describe the multistage credentialing process of the ABPP in a modest but thorough fashion, from initial review of the application to preparation and review of the work samples to the on-site observation by three Diplomate examiners of the candidate's professional work.

The same principle applies to publications. Experts who submit lengthy lists of professional publications may respond to the question, "Do you have any publications in your field?" with "Yes, I have many of them." However, it turns out that most or all of these are in forums such as the "*Lake County Bulletin of Reading Improvement.*" Knowledgeable attorneys routinely challenge experts' publications by asking whether they are in refereed professional or scientific journals. If, as a response to the question "How are articles for this publication screened?" the best that one can come up with is, "Well, they are always looking for good material," the publication should not be presented to the court as an indication of the expert's high professional standing.

In many situations, opposing counsel will attempt to limit or exclude the testimony of an expert on the grounds that the witness's experience and training, although generally establishing qualification as a psychologist, do not provide grounds for giving expert opinions on specific aspects of the case. This objection is typically raised in cases in which a child or adolescent is the subject of the expert's testimony and it is incumbent upon the expert to demonstrate a basis in either experience or training to render an opinion as to individuals in these age groups.

Other situations in which such objections are common include those cases involving the influences of drug and alcohol on behavior, battered woman syndrome testimony, neuropsychological issues (where opposing counsel will stress the organic component if the witness is not a neuropsychologist), and employment issues (where the witness does not have specific training or experience in industrial/organizational psychology).

Although challenges that are specific to the expert's qualifications relative to the Millon inventories are rare during voir dire (unless the expert is being called specifically to testify only as to issues about these tests), it enhances credibility when testifying about Millon inventory results to have had workshop or seminar training in theoretical and technical aspects of these instruments.

DIRECT TESTIMONY

Once the expert has been qualified as an expert by the court, the next major task is development of the actual testimony. In addition to adequate preparation, the expert will ensure that his or her testimony is accepted and considered if the main purpose of direct examination is kept in mind. According to one major legal text on trial preparation, direct testimony "should elicit from the witness, in a clear and logical progression, the observations and activities of the witness so that each of the jurors understands, accepts, and remembers his testimony" (Mauet, 1988, p. 75). Thus, direct testimony is generally characterized by the use of clearly organized and logical thinking, simple language that can be easily understood, explanations of vague or difficult-to-understand principles, and the outlining of everything the expert did to arrive at the final opinion in a way that a trier of fact can reconstruct in hindsight. Direct testimony can also be a time to acknowledge areas of weakness in one's opinion, if necessary.

When testifying on direct examination about the Millon inventories, there are several helpful guidelines to keep in mind. These apply equally well to other areas of testimony, but the Millon inventories are the major focus in this discussion.

The first principle to recognize is that such technical terms as scale names, profile codetypes, psychometric terms, and other similar concepts should be accurately and simply defined. This should be done the first time any such term is used (Mauet, 1988). As the following example illustrates, technical terms may confuse jurors if not defined early on in direct examination.

Q: Now, Doctor, you just described the MCMI-II to the jury. You relied on that test, in part, to formulate your opinion, did you not?

A: Yes, I did.

Q: What did the results of that test reveal about Mr. Smith's anxiety level?

A: Mr. Smith was experiencing an extremely high level of tension, worry, muscular tension, and other anxiety-related symptoms.

Q: How did you determine that his anxiety level was "extremely high," as you put it?

A: Mr. Smith's Anxiety Scale on the MCMI-II was above what is referred to as a base rate score of 85. This means that he scored in the same range as those individuals presenting for mental health treatment who are determined by their treating therapist to be experiencing anxiety as a prominent part of their clinical symptoms.

In this example, the expert generally defines what a base rate score is in practical terms. The jury is not likely to know what such a score is, so a simple and clear definition helps to establish how the psychologist derived the conclusion from the test profile.

An expert must also be cognizant of a second major principle that guides the process of direct testimony. Although the temptation to cover every possible detail on direct examination is great, the witness should stick to the subject at hand. Excessive discussion or explanations that are digressive run the risk that an expert will stray into an area in which he or she lacks expertise; irrelevant and minor details may cause confusion for jurors and the expert may inadvertently raise an issue about which he or she is unprepared to talk. Also remember that the content of cross-examination is limited to the issues that are raised during direct examination. Thus, if digressive material is brought up during direct testimony, the expert may have opened up the door for a barrage of attacking questions on cross-examination. Consider the following exchange during direct testimony of a psychologist testifying at a personal injury trial.

Q: So, the MCMI-II results were consistent with your clinical diagnosis of a major depression. Is that correct?

A: Yes.

Q: Would a person with major depression experience loss of appetite?

A: It is very common, yes, but this does not have to occur in every single case.

Q: Would a person with major depression experience difficulty sleeping?

A: Again, it is common, but does not have to be present in every case of major depression.

Q: How would you treat those symptoms?

A: There are a number of options . . . [the witness explains various behavioral techniques, then continues] . . . There are also various medications which could be considered. Some antidepressants are sedating, while others tend to be more activating. They affect different neurotransmitter systems in the central nervous system . . .

Unless the expert has qualified as an expert in psychopharmacology, there is a strong likelihood that the opposing attorney will make an issue out of this testimony on cross-examination. The expert has discussed details about antidepressant medication that can be attacked in various ways, including the lack of medical education for a psychologist and the fact that psychologists are not currently licensed to prescribe medication. If the expert limits his or her testimony only to the relevant facts and does not offer unnecessary details, there is greater confidence placed in the resulting opinion. In this example, the expert could have acknowledged the need for a medication consultation, the symptoms that would point to such a need, thus supporting a psychologist's diagnostic skills, and how a referral to an appropriate medical professional is standard psychological practice.

A third general guideline for providing direct testimony is to have respect for the jury. It may be tempting not only to use technical language to impress the court but also to become somewhat arrogant and condescending to a jury without any clear intention of appearing as such. This can happen even with highly skilled and experienced forensic practitioners. Direct testimony that respects the intelligence of jurors and their capacity to learn even the most technically complex of concepts should not be underestimated. Consider the following forms of response.

A: The concept of test validity is really a basic principle that is straightforward and easy to understand.

or

A: You actually need experience talking to someone with such a condition to really understand them.

or

A: Mrs. Jones's MCMI-II profile was easy to identify and classify as invalid.

In these examples, the jury may be quick to view the expert as arrogant. In the first answer, some jurors may feel that the witness views them as less capable of understanding the concept of test validity if there are aspects of the concept that they cannot clearly understand. Test validity can be complex and jurors may take exception to the witness's implications. In the same way, jurors do not want to hear that they may be incapable of understanding a particular concept or diagnosis if they do not possess specialized experience that the expert has. The purpose of direct testimony is to provide knowledge that the jury might not have, but which jurors are fully capable of comprehending. Thus, respect for the trier of fact is important in providing effective direct testimony.

Because the effectiveness of direct testimony depends in large part on the teaching ability of the expert, individual aids can also be employed during direct examination. Overhead diagrams of Millon inventory profiles, summarized data from the test manuals or research studies, and other visual aids can be extremely useful in simplifying and clarifying complex issues and material. The expert can prepare these visual aids in advance of trial and use them during direct testimony. Also, referral to notes and materials in a cue book, discussed earlier and in some detail by Blau (1984), can keep testimony accurate and clear. It should be kept in mind, however, that any materials brought to the witness stand and referred to during testimony can be entered as evidence and viewed by the court, jury, and both attorneys. Thus, the expert should avoid overheads, photocopied book pages, or hand-written notes that contain question marks, numerous qualifiers ("if," "but," "maybe," etc.), or other markings that create doubt about the expert's interpretations, analyses, and conclusions.

CROSS-EXAMINATION

General Issues

Although trial attorneys are taught to start the process of cross-examination with the basic question of whether or not a witness needs to be cross-examined (Mauet, 1988), experts in forensic psychology should always prepare their testimony with the expectation that they will be cross-examined. A good trial attorney will never pass up the opportunity to weaken the opposing side's case and cross-examination is one of the best techniques for achieving this goal.

According to Mauet (1988), there are two basic purposes of cross-examination and attorneys will attempt to achieve both of these goals. The first is to elicit favorable testimony that will support the case for the attorney conducting the cross-examination. Thus, the expert can expect to respond to hypothetical factual situations and be forced into conceding on points made during direct examination. A second goal of cross-examination, one that is generally associated with the procedure, is to discredit, minimize, or in other ways destroy the integrity and credibility of not only the expert's opinion and conclusions but also the expert.

When testifying on cross-examination, the expert can expect that the process will proceed from questions that attempt to elicit favorable admissions and testimony through a gradual change of tone to questions that are more attacking and challenging. The general reasoning behind this strategy is as follows:

> At the end of the direct examination, most witnesses will have testified in a plausible fashion and their credibility will be high. This is the time to extract favorable admissions and information from the witness, since the witness' credibility will enhance the impact of the admissions. Such admissions will have less impact, and be less likely to occur, if you have previously attacked the witness. (Mauet, 1988, p. 214)

Regardless of the actual tone in the initial parts of cross-examination, the expert must expect, but not be defensive about, the attacking nature of cross-examination. As one experienced forensic practitioner once quipped, "Good morning, Doctor!" is the last respectable thing you will probably hear from the cross-examiner.

In order to get the expert witness to provide testimony favorable to the case, an attorney on cross-examination will employ a number of tactics. First, he or she will attempt to highlight and focus on any direct testimony the expert offered that is either neutral or particularly helpful. In addition, the cross-examining attorney will use hypothetical examples, leading questions, and factual details which can support the opposing case. Under these circumstances, the expert should acknowledge any facts that have sound support but should not be quick to abandon conclusions, or adopt alternative conclusions, without careful reflection and thought. Hypothetical questions may require assumptions that conflict directly with known facts. In the same way, a leading question may require inferences that are likewise based on faulty presumptions. Consider the following exchange:

Q: Doctor, since the MACI is a self-administered test, you wouldn't know about other patients on the unit who helped Richard complete the test, thus influencing the results. The test would therefore be invalid, wouldn't it?

A: Well, there are two parts to your question . . .

Q: Please, just answer yes or no.

A: I cannot answer that question in a yes or no format.

Q: You mean you can't answer the question as to whether or not the MACI was valid?

A: Of course I can. You first asked about the administration of the test, which I monitored from start to finish. Richard did not experience any distractions, since I observed him complete the test alone. Secondly, I was able to determine that Richard's MACI was valid and interpretable.

In this example, the cross-examining attorney employed tactics that not only sought to elicit testimony favorable to her case but also attempted to discredit the witness's reliance on the MACI. The initial question contained an inference the witness knew to be false, namely, that the teenager in this case had other people help him with the test. Second, the attorney attempted to direct the witness to answer yes or no. In this example, the expert did not fall into the trap of answering in such a limited format. Just because an attorney orders a witness to respond in a particular fashion does not mean that the expert must respond in that manner. The witness should provide an answer that conveys exactly what is intended and should not be directed on how to respond. Judges will usually be sensitive to an expert's need to have latitude and will generally permit a qualification or explanation if the expert makes it clear that he or she cannot answer in a limited fashion.

Cross-examining attorneys will also employ other tactics to discredit a witness. One method is to impeach the witness by getting the expert to make contradictory statements and conclusions. Various resources are used for this technique and include getting the expert to testify to something on cross-examination that conflicts with testimony in the deposition or on direct examination, getting the expert to recognize a treatise as an established authority and then cite material from the treatise that conflicts with the expert, and other similar strategies. To avoid impeachment, the expert should always be aware of his or her prior testimony, depositions should be reviewed and reread before trial, and the expert should be cautious about what he or she accepts as authority. Remember, no matter how popular a text or paper is in the professional literature, the expert is under no obligation to accept any treatise as authoritative and one may qualify its acceptance by recognizing the treatise with certain stated qualifiers or exceptions.

Other attempts to discredit the expert on cross-examination include attacking the expert's biases, prejudices, and motives. Thus, the attorney will likely ask about the expert's fee, prior cases in which he or she has testified, or prior experiences as a witness for the attorney who originally called the expert to the stand. These matters are best handled in a straightforward yet precise manner. Thus, for example, the expert can state that he or she is being compensated at a particular rate for the *time spent* on a case, not the actual testimony; time, not testimony, is compensated in professional practice.

Cross-Examination and the Millon Inventories

One of the major sources from which attorneys draw questions for cross-examining expert witnesses in psychiatry and psychology is Ziskin and Faust's (1988) three-volume text *Coping with Psychiatric and Psychological Testimony*. These volumes have sections on a variety of issues about which experts testify and those professionals who provide expert testimony should become familiar with the material in this work. One of the sections deals explicitly with the MCMI. Below we outline some techniques for successfully meeting the challenges that can be raised on cross-examination.

There has been considerable debate about the points raised by Ziskin and Faust in their unwavering criticism of testimony by behavioral scientists and mental health professionals (Brodsky, 1989; Faust & Ziskin, 1988a, 1988b; Matarrazzo, 1991; Rogers, Bagby, & Perera, 1993;

Ziskin & Faust, 1991). Although the specifics of this debate touch on numerous issues, the basic fact remains that the Ziskin and Faust (1988) text represents a biased review of the professional literature with the intent being to help attorneys prepare cross-examination. Consider the following acknowledgment in their preface:

> The book consists almost entirely of literature which negates the expertise of mental health professionals. *There is literature not contained in this book that is supportive of forensic psychiatry and psychology* [emphasis added], although for some topics this literature may be slim or close to nonexistent. . . . The reason we exclude supportive literature is *not* [emphasis in original] so that readers will think it does not exist. As noted, it may or does exist. However, although perhaps of academic interest, we view such supportive evidence as largely irrelevant from a legal context. (p. xvii)

This passage taken from Ziskin and Faust is important to keep in mind when the expert encounters challenges and attacks from this source.

In keeping with this bias, Ziskin and Faust (1988) have outlined a strategy for attacking psychological tests, and the MCMI in particular; this strategy is likely to be extended to all the Millon inventories (see vol. 3, p. 162). Drawing from the suggestions made by these critics, an attorney is likely to challenge the Millon inventories with the following types of questions, which have been paraphrased from Ziskin and Faust (1988). In response, some strategies are provided for ways in which the psychologist can effectively defend the use of these instruments under cross-examination.

Q: Isn't it true that the [MCMI-II, MCMI-III, MACI, etc.] is a new test?

Response strategy. The length of time a commercial test has been on the market has little to do with the reliability, validity, and utility of the instrument. By analogy, just because a new medication has entered the market does not mean that consumers are taking their chances on its effectiveness and side effects. A large body of empirical research precedes approval of a drug by the Food and Drug Administration (FDA). In the same way, ethical preparation of commercial psychological tests requires much preliminary research and the test manual reports on this data. All the Millon inventories have detailed technical manuals which report on empirical findings pertaining to reliability, validity, and interpretation.

Q: But Doctor, there really hasn't been time to accumulate thousands of research studies on the Millon test as there has been with the MMPI, has there?

Response strategy. According to the Millon inventories' author, Theodore Millon, there have been well over 400 published studies and dissertations on the MCMI and MCMI-II alone (Theodore Millon, personal communication, September 1994). The real strength of empirical support for a test lies not in the quantity of studies but with the quality of the work. Craig (1993a) has brought together a number of chapters by experts who have summarized the body of research on the MCMI and the amount of research on the test is substantial. Reference to many of the chapters in Craig's text and review of the reference lists at the end of chapters would prepare any expert to cite a substantial body of literature.

Q: Research studies that have been negative about the test have appeared in the literature — is that true, Doctor?

Research strategy. This question is really meant to undermine the jury's confidence in the expert's reliance on the Millon inventories by highlighting any negative research that may exist. The expert can address this approach by emphasizing that as independent research is conducted, *both* negative and positive research is published; such research merely directs clinicians to where the strengths and weaknesses of a test are. If the expert bases his or her conclusions on aspects of the Millon inventory that are strengths established in the research literature, this question will allow the expert to highlight those strengths. Negative research generally reveals such specific weaknesses as an individual scale that may be of questionable utility in a given situation, how specific test results are interpreted, or the lack of correspondence between self-report measures and structured clinical interviews. These research findings can be qualified by noting any methodological weaknesses in a study; also, the results of a negative study do not have any bearing on the particular use made of the test if the practitioner did not make use of the test in a way that conflicts with the findings of the negative study. The forensic practitioner can develop any number of similar strategies for defending against such an attack. Remember that negative research findings may not necessarily pertain to a valid aspect of the test. For example, an attorney who states that no research supports the use of the MCMI for measuring neurological symptoms can be informed that the test was never intended for that particular purpose.

Q: Hasn't there been a substantial amount of negative scientific and professional literature on the Millon tests?

Response strategy. Many of the same responses to the previous question can be raised for this question. In addition, it can be pointed out that "negative professional literature" in the form of opinion and critique does not point to test invalidity. In fact, professional skepticism about the MCMI-I (Widiger et al., 1985) became the impetus to revise the test (Millon, 1985) and actually resulted in such improvements in the test as better validity statistics (McCann, 1991; Widiger & Corbitt, 1993). Thus, negative professional literature can serve to improve professional practice and technique and is part of the scientific process. In addition, because the MCMI-I is obsolete and the MCMI-II, MCMI-III, and MACI are the currently used tests, criticism based on the MCMI-I would likewise be obsolete.

Q: Doesn't the fact that the Millon inventories are continuously being revised mean that there are ongoing problems with these tests?

Response strategy. The Millon inventories undergo revision to keep the scales concurrent with changes in DSM diagnostic criteria and syndromes, which also undergo modification and challenge. Scientific inquiry and empirical investigation do not rest on the fact that we live in a static, unchanging world. Quite the contrary, scientific observations are changing as well, as our world becomes more complex and the technology we possess for making scientific discoveries is changing and improving. Thus, the Millon inventories merely reflect this process and undergo revisions to keep current with advances in the fields of clinical psychology, psychiatry, and psychodiagnosis, as well as with improvements in psychological measurement procedures.

Q: Isn't there a study [perhaps a reference is cited] showing that . . . [e.g., the MCMI overdiagnoses abnormality, there is a particular scale which shows poor concordance with clinician diagnosis, etc.]?

Response strategy. Most of the studies cited in the literature showing negative findings (e.g., Repko & Cooper, 1985; DeWolfe, Larson, & Ryan, 1985; Piersma, 1987a, 1987b) apply to the MCMI-I and can be countered by noting improvements with the MCMI-II and MCMI-III. In some instances, a specific MCMI-II study may be cited that has negative implications (e.g., delRosario, McCann, & Navarra, 1994). There are a number of ways to respond to such attacks. If specific scales on the Millon inventory are not relied on in formulating a conclusion, diagnosis, or opinion, then any reference to negative research that attacks an unused scale would be irrelevant. The expert could point to positive, supportive research on the scales or indices relied upon. For example, if the MCMI-II is utilized to assess for possible malingering of psychosis in a murder trial where insanity has been raised as a defense and an attorney attacks the Thought Disorder Scale (SS) on cross-examination, the expert can point out the validity of the MCMI-II's modifier indices as measures of response style, including malingering. Another strategy for defending against attacks with negative research is to point out that studies often interpret Millon inventory results dichotomously; that is, the scales are used to make a diagnostic decision on an "either–or" basis—either the diagnosis is present or it is not. Such an interpretive approach has numerous limitations, because it fails to view the scales as dimensional measures of traits, personality characteristics, and clinical states (Flynn, McCann, & Fairbank, 1995). Specifically, not only are Millon inventory scale elevations diagnostically relevant, but they reveal aspects of the person being evaluated that can be descriptively useful and provide a richer set of descriptive features other than diagnostic labels. Finally, negative research findings on the Millon inventories can be met with attacks on the methodological design of these studies. One can also highlight the difficulties in generalizing results from some studies to the current application of the test. Also, the particular defendant or litigant being evaluated may not be representative of the subject sample contained in a particular study which has a negative implication.

CONCLUSION

The process of testifying in open court is intimidating to many and even experienced forensic professionals find the act anxiety provoking at times. At the heart of any sound testimony is advance preparation by the expert. Preparation is essential to conducting a thorough forensic evaluation; to providing clear, coherent, and useful direct testimony; and to withstanding even the harshest of cross-examinations. This chapter provides detailed information about how direct and cross-examination is developed by attorneys and suggestions are made for dealing with problems that arise when an expert takes the witness stand. Specific suggestions are made for developing direct testimony on the Millon inventories and specific cross-examination questions are presented to help experts prepare for defending against attacks that may be made on their use of these instruments. With adequate preparation and familiarity with the literature on these instruments, the expert will be able to stand up to attacks and challenges.

EIGHT

Use of Computerized Reports in Court

The exponential growth of computer technology over the last few decades is evident in almost every aspect of daily life. Psychological testing, and personality assessment in particular, is an area of clinical practice that has not escaped the impact of computers. In particular, objective personality tests such as the MCMI and MACI are ideally suited for computer applications, given the unambiguous nature of test administration and the clear-cut scoring rules and procedures that apply. In addition, the use of computers to generate interpretive statements and descriptive summaries has grown rapidly.

In light of the expansion of our knowledge about and acclimation to a computer-assisted information processing technology, the original model of computerized test interpretation based on the mimicking of a psychological report written by an individual clinician seems rather dated. Indeed, at the time such programs were developed, starting in the late 1960s, psychologists knew relatively little about the strengths and limitations of computers but were intrigued by the capacity of the machine to perform what had until that time been a task limited to individuals who had years of specialized experience and training in test interpretation. The model of an individual clinician preparing a psychological report specifically for an individual client was the only method available.

In today's information processing jargon, that model is classified as an expert system. An expert system is one in which the judgment processes of an expert are modeled and the computer program is designed to provide assessments that represent what the expert would decide, given the input data. Roid (1986) discusses various types of expert systems in psychology, ranging from the subjective to the scientific. At the lower end of this continuum lies the plain scoring system that provides only a printout of the numerical scores with no interpretive statements at all. Next in the hierarchy is the descriptive program, which provides brief descriptive phrases such as "above average" or "possible organic problems" in response to score configurations. Next comes the interpretive program, which is simply a model of the expert judgment of a clinician based on that individual's personal experience with the instrument. This type of program may tie together various components of the test into a series of interpretive statements that are logically cohesive. The underlying model for such a program is sometimes termed "rational validity" in that the interpretations are based on logical connections among sets of score patterns, relying heavily on the assumption of construct validity for the individual scales of the instrument. At the top of the hierarchy we have the clinician-actuarial program, which contains not only subjective interpretations but also statements based on actuarial data for individual scales. Thus, hypothetically, such a program would contain such standard clinical interpretations as "This patient is likely to react in an impulsive and hostile manner to perceived slights and insults" and also such statements as "Research has demonstrated that patients with the subject's score profile are three times as likely as other subjects to violate parole within a six-month period."

Roid (1986) stresses that truth in labeling these programs is essential in order for the psychologist to be able to determine the degree of confidence to place in any individual interpretive statement. Whereas Roid's discussion addressed the needs of clinical practitioners primarily, the issue of truth in labeling is vital in forensic situations in which the expert is likely to be asked in detail for the research data supporting particular statements based on test score configurations. It is one thing to respond that the interpretation relies on the opinion of a single expert modeled by a computer program and another to be able to state that the interpretation reflects a specific empirical research finding. Roid recommends that the basis for each statement should be stated explicitly in the test manual or in the printout, which would be of value to clinicians and extremely helpful to forensic psychologists who brave the pitfalls of using computerized narrative reports and rely on them while giving opinions on the witness stand. This position is echoed in the American Psychological Association's (APA) guidelines for computer-based tests and interpretations (American Psychological Association, 1986).

Although computerized administration and scoring of psychological tests has generated relatively little controversy, the application of advanced technology to the interpretation of test results has been a source of considerable professional debate. It should come as no surprise, then, that computerized interpretive summaries can create a great deal of controversy in courtroom settings. Moreover, the use of such reports is fraught with potential pitfalls. When using interpretive reports in forensic settings, the well-informed clinician should be aware of the advantages and limitations of computer-assisted assessment techniques in clinical settings, how the interpretive reports for the Millon inventories were derived, and the specific problems that can arise when computer applications are extended to forensic cases. The chapter concludes by recommending either computer-generated profiles or hand scoring of the Millon inventories.

ADVANTAGES OF COMPUTER-BASED INTERPRETATION

Strictly from a practical standpoint, automated test interpretation provides a highly useful "outside opinion" of the patient's problems (Butcher, 1990). Moreover, the time ordinarily spent integrating, preparing, and coordinating test data can be spent on other important matters. In addition, the large database that often forms the pool from which interpretive summaries are drawn provides for comprehensive coverage of the major inferences for particular test profiles. In other words, computer-generated summaries are more likely to include information that may otherwise be unavailable to or overlooked by the clinician who interprets the profile. The major drawback with this approach is that an expert witness is often chosen to perform an evaluation and to render his or her own opinion. Thus, use of an "external" supportive opinion may be viewed by opposing counsel with scorn.

Another advantage to computer-generated test interpretation lies in the fact that the reports, particularly the MCMI-II and MACI interpretive reports from NCS, are modeled after those written by professional clinical psychologists. Thus, the summaries provide a useful guide for assisting the psychologist in writing reports that are individualized for a particular client or patient, as well as organizing feedback to attorneys and judges.

It has been suggested that the conclusions derived from statistically derived and actuarially based inferences are subject to less interpretive error than are those deduced by clinical inference only (Meehl, 1954). Computer databanks often provide a vast resource of clinical information about test patterns that might not otherwise be available to the average clinician. When unique or novel test results are encountered, computer programs can derive interpretive summaries from a pool of comparable cases (e.g., Lanyon, 1968). In these instances, the human interpreter must resort to speculation and tenuous hypotheses. Thus, an actuarial computer system is likely to yield reports that are as good as those of the typical user of the test.

Other advantages in using computer technology for psychological assessment include the assurance of accuracy and consistency in scoring and the implementation of specific decision rules for deriving interpretive statements (Jackson, 1985). Moreover, computers allow for virtually unlimited storage and retrieval of novel and innovative information on the correlates of test indicators. Consequently, new algorithms and interpretive rules can be developed and there is the greater likelihood that analyses of extensive normative databases can be carried out with the assistance of computers (Jackson, 1985; Krug, 1987).

LIMITATIONS OF
COMPUTER-BASED INTERPRETATION

Despite the advantages computerized test reports offer, there are several limitations and professional concerns, which have been the focus of considerable debate (Butcher, 1990; Fowler & Butcher, 1986; Matarazzo, 1986; Snyder, Widiger, & Hoover, 1990). One overriding concern has been the lack of substantial research data supporting the validity of statements made in a given report. This can be a particularly difficult criticism to defend on cross-examination. Related to this issue is the fact that many multiscale inventories and tests have a large range of profiles that are possible. However, there are insufficient actuarial data on many of the less common configurations, yielding a small catalog of external correlates. Thus, interpretive systems are often largely dependent on the expertise and skill of the program developer (Butcher, 1990). Because of this issue, forensic practitioners need to be aware of how narrative summaries have been derived for the instrument they are using when providing testimony in court.

A second major limitation of automated reports lies in the fact that they are often general and describe personality and syndromal prototypes. Thus, there is a lack of statements directed specifically to the individual. In forensic cases, often the most useful expert testimony is that which directs the assessment to specific questions and not to general or global inferences. Although reports strive to be broad and comprehensive, they often fail to give the subtle differences that exist from case to case. Thus, the task of answering narrow referral questions may be frustrated when broad-based interpretations are provided in computerized reports. As a result, confusion can arise in testimony if an issue is made as to the validity or certainty of a tangential or unrelated issue raised in a computerized summary.

Furthermore, moderator variables such as setting-specific base rates and demographic variables are often not considered. The report user must then go through a decision-making process whereby it has to be established whether the report is a "good fit" or whether it does not apply to what is known about the patient. In this latter instance, the report might provide information that is correct, but the clinician is unaware of it. On the other hand, other variables such as response sets, setting-specific base rates, or some other factor may affect the report's validity for the specific case.

Another important set of concerns lies in the ethical and legal issues over control of access to computerized narrative reports. Because of the relative ease in use, computer reports tend to remove the critical process of integrating assessment data. That is, automated reports may be used by those who are not well trained in the theory and practice of test development and psychometric principles. Thus, reports become a definitive statement for some and not just part of a larger psychological assessment approach. Moreover, reports are generated for use by professionals and often focus on the problematic and pathological aspects of the individual. Because patients are frequently interested in their test results and may want a copy of their test report, they can be confronted with statements or descriptions about themselves that are either upsetting or stated in language that is difficult to understand. In this instance, reports can be easily misinterpreted if not used by an appropriately trained professional.

Generally, computerized reports are best viewed as a set of hypotheses that may be useful in clinical settings where symptom relief and effective treatment are the major goals. Even in clinical settings, however, such reports should be evaluated in light of additional sources of information. Such external sources would include other test data, behavioral observations, documented history, and reports provided by the patient and collateral interviews. As more external data support the report's statements, greater confidence is placed in its validity. On the other hand, hypotheses from the report can be rejected if such outside information disconfirms these suppositions. Ultimately, the clinician must rely on sound clinical skills and decision making in arriving at conclusions about the patient.

In forensic settings, however, computerized reports create a number of problems, and even the advantages that may support their use clinically are at odds with forensic goals. Another issue that looms large for forensic psychologists but does not appear to be addressed by either the Millon inventories or any other major series of clinical personality tests is disclosure of the specific score configuration that triggers particular interpretive statements. It is essential for expert witnesses to know this information in order to be prepared to respond to questions regarding the nexus between how the subject responded and the resulting interpretations. The APA standards state that in order to be able to evaluate a computer-based interpretation, the test user must know the relationship between test responses and interpretations (American Psychological Association, 1986, p. 21). The APA standards recommend that developers provide references for statements in the report or provide in the manual all the interpretive statements in the program library along with the scales and research on which they are based (p. 22).

One area cited by Roid (1985) as a source of frequent clinician error has been effectively addressed by the Millon inventories, although on a somewhat more basic level than Roid envisioned. The problem of errors relating to neglect of BR data is of such importance that Roid recommends that all computerized test interpretive programs include a segment explaining the proper use of BR predictions. He cites the temptation for clinicians, even seasoned ones, to place excessive weight on case-specific information and to ignore BR data unless reminded by an outside aide such as a computerized interpretive program. Of course, there is no need for such an educational segment in the narrative report of the Millon inventories because the scores themselves are adjusted for BR data; users who have familiarized themselves with the test manual will have already grasped this concept.

Returning to the theme of a seemingly individualized clinical report as being an outmoded model for employing computer technology in interpreting psychological test data, the APA standards comment, "A major concern about computer-generated reports is that they may not be as individualized as those generated in the conventional manner" (p. 12). In truth, they are not individualized but represent conclusions that are generated in the absence of any input concerning the specifics of the client's situation. The optimal method of making sense out of test data is for the clinician to integrate the test findings with specific and unique features of the case at hand in order to address specific referral questions that come up in virtually every case. The optimal situation for the clinician or forensic psychologist engaged in this task is to have at hand a research assistant to provide empirical findings and well-accepted test score configuration interpretations in response to the user's specific inquiries.

Roid (1985) recommends a shift from the expert-system model to the research-assistant model, which allows users to take advantage of the enormous retrieval capacities of computer programs. Under the research-assistant model, the paradigm changes from the user's appealing to a virtual expert for a consultation on the case to one in which the user becomes the expert and employs the computer as a source of retrieval of relevant empirical findings in an adaptive, interactive mode that employs the software to its full advantage. This model also obviates generating reams of superfluous interpretive statements that merely provide fodder for cross-examination and allows the forensic expert to concentrate on the specific questions of interest in any given case. Roid further states that this paradigm can easily combine fuzzy logic and probabilistic methods to produce interpretations that are more consistent with the state of our scientific knowledge than the type of "yes–no" statements commonly found in virtually all present report formats.

Under the research-assistant paradigm, therefore, the experience of the user would not be at all like receiving a tailor-made report from an expert colleague to whom one has referred the client for a consultation but more akin to posting inquiries on the Internet and receiving immediate feedback from a huge database, with various responses branching out to further questions unique to each individual inquiry. The user-friendly dialogue might run something like this:

User: List interpretations of Scales S > 75 and 1 > 85 and 2 > 85

Program: Chances are 8 out of 10 that the subject qualifies for a diagnosis of Schizophrenia, Chronic Undifferentiated Type, regardless of whether Scale SS is elevated or not . . . No studies available on this three scale configuration . . . Subjects with Scales S > 75 and 1 > 85 have been found to display very severe deficits in social competency (Smith, XXXX) as well as very severe intrusion of primary process into normal stream of consciousness (Jones, XXXX) . . . Subjects with Scales S > 75 and 2 > 85 have been found to be more likely to set fires than subjects with S < 76 and 2 < 86 (Brown, XXXX) . . . See supplementary CD-ROM for more recent findings.

Such a system would remove, or at least alleviate, a current problem among some practitioners who come to the attention of state psychology boards, namely, the absolute and naive reliance on the narrative computer-generated report.

In one well-publicized case, a psychologist routinely used the MMPI as his only psychometric measure in performing child custody assessments on parents referred by the courts. He relied on the computer-generated report in an extremely literal fashion without possessing any significant independent capability for interpreting the scale scores. This practice resulted in several destructive recommendations. The practitioner's license to practice was revoked after the state psychology board initiated proceedings in response to a total of 22 complaints filed against him by disgruntled litigants. The state guidelines for performing such assessments, developed subsequent to this case, explicitly state that it is malpractice to employ a computerized narrative report for an assessment instrument unless one has an independent capability to interpret the scales of that instrument.

The following case did not result in as extreme a result as the previous example, but it illustrates some of the problems that can arise for the attorney calling the expert when computerized interpretation is utilized in legal settings. The importance of carefully integrating computer-generated interpretive statements with the clinician's own professional judgment and knowledge of the case was ignored. As a result, the expert witness was effectively rendered helpless and his testimony was completely disregarded. The facts are from an actual case.

CASE 8.1. IMPEACHED TESTIMONY

Dr. Z. was asked to perform an evaluation on Mr. P. in the context of a child custody evaluation. As part of his assessment, Dr. Z. administered the MCMI to Mr. P. and utilized an "in-house" interpretive program which his group practice used in the regular course of it clinical assessment procedures. The computer program generated a summary about the individual, once the base rate scores had been obtained via profile scoring through NCS.

The group in which Dr. Z. practiced had designed the program to be quite comprehensive and it generated several pages of information. Every conceivable psychological process or personality dimension was described within a 14-page report consisting only of test interpretation. To save time, the summary was printed out in such a manner that it was represented as the clinical report of Dr. Z. on his evaluation of Mr. P. No attempt was made to edit or modify the printout based on information made available from other sources.

While on the witness stand, Dr. Z. was being cross-examined by the attorney for Mr. P.'s adversary, Mrs. P. The attorney had a copy of Dr. Z.'s "report," which was the computerized interpretive summary. Contained in the report were two key statements which conflicted directly with the testimony provided by Dr. Z. In response, Dr. Z. attempted to explain how the report was really a computerized summary of hypotheses about the individual and did not represent his formal report or opinion. Dr. Z. attempted to explain the limitations of computerized test interpretation and further offered that such reports need to be considered in light of other pieces of data. The judge ruled that because Dr. Z. had put his name on the summary and represented it as his interpretation, the document constituted an official opinion. As a result, the report was used effectively by Mrs. P.'s attorney to impeach Dr. Z.'s testimony. That is, because Dr. Z. had introduced two different pieces of evidence (one being his report and the other being his testimony in court) which conflicted with one another, the court held that he was an unreliable witness. Dr. Z.'s testimony was completely disregarded by the court.

———◆———

This case illustrates clearly the need for good clinical judgment and decision making when providing conclusions that are offered as expert testimony.

COMPUTERS AND THE MILLON INVENTORIES

The use of computers for scoring, as opposed to interpreting, the Millon inventories can save time and resources and can also reduce the likelihood of the errors and miscalculations that are possible with hand scoring. However, a careful reading of the test manual for the particular Millon inventory being used is strongly recommended so that the forensic psychologist can comfortably explain the scoring procedures and algorithms if needed. Automated services for scoring and interpretation are available through NCS and two computer output formats are available. One product consists of the profile report, which is a printout of the profile, scale scores, a set of introductory paragraphs on the limitations and restrictions of test use, and a judgment of the probable validity and reliability of the test data. Figure 8.1 provides a sample profile report for the MCMI-II. Although these reports provide a professional-looking, easy-to-read profile, there is no information given on test interpretation. This format is generally preferable in forensic cases because it eliminates the potential problems of having to defend one's opinion in light of possible contradictory hypotheses that may be contained in a computer-generated report.

For the practitioner who chooses to forego the recommendation of utilizing "profile-only" reports or hand scoring and instead uses the interpretive reports, it must be recognized that the report will need to be defended on cross-examination. To meet the challenge of such questioning, the forensic practitioner must be familiar not only the with content of the report obtained on a particular individual but also with how the reports in general were constructed and derived during validation of the Millon instruments. The following discussion is offered

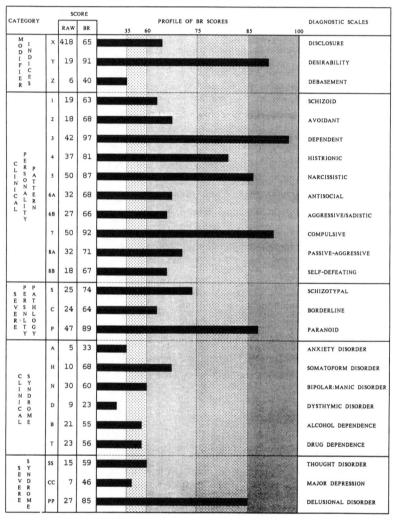

FIGURE 8.1. Profile report for the MCMI-II. MCMI-II/Copyright 1987 by Theodore Millon. Reprinted by permission.

MCMI-II reports are normed on patients who were in the early
phases of assessment or psychotherapy because of emotional
discomforts or social difficulties. Respondents who do not fit
this normative population or who have inappropriately taken the
MCMI-II for nonclinical purposes may have distorted reports. To
optimize clinical utility, the report highlights pathological
characteristics and dynamics rather than strengths and positive
attributes. This focus should be kept in mind by the referring
clinician reading the report.

Based on theoretical inferences and probabilistic data from
actuarial research, the MCMI-II report cannot be judged
definitive. It must be viewed as only one facet of a
comprehensive psychological assessment, and should be evaluated in
conjunction with additional clinical data (e.g., current life
circumstances, observed behavior, biographic history, interview
responses, and information from other tests). To avoid its
misconstrual or misuse, the report should be evaluated by mental
health clinicians trained in recognizing the strengths and
limitations of psychological test data. Given its limited data
base and pathologic focus, the report should not be shown to
patients or their relatives.

INTERPRETIVE CONSIDERATIONS

In addition to the preceding considerations, the interpretive
narrative should be evaluated in light of the following
demographic and situational factors. This 22 year old separated
white woman with less than a high school education, currently seen
professionally as an outpatient, did not identify specific
problems and difficulties of an Axis I nature in completing the
demographic portion of this test.

Unless this patient is a demonstrably well-functioning adult who
is currently facing minor life stressors, her responses suggest
(1) a well-established need for social approval and commendation,
evident in tendencies to present oneself in a favorable light, or
(2) a general naivete about psychological matters, including a
deficit in self- insight that derives from a long-standing habit
of attending to superficial appearances. The interpretation of
this profile should be made with these characteristics in mind.

FIGURE 8.1. *(cont.)*

as a brief guide to both explaining the development of the reports during direct testimony and formulating questions by opposing counsel for cross-examination of the practitioner who offers an interpretive report into evidence. Although there may be other commercial interpretive systems available for the Millon inventories, the following discussion applies only to the development of the reports generated by NCS, the test publisher. This discussion is a summary of information provided by Millon (1987, 1993, 1994a) and Millon and Green (1989).

Derivation of NCS Interpretive Reports

All automated report systems employ a series of rules for assigning specific interpretive statements to certain scale elevations or profile configurations. Some of these rules may be based strictly on actuarial data that have fixed rules (e.g., Gilberstadt & Duker, 1965; Marks & Seeman, 1963). Other systems have rules that are based on clinical judgment and literature reviews, allowing a degree of flexibility when matching descriptive statements to particular profile configurations (e.g., Finney, 1966; Fowler, 1965). In general, computerized interpretive systems assume that there is an empirically demonstrated relationship between test scores and the description of clinical symptoms and personality style. The Millon inventory system is, in part, an actuarial system based on results from descriptive ratings obtained through a series of empirical studies (Millon, 1993, 1994a). In addition, the MCMI and MACI systems rest heavily on hypotheses and descriptions that are formulated through a systematic clinical theory (Millon, 1969, 1981, 1986a, 1986b).

Creation of the interpretive reports was undertaken concurrently with the construction and validation stages for the particular Millon test being developed. Initial stages of development sought to identify 10, and later 11, basic personality styles which were derived from the theory on which the test is based (Millon, 1986a, 1986b, 1993, 1994a). Using research that was conducted during development of the test, clinical judgment data were utilized to identify groups of test profiles that were significant variants of these basic personality prototypes. An important criteria needed for a profile to be viewed as representative of a basic character style was that the profile be consistent with the underlying theory and with DSM-III-R and DSM-IV formulations for the personality style.

The second stage in development of the interpretive system consisted of a systematic compilation of descriptive paragraphs and statements made through clinical ratings and which comprise part of the database for validation studies. The most frequent and clinically meaningful combination of these ratings formed the major set of descriptors for each profile. Additional information on each particular codetype was taken from theory-based descriptions for the personality type represented by the codetype; this material was integrated with the empirically derived descriptors.

The final stage in developing a fully functional interpretive system consisted of constructing a computer program that would select appropriate descriptive statements for a given MCMI or MACI profile. The computer facilities at NCS provide a fully automated system that arranges statements in the form of a narrative interpretive report. Given this method of development, the report reflects both empirically and theoretically derived descriptor–profile relationships.

Research Findings on Interpretive Reports

Given some of the controversy that has surrounded computerized test interpretation, increased attention has been paid to studying the validity and accuracy of computer-generated interpretive reports. Several methodological issues complicate this area of research. For instance, there are two general types of studies aimed at validating computerized reports: the cusumer-satisfaction study, in which test consumers rate the accuracy of a report, and external-criterion studies, in which computer-generated statements are compared with independent sources of information (Snyder et al., 1990). Because external-criterion studies are often difficult and costly to conduct, most investigations into computer-based test reports have consisted of consumer-satisfaction studies. This research approach has been the most common for Millon inventory reports. There are no studies examining MCMI-II, MCMI-III, and MACI reports specifically, creating a major problem for the practitioner who uses computerized reports for these instruments. Those studies conducted on the MCMI-I and MAPI, both predecessors to the more current versions, may be relevant and applicable to the issue of MCMI-II and MACI report validity because the test author is responsible for the content of reports for all versions of the instruments.

In one of the first investigations on the utility and accuracy of the MCMI reports, Green (1982) compared MCMI-I and MMPI reports for 100 patients being treated by 23 mental health professionals. The clinicians were asked to rate the adequacy of information obtained in the reports, the descriptive accuracy of the narrative summary, and the usefulness of the report format. Overall, the results showed that clinicians rated the MCMI reports as both valid and useful and as superior to the MMPI reports in assessing the specific areas of interpersonal relationships, personality traits, and coping styles. In light of the fact that personality processes form one of the cornerstones of the theory guiding MCMI development, it is not surprising that information related to these issues would be rated more highly for the MCMI profile.

Siddall (1986) and Gualtieri, Gonzalas, and Baldwin (1987) have examined the use of the MCMI report with substance abusing populations. Again, these surveys revealed that clinicians rated the MCMI report as accurate in describing substance abuse cases. The narrative summaries were viewed as useful in clarifying case issues, adding additional relevant information, and confirming knowledge about the patient (Siddall, 1986). Interpretive reports for the MCMI have also been found to be accurate in describing patients' status apart from pathology that is chemically induced (Gualtieri et al., 1987). These findings support the utility and accuracy of MCMI reports across a variety of clinical populations.

In an investigation on the utility of the MAPI, Rubenzer (1992) compared the computer-generated interpretive reports with traditional psychological evaluation reports typically written by clinicians. Each type of report (MAPI vs. traditional) was evaluated by therapists and nursing staff in an inpatient hospital setting for adolescents. Specifically, the reports were rated on such variables as whether the written summary confirmed working clinical hypotheses, clarity, repetition, consistency, inclusion of trivial or misleading information, and other such variables. Overall, there was no difference between the rated accuracy of MAPI interpretive reports and clinician-generated reports on patients. Both types of reports were viewed as "mediocre" in accuracy and usefulness, with MAPI reports rated as more specific in their interpretations and as superior in quality of writing.

Despite evidence of consumer satisfaction with the utility and accuracy of MCMI and MAPI narrative reports, these findings have a major methodological weakness. Because studies on the reports often lack comparison groups, some may argue that satisfaction with the interpretive summaries reflects the Barnum effect (i.e., statements reflecting trivial yet very common characteristics are readily accepted by the report user). Two more recent studies have attempted to assess for possible Barnum effects using simulated, "random" reports on patients as a comparison with the actual MCMI report (Moreland & Onstad, 1987; Sandberg, 1987).

Sandberg (1987) had graduate students in clinical psychology simulate MCMI responses for two different patients they were treating and with whom they had some degree of familiarity. The students were then provided with a narrative report for each patient. One report consisted of randomly selected statements that were "erroneous" for one patient and an accurate report on the other patient. Each MCMI narrative summary was then evaluated according to the same questionnaires used by Green (1982). Results showed that any potential Barnum effects were minimal in evaluation of the reports by the graduate clinicians.

Using doctoral-level clinical psychologists, Moreland and Onstad (1987) found similar results. Eight psychologists were used to rate the accuracy of a pair of computer-generated reports for each of 99 patients. One of the reports was an "accurate" report, while another was generated in random fashion. Seven sections of the report were rated separately for accuracy, including Axis II narratives, Axis I narratives, Axis I and Axis II diagnoses, Axis IV stressors, severity of condition, and therapeutic implications. Five of these seven sections were rated as significantly more accurate for the "actual" reports and the overall accuracy rating of the genuine reports was significantly higher than the rating for the random reports. These results were taken to show that MCMI reports are more accurate than the random generation of clinical symptoms or personality traits, lending support to the conclusion that Barnum effects are not a major factor in rating the utility of the reports.

Of greater concern to the forensic practitioner who utilizes computerized reports for the Millon inventories is the lack of research that supports the validity of the diagnostic suggestions provided in the reports. DeWolfe et al. (1985), for example, examined the accuracy of the MCMI-I reports for diagnosing bipolar affective disorder. In their sample of 48 patients with a discharge diagnosis of bipolar disorder, the MCMI-I correctly identified only 27% of the patients. Many possible explanations for such a low hit rate can be offered. These include the low sample size, the higher base rate of bipolar disorder in DeWolfe's inpatient sample relative to the lower base rate in the MCMI-I normative sample, and the lack of a standardized method for obtaining a clinical diagnosis to serve as the validating criterion. In a similar study, Piersma (1987b) examined the diagnostic accuracy of the MCMI report in patients with anxiety and depressive disorders. Again, the MCMI-I reports did not provide accurate diagnoses, with anxiety disorders being overdiagnosed and depressive disorders underdiagnosed.

It has been suggested by Moreland (1993) that the results from these studies can be explained in terms of the differences between the samples used in studying diagnostic accuracy of the reports and the normative sample for the MCMI-I. Moreland concludes that MCMI computerized reports "are most likely to be accurate if used with outpatients" (p. 229). This conclusion paints the practitioner who relies on diagnostic suggestions in the report into a corner that is difficult to escape. Many forensic cases involve individuals who are not currently in outpatient treatment or who have a history of inpatient care. An attorney who attacks the computer-generated diagnoses by citing these studies will make it difficult to defend the use of a computerized report.

CONCLUSION

The use of computerized interpretive reports for the Millon inventories is not recommended in forensic settings. Instead, the forensic practitioner is encouraged to use either hand scoring or computer-generated profile-only reports. The reasons for this position become clearer when the advantages and limitations of computerized interpretation discussed earlier are given careful analysis.

All the advantages of computerized test interpretation might support the use of this technique in clinical settings, but there are no advantages in forensic cases. Specifically, whereas a computerized report may serve as a form of "outside opinion" or set of clinical hypotheses, the forensic examiner is sought to provide conclusions, not hypotheses, in legal settings. Moreover, the expert witness is generally retained for his or her own opinions, not those of other professionals. Thus, defending the use of computerized interpretive reports as "outside consultation" may weaken the witness's credibility.

In the same way, when computer-based actuarial information is used to interpret unique or novel profiles, the resulting statements may not be adequately researched or validated to withstand strict scrutinization in a legal setting. A forensic expert must be aware of how interpretive statements are derived from test data; novel or unique computer algorithms may create difficulties in establishing the validity of innovative interpretive methods.

Finally, the reliance on standard, clear-cut decision rules for generating interpretive statements prevents the forensic practitioner from narrowing the conclusions drawn from the data to specific questions being asked. As has been noted in earlier chapters, forensic assessment requires a careful clarification of the referral questions. If the examiner is clear on what is being asked, he or she can examine the test data with these specific questions in mind rather than relying on a broad-based interpretation that can provide information unrelated to the task at hand. Computer reports often contain more information than is necessary for many forensic evaluations. Consequently, excessive interpretation can create confusion or doubt for the court, or, as Case 8.1 illustrates, it can create potential conflict in testimony that renders the expert ineffective.

The advantages of computer-based interpretation that support the use of this technology in clinical settings all but disappear in forensic settings. One is then left with the limitations mentioned earlier, such as weak validity data on the interpretive statements and diagnostic conclusions themselves, the nonspecificity of computerized reports generally, and the impact of moderator variables on specific test results. Thus, although computer-based test interpretation may have a place in clinical practice, where ongoing case conceptualization and implementation of effective treatment strategies are the primary goals, its use in forensic settings is plagued with difficulties. The nature of the problems lends support to the argument that the use of such reports in the legal arena should be avoided.

An Interpretive
Strategy for the
Millon Inventories
in Forensic Cases

Using the information in a Millon inventory profile requires a series of interpretive stages, each aimed at providing a useful piece of information in the overall assessment. The primary value of the Millon inventories for forensic psychologists lies in their ready applicability to fact-specific referral questions beyond the general diagnosis. As noted earlier, the Millon inventories are the only major clinical personality assessment instruments that rest on a basis of well-articulated theory. Furthermore, this theory is documented by several thorough reviews of the literature that integrate various psychoanalytic, neurobiological, interpersonal, cognitive, behavioral, and statistical models of personality (Millon, 1981; Millon & Davis, 1996). Thus, although specific interpretations based on the theory have not been validated empirically (and could not possibly be, given the virtually limitless number of specific referral questions that arise in complex legal matters), there is solid "rational" or "clinical" validity support for such interpretations and a great deal of tangential empirical validity research that has been reviewed elsewhere (cf. Craig, 1993b). These factors provide a scientifically acceptable basis for applying Millon inventory results to specific questions concerning a person's interpersonal issues, cognitive style, behavioral dynamics, and other questions that typically arise in the practical daily work of forensic psychologists.

Other than scientific adequacy, the other major consideration is acceptability of a procedure in a legal forum. As discussed earlier, DSM-

IV has assumed the status of the ultimate mental health learned treatise. By nearly universal consensus, attorneys and judges rely on DSM-
IV as the framework from which to view mental health issues before
the court. Theodore Millon, who served on the Personality Disorders
Work Group of both DSM-III and DSM-IV, designed the inventories
to coordinate with DSM multiaxial diagnostic system. The MCMI-II has
substantial content validity against DSM-III-R and to a large extent
against DSM-IV because many personality disorder criteria have undergone little or no change between these two versions of the diagnostic classification system. Unfortunately, the MCMI-III, which has a high
degree of content validity against DSM-IV, does not, at the time of this
writing, have sufficient criterion-related or factorial validity support
to warrant its use in forensic contexts. For most situations, the MCMI-
II and MACI are sufficiently related to DSM-IV that their diagnostic
framework dovetails with that of the de facto ultimate treatise, making
them readily understandable and acceptable to attorneys and judges.

Millon's descriptions of individual personality disorders, and various combinations of personality disorders that have a high comorbidity
as presented in his work (Millon, 1981; Millon & Davis, 1996), stand
as classic syntheses of voluminous research on these disorders span-
ning several decades. These descriptions have since been further elaborated by organizing the various dimensions that define personality
according to characteristics that are associated with each personality
disorder under various domains of clinical observations and inferences
(see Tables 9.1–9.14 at the end of this chapter). These characteristics
include both functional attributes, referring to fluid and dynamic
processes of a person's adaptation, and structural attributes, defined
as quasi-stable characteristics that endure over time and serve to explain consistency in behavior and personality.

There are four classes of domains as outlined in Tables 9.1–9.14.
The *behavioral level* includes expressive acts (a functional attribute sub-
suming the observables of behavior) and interpersonal conduct (a functional attribute which refers to a person's characteristic style of
interacting with others). The *phenomenological level* includes cognitive
style (a functional attribute describing the individual's manner of
processing information arising from both internal and external
sources), object representations (a structural attribute referring to the
enduring thoughts, feelings, and attitudes that serve as a template for
guiding future interpersonal relationships), and self-image (a structural attribute defining the lasting feelings and perceptions people have
of themselves). The *intrapsychic level* includes regulatory mechanisms
(a functional attribute defined as the methods for defending against
internal conflict and turmoil) and morphologic organization (a struc-

tural attribute that is defined as the manner in which a person's internal emotions, thoughts, and personality structure is organized and interconnected). Finally, the *biophysical level* includes the structural attributes of mood and temperament, which are biophysically based levels of emotional arousability and sensitivity.

In Tables 9.1–9.14, there is a key descriptive label for each personality disorder on each domain component. For example, the major regulatory mechanism for paranoid personality disorder in Table 9.14 is projection, whereas the regulatory mechanism for obsessive–compulsive personality disorder in Table 9.9 is reaction formation. Each descriptor is followed by a brief explanatory passage. All this information represents a synthesis of voluminous research for each of the disorders and is consistent with the descriptions of the disorders as presented in DSM-III-R, with enormous overlap with DSM-IV. *The value of these tables for the forensic psychologist is that the domains in these tables provide a virtual organized menu of traits, dynamics, and other attributes that constitute a research based supplement to the individual opinion of the expert. Via the DSM-III-R/DSM-IV nexus we can relate specific psychometric test findings to specific referral questions on nearly any aspect of psychological functioning, with the interpretive algorithm, so to speak, perfectly accessible in tabular form.*

To make adequate use of the interpretive information to be derived from the Millon inventories and these tables and to apply it to fact-specific referral questions, we recommend the following steps.

Step 1: Examine the Validity scale and modifier indices. The base rate scores found in the Millon inventory profile report have already been adjusted to compensate for deviant response styles. However, experience has shown that it is important to pay attention to the examinee's response set in interpreting the adjusted scores and not to rely on the score modifications as constituting the final word on the subject's possible defensiveness, malingering, confusion, or other response set.

Step 2: Review the clinical syndrome scales. After inspecting the modifier indices, the practitioner should review the Axis I clinical syndrome sections for information regarding any symptoms or diagnoses that may be affecting the examinee. In forensic contexts, drug abuse, alcohol abuse, depression, thought disorder, and delusional thinking typically play a role in the assessment. In addition, in personal injury and disability cases, anxiety and somatization (Scale H) often figure prominently, as discussed in Chapter 5.

Step 3: Review the personality disorder scales. The basic and severe personality disorder scales should be inspected. Individuals with a BR score of 75 and above on any scale may be considered at least to present traits associated with that disorder, with scores increasing above this level reflecting a greater likelihood of a diagnosable personality disorder.

Step 4: Refer to domain tables for specifics. The material reproduced in Tables 9.1–9.14 should be reviewed for characteristics associated with the subject's diagnosed personality disorder(s) or traits. The domains will help to organize the clinical picture of the client and specific attributes associated with relevant domains may be applied to address specific referral questions.

The following cases are interpretive examples of the application of the Millon inventories in forensic cases.

CASE 9.1. DEPENDENT PERSONALITY DISORDER AND PLAUSIBILITY OF CHARGES

[Note: This example is based on a case in which the defendant was diagnosed as having dependent personality disorder; however, she was considered too limited educationally and cognitively to take the MCMI-II.]

Anna R., a 45-year-old woman, was accused of masterminding an arson in which two people were killed. Anna's two sons were the actual perpetrators of the act, which they admitted under police questioning. An accomplice of the two young men, unrelated to them, implicated Anna as the person who planned the crime and coerced her sons into committing it. Had Anna been capable of taking the MCMI-II, her record surely would have contained a major elevation on Scale 3 (Dependent). For purposes of this interpretation, however, it is necessary only for the defendant to have been diagnosed clinically as having dependent personality disorder. Turning to the domains at the behavioral level in Table 9.4, we find under expressive acts that individuals with this disorder are characterized as incompetent. Specifically, the accompanying text indicates that dependent persons lack functional skills, avoid self-assertion, and withdraw from adult responsibilities. The other domain at the behavioral level in Table 9.4 is interpersonal conduct. The key descriptor for dependent personality disorder under this domain is submissive. The explanatory text indicates that these individuals are compliant, placating, and conciliatory. They subordinate their needs to a nurturing figure.

The application of this information is a delicate matter in that, as cautioned in Chapter 4, one should avoid any testimony that appears to be profile evidence. That is, one should refrain from statements to the effect that it is either more or less likely that an individual committed a given offense because that individual does or does not fit the "profile" associated with such offenders. In this case, the expert was not required to supply any connection between the defendant's characteristics and any purported scientifically determined likelihood that she committed the alleged offense. The task was merely to demonstrate that the defendant, instead of being a cunning, controlling, coercive woman who was capable of manipulating her grown sons into committing a serious criminal offense, as the prosecutor depicted her, was in fact the opposite. The witness described Anna R. as a submissive woman who preferred to give in to others, rather than risk their rejection, and was compliant with their demands. Further, by virtue of her personality disorder, Anna was lacking in adequate functional skills and avoided self-assertion. This characterization of the defendant was entirely consistent with the picture that she presented during her testimony and it was left to the good sense of the jury to decide whether this dependent, socially inept woman was really the "brains" and motive force behind a fatal arson.

CASE 9.2. SPECIFIC QUESTIONS REGARDING PARENTAL FITNESS

Michaela S. is a 24-year-old mother of four whose history includes giving up on her defiant 2-year-old son and sending him to his birth father, only to stop by the father's house several weeks later to demand the immediate return of the child. This behavior created a scene with the father's new wife and resulted in Michaela's filing a complaint with the police alleging that her ex-husband had kidnapped that child.

Michaela's two older children were removed when her paramour broke her 6-year-old daughter's arm while disciplining her. Michaela and the paramour displayed token compliance with the child protective services' order that they receive counseling and were seeking a return of the children. The birth father of the oldest two was seeking custody of those two children. One of the specific referral questions to be addressed in Michaela's examination was whether she was capable of responding to her 6-year-old daughter's emotional needs, including the child's feelings concerning her mother's paramour, who had abused her, and Michaela's denial of the abuse. It was noted that both Michaela and her boyfriend continued to explain the child's fractured arm as being the result of an accident, despite the fact that the girl gave a detailed account of the abuse that was entirely consistent with the nature of the injury as determined by a physician specializing in children's traumatic injuries.

Michaela's MCMI-II record was a follows: 7 ** 5 * 4 6A + 3 6B " 1 2 8A 8B " // . ** . * // . ** . * // . ** . * //. It is also important in evaluating this record to note that the BR score for Scale X (Disclosure) was 15, Scale Y (Desirability) was 75, and Scale Z (Debasement) was 0. The only clinical elevations here are on the Compulsive (7) and Narcissistic (5) scales. Although it is not uncommon to see an elevation on Scale 7 in this type of record, which is in large measure a reflection of the subject's defensive response set, it is noted that the elevation in this particular profile is greater than 85 and that the fact that it is accompanied by a high Scale 5 (Narcissistic) score points in a direction away from a purely defensive record. The interpretive picture that emerges when the two elevations are considered together, namely, that of a rigid, perfectionistic, self-centered individual, is consistent with other clinical impressions of this individual.

Turning to the specific referral question of capacity to appreciate and respond appropriately to her daughter's emotional needs, we consider the domains of expressive acts and interpersonal conduct. The key descriptor for narcissistic personality disorder in Table 9.6 is "haughty," with the explanatory text including statements such as "acts in an arrogant . . . and disdainful manner" and "indifference to the rights of others." Under the compulsive personality disorder in the same domain in Table 9.9, we find the characteristic "disciplined" with the accompanying text "perfectionism interferes with decision making and task completion." Under the other behavioral level domain, interpersonal conduct, we find that the key descriptor for narcissistic personality disorder is "exploitative," with additional text indicating that this type of subject is not empathic and takes others for granted without reciprocating. Thus, in addressing the specific referral question of appropriate behavior toward the child, we can expect that if the child were to be returned at the present time, she would encounter little empathic attunement to her emotional needs and that her right to have her parent protect and support her would be subordinated to her mother's need to preserve the illusion of a perfect relationship with the abusive stepfather. She would be exploited in the sense of being forced to endorse the family's version of events regarding any new instances of abuse and she would be expected to conform to her mother's inappropriately perfectionistic behavioral expectations of her.

Each of the interpretive statements can be defended on the basis of cumulative research results and clinical observations. That is, the interpretation of Millon inventory results and description of clinically diagnosed personality disorders according to the characteristics outlined in Tables 9.1–9.14 must be integrated from an analysis of the data obtained from the clinical interview, psychosocial history, review of supporting documents, statements from collateral resources, and other information typically relied on in forensic assessment. The specific descriptors in these tables are linked to DSM diagnostic categories, as elaborated in the carefully documented work of Millon (1981, 1986a, 1986b; Millon & Davis, 1996), and are further linked to the examinee's own statements as recorded in Millon inventory responses, with this link resting upon a foundation of the Millon inventories' demonstrated empirical validity.

TABLE 9.1. Clinical Domains for Scale 1: Schizoid/Introversive

Behavioral level

(F) Expressively Impassive (e.g., appears to be in an inert emotional state, life-less, undemonstrative, lacking in energy and vitality; is unmoved, unanimated, robotic, phlegmatic, displaying deficits in activation, motoric expressiveness, and spontaneity).

(F) Interpersonally Unengaged (e.g., seems indifferent and remote, rarely responsive to the actions or feelings of others, chooses solitary activities, possesses minimal "human" interests; fades into the background, is aloof or unobtrusive, neither desires nor enjoys close relationships, prefers a peripheral role in social, work, and family settings).

Phenomenological level

(F) Cognitively Impoverished (e.g., seems deficient across broad spheres of human knowledge and evidences vague and obscure thought processes, particularly about social matters; communication with others is often unfocused, loses its purpose or intention, or is conveyed via a loose or circuitous logic).

(S) Complacent Self-Image (e.g., reveals minimal introspection and awareness of self; seems impervious to the emotional and personal implications of everyday social life, appearing indifferent to the praise or criticism of others).

(S) Meager Objects (e.g., internalized representations are few in number and minimally articulated, largely devoid of the manifold percepts and memories of relationships with others, possessing little of the dynamic interplay between drives and conflicts that typify well-adjusted individuals).

Intrapsychic level

(F) Intellectualization Mechanism (e.g., describes interpersonal and affective experiences in a matter-of-fact, abstract, impersonal, or mechanical manner; pays primary attention to formal and objective aspects of social and emotional events).

(S) Undifferentiated Organization (e.g., given an inner barrenness, a feeble drive to fulfill needs, and minimal pressures either to defend against or resolve internal conflicts or cope with external demands, internal morphologic structures may best be characterized by their limited framework and sterile pattern).

Biophysical level

(S) Apathetic Mood (e.g., is emotionally unexcitable, exhibiting an intrinsic unfeeling, cold, and stark quality; reports weak affectionate or erotic needs, rarely displaying warm or intense feelings, and is apparently unable to experience most affects—pleasure, sadness, anger—in any depth).

Note. (F), functional attribute; (S), structural attribute. Taken from the *Millon Clinical Multiaxial Inventory–III Manual,* by Theodore Millon, 1994, Minneapolis, MN: National Computer Systems. Copyright 1994 by Theodore Millon. Reprinted by permission.

TABLE 9.2. Clinical Domains for Scale 2A: Avoidant/Inhibited

Behavioral level

(F) Expressively Fretful (e.g., conveys personal unease and disquiet, a constant timorous, hesitant, and restive state; overreacts to innocuous events and anxiously judges them to signify ridicule, criticism, and disapproval).

(F) Interpersonally Aversive (e.g., distances self from activities that involve intimate personal relationships and reports extensive history of social pananxiety and distrust; seeks acceptance, but is unwilling to get involved unless certain to be liked, maintaining distance and privacy to avoid being shamed and humiliated).

Phenomenological level

(F) Cognitively Distracted (e.g., warily scans environment for potential threats and is preoccupied by intrusive and disruptive random thoughts and observations; an upwelling from within of irrelevant ideation upsets thought continuity and interferes with social communication and accurate appraisals).

(S) Alienated Self-Image (e.g., sees self as socially inept, inadequate, and inferior, thereby justifying his or her isolation and rejection by others; feels personally unappealing, devalues achievements, and reports persistent sense of aloneness and emptiness).

(S) Vexatious Objects (e.g., internalized representations are composed of readily reactivated, intense, and conflict-ridden memories of problematic early relations; limited avenues for experiencing or recalling gratification, and few mechanisms to channel needs, bind impulses, resolve conflicts, or deflect external stressors).

Intrapsychic level

(F) Fantasy Mechanism (e.g., depends excessively on imagination to achieve need gratification, confidence building, and conflict resolution; withdraws into reveries as a means of safely discharging frustrated affectionate and angry impulses).

(S) Fragile Organization (e.g., a precarious complex of tortuous emotions depends almost exclusively on a single modality for its resolution and discharge, that of avoidance, escape, and fantasy and, hence, when faced with personal risks, new opportunities, or unanticipated stress, few morphologic structures are available to deploy and few back-up positions can be reverted to, short of regressive decompensation).

Biophysical level

(S) Anguished Mood (e.g., describes constant and confusing undercurrent of tension, sadness, and anger; vacillates between desire for affection, fear of rebuff, embarrassment, and numbness of feelings).

Note. (F), functional attribute; (S), structural attribute. Taken from the *Millon Clinical Multiaxial Inventory–III Manual,* by Theodore Millon, 1994, Minneapolis, MN: National Computer Systems. Copyright 1994 by Theodore Millon. Reprinted by permission.

TABLE 9.3. Clinical Domains for Scale 2B: Depressive/Doleful

Behavioral level

(F) Expressively Disconsolate (e.g., appearance and posture convey an unrelievably forlorn, somber, heavy-hearted woebegone if not grief-stricken quality; irremediably dispirited and discouraged, portraying a sense of permanent hopelessness and wretchedness).

(F) Interpersonally Defenseless (e.g., owing to feeling vulnerable, assailable, and unshielded, will beseech others to be nurturant and protective; fearing abandonment and desertion, will not only act in an endangered manner but will seek, if not demand, assurances of affection, steadfastness, and devotion).

Phenomenological level

(F) Cognitively Pessimistic (e.g., possesses defeatist and fatalistic attitudes about almost all matters, sees things in their blackest form and invariably expects the worst; feeling weighed down, discouraged, and bleak, gives the gloomiest interpretation of current events, despairing as well that things will never improve in the future).

(S) Worthless Self-Image (e.g., judges self to be of no account, valueless to self or others, inadequate and unsuccessful in all aspirations; barren, sterile, impotent, sees self as inconsequential and reproachable, if not contemptible, a person who should be criticized and derogated; feels guilty for possessing no praiseworthy traits or achievements).

(S) Forsaken Objects (e.g., internalized representations of the past appear jettisoned, as if life's early experiences have been depleted or devitalized, either drained of their richness and joyful elements, or withdrawn from memory, leaving one to feel abandoned, bereft, discarded, cast off, and deserted).

Intrapsychic level

(F) Asceticism Mechanism (e.g., engages in acts of self-denial, self-punishment, and self-torment, believing that one should exhibit penance and be deprived of life's bounties; there is a repudiation of pleasures, harsh self-judgments, and self-destructive acts).

(S) Depleted Organization (e.g., the foundation for morphologic structures is markedly weakened, with coping methods enervated and defensive strategies impoverished, emptied, and devoid of their vigor and focus, resulting in a diminished if not exhausted capacity to initiate action and regulate affect, impulse, and conflict).

Biophysical level

(S) Melancholic Mood (e.g., is typically woeful, gloomy, tearful, joyless, and morose; characteristically worrisome and brooding, the low spirits and dysphoric state rarely remit).

Note. (F), functional attribute; (S), structural attribute. Taken from the *Millon Clinical Multiaxial Inventory–III Manual,* by Theodore Millon, 1994, Minneapolis, MN: National Computer Systems. Copyright 1994 by Theodore Millon. Reprinted by permission.

TABLE 9.4. Clinical Domains for Scale 3: Dependent/Submissive

Behavioral level

(F) Expressively Incompetent (e.g., withdraws from adult responsibilities by acting helpless and seeking nurturance from others; is docile and passive, lacks functional competencies, and avoids self-assertion).

(F) Interpersonally Submissive (e.g., needs excessive advice and reassurance; subordinates self to stronger, nurturing figure, without whom may feel anxiously alone and helpless; is compliant, conciliatory, and placating, fearing being left to care for self).

Phenomenological level

(F) Cognitively Naive (e.g., rarely disagrees with others and is easily persuaded, unsuspicious, and gullible; reveals a Pollyanna attitude toward interpersonal difficulties, watering down objective problems and smoothing over troubling events).

(S) Inept Self-Image (e.g., views self as weak, fragile, and inadequate; exhibits lack of self-confidence by belittling own attitudes and competencies; hence not capable of doing things on one's own).

(S) Immature Objects (e.g., internalized representations are composed of infantile impressions of others, unsophisticated ideas, incomplete recollections, rudimentary drives, childlike impulses, and minimal competencies to manage and resolve stressors).

Intrapsychic level

(F) Introjection Mechanism (e.g., is firmly devoted to another to strengthen the belief that an inseparable bond exists between them; jettisons independent views in favor of those of others to preclude conflicts and threats to relationship).

(S) Inchoate Organization (e.g., owing to entrusting others with the responsibility to fulfill needs and to cope with adult tasks, there is both a deficient morphologic structure and a lack of diversity in internal regulatory controls, leaving a miscellany of relatively undeveloped and undifferentiated adaptive abilities, and an elementary system for functioning independently).

Biophysical level

(S) Pacific Mood (e.g., is characteristically warm, tender, and noncompetitive; timidly avoids social tension and interpersonal conflicts).

Note. (F), functional attribute; (S), structural attribute. Taken from the *Millon Clinical Multiaxial Inventory–III Manual,* by Theodore Millon, 1994, Minneapolis, MN: National Computer Systems. Copyright 1994 by Theodore Millon. Reprinted by permission.

TABLE 9.5. Clinical Domains for Scale 4: Histrionic/Dramatizing

Behavioral level

(F) Expressively Dramatic (e.g., is overreactive, volatile, provocative, engaging, intolerant of inactivity, resulting in impulsive, highly emotional, and theatrical responsiveness; describes penchant for momentary excitement, fleeting adventures, and short-sighted hedonism).

(F) Interpersonally Attention-Seeking (e.g., actively solicits praise and manipulates others to gain needed reassurance, attention, and approval; is demanding, flirtatious, vain, and seductively exhibitionistic, especially when wishing to be the center of attention).

Phenomenological level

(F) Cognitively Flighty (e.g., avoids introspective thought, is overly suggestible, attentive to fleeting external events, and speaks in impressionistic generalities; integrates experiences poorly, resulting in scattered learning and thoughtless judgments).

(S) Gregarious Self-Image (e.g, views self as sociable, stimulating, and charming; enjoys the image of attracting acquaintances by physical appearance and by pursuing a busy and pleasure-oriented life).

(S) Shallow Objects (e.g., internalized representations are composed largely of superficial memories of past relations, random collections of transient and segregated affects and conflicts, and insubstantial drives and mechanisms).

Intrapsychic level

(F) Dissociation Mechanism (e.g., regularly alters and recomposes self-presentations to create a succession of socially attractive but changing facades; engages in self-distracting activities to avoid reflecting on and integrating unpleasant thoughts and emotions).

(S) Disjointed Organization (e.g., there exists a loosely knit and carelessly united morphologic structure in which processes of internal regulation and control are scattered and unintegrated, with ad hoc methods for restraining impulses, coordinating defenses, and resolving conflicts, leading to mechanisms that must, of necessity, be broad and sweeping to maintain psychic cohesion and stability, and, when successful, only further isolate and disconnect thoughts, feelings, and actions).

Biophysical level

(S) Fickle Mood (e.g., displays rapidly shifting and shallow emotions; is vivacious, animated, and impetuous and exhibits tendencies to be easily excited and as easily angered or bored).

Note. (F), functional attribute; (S), structural attribute. Taken from the *Millon Clinical Multiaxial Inventory–III Manual*, by Theodore Millon, 1994, Minneapolis, MN: National Computer Systems. Copyright 1994 by Theodore Millon. Reprinted by permission.

TABLE 9.6. Clinical Domains for Scale 5: Narcissistic/Egotistic

Behavioral level

(F) Expressively Haughty (e.g., acts in an arrogant, supercilious, pompous, and disdainful manner, flouting conventional rules of shared social living, viewing them as naive or inapplicable to self; reveals a careless disregard for personal integrity and a self-important indifference to the rights of others).

(F) Interpersonally Exploitative (e.g., feels entitled, is unempathic, and expects special favors without assuming reciprocal responsibilities; shamelessly takes others for granted and uses them to enhance self and indulge desires).

Phenomenological level

(F) Cognitively Expansive (e.g., has an undisciplined imagination and exhibits a preoccupation with immature and self-glorifying fantasies of success, beauty, or love; is minimally constrained by objective reality, takes liberties with facts, and often lies to redeem illusions).

(S) Admirable Self-Image (e.g., believes self to be meritorious, special, deserving of great admiration; acts in a grandiose or self-assured manner, often without commensurate achievements; has a sense of high self-worth, despite being seen by others as egotistic, inconsiderate, and arrogant).

(S) Contrived Objects (e.g., internalized representations are composed far more than usual of illusory and changing memories of past relationships; unacceptable drives and conflicts are readily refashioned as the need arises, others are often simulated and pretentious).

Intrapsychic level

(F) Rationalization Mechanism (e.g., is self-deceptive and facile in devising plausible reasons to justify self-centered and socially inconsiderate behavior; offers alibis to place self in the best possible light, despite evident shortcomings or failures).

(S) Spurious Organization (e.g., morphologic structures underlying coping and defensive strategies tend to be flimsy and transparent, appear more substantial and dynamically orchestrated than they are in fact, regulating impulses only marginally, channeling needs with minimal restraint, and creating an inner world in which conflicts are dismissed, failures are quickly redeemed, and pride is effortlessly reasserted).

Biophysical level

(S) Insouciant Mood (e.g., manifests a general air of nonchalance, imperturbability, and feigned tranquility; appears cooly unimpressionable or buoyantly optimistic, except when narcissistic confidence is shaken, at which time either rage, shame, or emptiness is briefly displayed).

Note. (F), functional attribute; (S), structural attribute. Taken from the *Millon Clinical Multiaxial Inventory–III Manual,* by Theodore Millon, 1994, Minneapolis, MN: National Computer Systems. Copyright 1994 by Theodore Millon. Reprinted by permission.

TABLE 9.7. Clinical Domains for Scale 6A: Antisocial/Unruly

Behavioral level

(F) Expressively Impulsive (e.g., is impetuous and irrepressible, acting hastily and spontaneously in a restless, spur-of-the-moment manner; is short-sighted, incautious, and imprudent, failing to plan ahead or consider alternatives, no less heed consequences).

(F) Interpersonally Irresponsible (e.g., is untrustworthy and unreliable, failing to meet or intentionally negating personal obligations of a marital, parental, employment, or financial nature; actively intrudes upon and violates the rights of others; transgresses established social codes through deceitful or illegal behavior).

Phenomenological level

(F) Cognitively Deviant (e.g., construes events and relationships in accord with socially unorthodox beliefs and morals; is disdainful of traditional ideals, fails to conform to social norms, and is contemptuous of conventional values).

(S) Autonomous Self-Image (e.g., sees self as unfettered by the restrictions of social customs and the constraints of personal loyalties; values the image and enjoys the sense of being free, unencumbered, and unconfined by persons, places, obligations, or routines).

(S) Debased Objects (e.g., internalized representations include degraded and corrupt relationships that spur vengeful attitudes and restive impulses, which are driven to subvert established cultural ideals and mores and to devalue personal sentiments and to sully, but intensely covet, the material attainments of society denied them).

Intrapsychic level

(F) Acting-Out Mechanism (e.g., inner tensions that might accrue by postponing the expression of offensive thoughts and malevolent actions are rarely constrained; socially repugnant impulses are not refashioned in sublimated forms, but are discharged directly in precipitous ways, usually without guilt).

(S) Unruly Organization (e.g., inner morphologic structures to contain drive and impulse are noted by their paucity, as are efforts to curb refractory energies and attitudes, leading to easily transgressed controls, low thresholds for hostile or erotic discharge, few subliminal channels, unfettered self-expression, and a marked intolerance of delay or frustration).

Biophysical level

(S) Callous Mood (e.g., is insensitive, irritable, and aggressive, as expressed in a wide-ranging deficit in social charitableness, compassion, or remorse; exhibits a coarse incivility and an offensive if not reckless disregard for the safety of self or others).

Note. (F), functional attribute; (S), structural attribute. Taken from the *Millon Clinical Multiaxial Inventory–III Manual* by Theodore Millon, 1994, Minneapolis, MN: National Computer Systems. Copyright 1994 by Theodore Millon. Reprinted by permission.

**TABLE 9.8. Clinical Domains for Scale 6B:
Aggressive (Sadistic)/Forceful**

Behavioral level

(F) Expressively Precipitate (e.g., is disposed to react in sudden abrupt out-bursts of an unexpected and unwarranted nature; recklessly reactive and daring, attracted to challenge, risk, and harm; unflinching, undeterred by pain, and undaunted by danger and punishment).

(F) Interpersonally Abrasive (e.g., reveals satisfaction in intimidating, coerc-ing, and humiliating others; regularly expresses verbally abusive and deri-sive social commentary; exhibits vicious if not physically brutal behavior).

Phenomenological level

(F) Cognitively Dogmatic (e.g., is strongly opinionated and close-minded, un-bending, and obstinate in holding to preconceptions; exhibits a broad-ranging authoritarianism, social intolerance, and prejudice).

(S) Combative Self-Image (e.g., proudly characterizes self as assertively com-petitive, vigorously energetic, and militantly hard-headed; values aspects of self that present pugnacious, domineering, and power-oriented image).

(S) Pernicious Objects (e.g., internalized representations of the past are dis-tinguished by early relationships that have generated strongly driven ag-gressive energies and malicious attitudes, as well as by a contrasting paucity of sentimental memories, tender affects, internal conflicts, shame, or guilt).

Intrapsychic level

(F) Isolation Mechanism (e.g., can be cold-blooded and remarkably detached from an awareness of the impact of own destructive acts; views objects of violation impersonally, as symbols of devalued groups devoid of human sensibilities).

(S) Eruptive Organization (e.g., despite a generally cohesive morphologic struc-ture composed of routinely adequate modulating controls, defenses, and expressive channels, surging powerful and explosive energies of an aggres-sive and sexual nature threaten to produce precipitous outbursts that peri-odically overwhelm and overrun otherwise competent restraints).

Biophysical level

(S) Hostile Mood (e.g., has an excitable and irritable temper that flares readi-ly into contentious arguments and physical belligerence; is cruel, mean-spirited, and fractious, willing to do harm, even persecute others to get own way).

Note. (F), functional attribute; (S), structural attribute. Taken from the *Millon Clinical Mul-tiaxial Inventory–III Manual,* by Theodore Millon, 1994, Minneapolis, MN: National Com-puter Systems. Copyright 1994 by Theodore Millon. Reprinted by permission.

TABLE 9.9. Clinical Domains for Scale 7: Compulsive/Conforming

Behavioral level

(F) Expressively Disciplined (e.g., maintains a regulated, highly structured, strictly organized life; perfectionism interferes with decision making and task completion).

(F) Interpersonally Respectful (e.g., exhibits unusual adherence to social conventions and proprieties; is scrupulous and overconscientious about matters of morality and ethics; prefers polite, formal, and correct personal relationships, usually insisting that subordinates adhere to personally established rules and methods).

Phenomenological level

(F) Cognitively Constricted (e.g., constructs world in terms of rules, regulations, schedules, and hierarchies; is rigid, stubborn, and indecisive and notably upset by unfamiliar or novel ideas and customs).

(S) Conscientious Self-Image (e.g., sees self as devoted to work, industrious, reliable, meticulous, and efficient, largely to the exclusion of leisure activities; fearful of error or misjudgment and hence overvalues aspects of self that exhibit discipline, perfection, prudence, and loyalty).

(S) Concealed Objects (e.g., only those internalized representations, with their associated inner affects and attitudes that can be socially approved, are allowed conscious awareness or behavioral expression; as a result, actions and memories are highly regulated, forbidden impulses sequestered and tightly bound, personal and social conflicts defensively denied, kept from awareness, and maintained under stringent control).

Intrapsychic level

(F) Reaction Formation Mechanism (e.g., repeatedly presents positive thoughts and socially commendable behavior that are diametrically opposed to deeper contrary and forbidden feelings; displays reasonableness and maturity when faced with circumstances that evoke anger or dismay in others).

(S) Compartmentalized Organization (e.g., morphologic structures are rigidly organized in a tightly consolidated system that is clearly partitioned into numerous, distinct, and segregated constellations of drive, memory, and cognition, with few open channels to permit interplay among these components).

Biophysical level

(S) Solemn Mood (e.g., is tense, joyless, and grim; restrains warm feelings and keeps most emotions under tight control).

Note. (F), functional attribute; (S), structural attribute. Taken from the *Millon Clinical Multiaxial Inventory–III Manual*, by Theodore Millon, 1994, Minneapolis, MN: National Computer Systems. Copyright 1994 by Theodore Millon. Reprinted by permission.

TABLE 9.10.   Clinical Domains for Scale 8A: Negativistic/Oppositional

Behavioral level

(F) Expressively Resentful (e.g., resists fulfilling expectations of others, frequently exhibiting procrastination, inefficiency, and obstinate, contrary, and irksome behavior; reveals gratification in demoralizing and undermining the pleasure and aspirations of others).

(F) Interpersonally Contrary (e.g., assumes conflicting and changing roles in social relationships, particularly dependent and contrite acquiescence and assertive and hostile independence; conveys envy and pique toward those who are more fortunate; is actively concurrently or sequentially obstructive and intolerant of others, expressing either negative or incompatible attitudes).

Phenomenological level

(F) Cognitively Skeptical (e.g., is cynical, doubting, and untrusting, approaching positive events with disbelief and future possibilities with pessimism, anger, and trepidation; has a misanthropic view of life, whines and grumbles, voicing disdain and caustic comments toward those who experience good fortune).

(S) Discontented Self-Image (e.g., sees self as misunderstood, luckless, unappreciated, jinxed, and demeaned by others; recognizes being characteristically embittered, disgruntled, and disillusioned with life).

(S) Vacillating Objects (e.g., internalized representations of the past include a complex of countervailing relationships, setting in motion contradictory feelings, conflicting inclinations, and incompatible memories that are driven by the desire to degrade the achievements and pleasure of others, without necessarily appearing to do so).

Intrapsychic level

(F) Displacement Mechanism (e.g., discharges anger and other troublesome emotions either precipitously or by employing unconscious maneuvers to shift them from their instigator to settings or persons of lesser significance; vents disapproval by substitute or passive means, such as by acting inept or perplexed or behaving in a forgetful or indolent manner).

(S) Divergent Organization (e.g., there is a clear division in the pattern of morphologic structures such that coping and defensive maneuvers are often directed toward incompatible goals, leaving major conflicts unresolved and full psychic cohesion often impossible by virtue of the fact that fulfillment of one drive or need inevitably nullifies or reverses another).

Biophysical level

(S) Irritable Mood (e.g., frequently touchy, temperamental, and peevish, followed in turn by sullen and moody withdrawal; is often petulant and impatient; unreasonably scorns those in authority and reports being easily annoyed or frustrated).

Note. (F), functional attribute; (S), structural attribute. Taken from the *Millon Clinical Multiaxial Inventory–III Manual*, by Theodore Millon, 1994, Minneapolis, MN: National Computer Systems. Copyright 1994 by Theodore Millon. Reprinted by permission.

TABLE 9.11. Clinical Domains for Scale 8B: Self-Defeating/Self-Demeaning

Behavioral level

(F) Expressively Abstinent (e.g., presents self as nonindulgent, frugal, and chaste; is reluctant to seek pleasurable experiences, refraining from exhibiting signs of enjoying life; acts in an unassuming and self-effacing manner, preferring to place self in an inferior light or abject position).

(F) Interpersonally Deferential (e.g., distances self from those who are consistently supportive, relating to others by being self-sacrificing, servile, and obsequious, allowing [if not encouraging] them to exploit, mistreat, or take advantage; renders ineffectual the attempts of others to be helpful and solicits condemnation by accepting undeserved blame and courting unjust criticism).

Phenomenological level

(F) Cognitively Diffident (e.g., hesitant to interpret observations positively for fear that, in doing so, they may take problematic forms or achieve troublesome and self-denigrating outcomes; as a result, there is a habit of repeatedly expressing attitudes and anticipation contrary to favorable beliefs and feelings).

(S) Undeserving Self-Image (e.g., is self-abasing, focusing on the very worst personal features, asserting thereby worthiness of being shamed, humbled, and debased; considers self a failure at living up to the expectations of others and hence deserves to suffer painful consequences).

(S) Discredited Objects (e.g., object representations are composed of failed past relationships and disparaged personal achievements, of positive feelings and erotic drives transposed into their least attractive opposites, of internal conflicts intentionally aggravated, of mechanisms for reducing dysphoria subverted by processes that intensify discomfort).

Intrapsychic level

(F) Exaggeration Mechanism (e.g., repetitively recalls past injustices and anticipates future disappointment as a means of raising distress to homeostatic levels; undermines personal objectives and sabotages good fortune so as to enhance or maintain accustomed level of suffering and pain).

(S) Inverted Organization (e.g., owing to a significant reversal of the pain–pleasure polarity, morphologic structures have contrasting and dual qualities — one more or less conventional, the other its obverse — resulting in a repetitive undoing of affect and intention, a transposing of channels of need gratification with those leading to frustration, and engaging in actions that produce antithetical, if not self-sabotaging, consequences).

Biophysical level

(S) Dysphoric Mood (e.g., experiences a complex mix of emotions, at times anxiously apprehensive, at others forlorn and mournful; feels anguished and tormented; intentionally displays a plaintive and wistful appearance, frequently to induce guilt and discomfort in others).

Note. (F), functional attribute; (S), structural attribute. Taken from the *Millon Clinical Multiaxial Inventory–III Manual*, by Theodore Millon, 1994, Minneapolis, MN: National Computer Systems. Copyright 1994 by Theodore Millon. Reprinted by permission.

TABLE 9.12. Clinical Domains for Scale S: Schizotypal

Behavioral level

(F) Expressively Eccentric (e.g., exhibits socially gauche and peculiar mannerisms; is perceived by others as aberrant, disposed to behave in an unobtrusively odd, aloof, curious, or bizarre manner).

(F) Interpersonally Secretive (e.g., prefers privacy and isolation, with few highly tentative attachments and personal obligations; has drifted over time into increasingly peripheral vocational roles and clandestine social activities).

Phenomenological level

(F) Cognitively Autistic (e.g., capacity to "read" thoughts and feelings of others is markedly dysfunctional; mixes social communication with personal irrelevancies, circumstantial speech, ideas of reference, and metaphorical asides; often ruminative, appearing self-absorbed and lost in daydreams with occasional magical thinking, bodily illusions, obscure suspicion, odd beliefs, and a blurring of reality and fantasy).

(S) Estranged Self-Image (e.g., exhibits recurrent social perplexities and illusions; experiences depersonalization, derealization, and dissociation; sees self as forlorn, with repetitive thoughts of life's emptiness and meaninglessness).

(S) Chaotic Objects (e.g., internalized representations consist of a piecemeal jumble of early relationships and affect, random drives and impulses, and uncoordinated channels of regulation that are only fitfully competent for binding tensions, accommodating needs, and mediating conflicts).

Intrapsychic level

(F) Undoing Mechanism (e.g., bizarre mannerisms and idiosyncratic thoughts appear to reflect a retraction or reversal of previous acts or ideas that have stirred feelings of anxiety, conflict, or guilt; ritualistic or magical behavior serves to repent for or nullify assumed misdeeds or "evil" thoughts).

(S) Fragmented Organization (e.g., possesses permeable ego boundaries; coping and defensive operations are haphazardly ordered in a loose assemblage of morphologic structures, leading to desultory actions in which primitive thoughts and affects are discharged directly, with few reality-based sublimations and significant further disintegration into a psychotic structural level, probably under even modest stress).

Biophysical level

(S) Distraught or Insentient Mood (e.g., excessively apprehensive and ill-at-ease, particularly in social encounters; agitated and anxiously watchful, evincing distrust of others and suspicion of their motives that persists despite growing familiarity; or, e.g., manifests drab, apathetic, sluggish, joyless, and spiritless appearance; reveals marked deficiencies in face-to-face rapport and emotional expression).

Note. (F), functional attribute; (S), structural attribute. Taken from the *Millon Clinical Multiaxial Inventory–III Manual,* by Theodore Millon, 1994, Minneapolis, MN: National Computer Systems. Copyright 1994 by Theodore Millon. Reprinted by permission.

TABLE 9.13. Clinical Domains for Scale C/9: Borderline

Behavioral level

(F) Expressively Spasmodic (e.g., displays a desultory energy level with sudden, unexpected, and impulsive outbursts; abrupt, endogenous shifts in drive state and inhibitory controls; not only places activation and emotional equilibrium in constant jeopardy, but engages in recurrent suicidal or self-mutilating behavior).

(F) Interpersonally Paradoxical (e.g., although needing attention and affection, is unpredictably contrary, manipulative, and volatile, frequently eliciting rejection rather than support; frantically reacts to fears of abandonment and isolation, but often in angry, mercurial, and self-destructive ways).

Phenomenological level

(F) Cognitively Capricious (e.g., experiences rapidly changing, fluctuating, and antithetical perceptions or thoughts concerning passing events; experiences contrasting emotions and conflicting thoughts toward self and others, notably love, rage, and guilt; vacillating and contradictory reactions are evoked in others by virtue of behavior, creating, in turn, conflicting and confusing social feedback).

(S) Uncertain Self-Image (e.g., experiences the confusion of an immature, nebulous, or wavering sense of identity, often with underlying feelings of emptiness; seeks to redeem precipitate actions and changing self-presentations with expressions of contrition and self-punitive behaviors).

(S) Incompatible Objects (e.g., internalized representations include rudimentary and extemporaneously devised but repetitively aborted learning, resulting in conflicting memories, discordant attitudes, contradictory needs, antithetical emotions, erratic impulses, and clashing strategies for conflict reduction).

Intrapsychic level

(F) Regression Mechanism (e.g., retreats under stress to developmentally earlier levels of anxiety tolerance, impulse control, and social adaptation).

(S) Split Organization (e.g., inner structures exist in a sharply segmented and conflicted configuration in which a marked lack of consistency and congruency is seen among elements, levels of consciousness often shift and result in rapid movements across boundaries that usually separate contrasting percepts, memories, and affect, all of which lead to periodic schisms in what limited psychic order and cohesion may otherwise be present, often resulting in transient, stress-related psychotic episodes).

Biophysical level

(S) Labile Mood (e.g., fails to accord unstable mood level with external reality; has either marked shifts from normality to depression to excitement, or has periods of dejection and apathy interspersed with episodes of inappropriate and intense anger and brief spells of anxiety or euphoria).

Note. (F), functional attribute; (S), structural attribute. Taken from the *Millon Clinical Multiaxial Inventory–III Manual*, by Theodore Millon, 1994, Minneapolis, MN: National Computer Systems. Copyright 1994 by Theodore Millon. Reprinted by permission.

TABLE 9.14. Clinical Domains for Scale P: Paranoid

Behavioral level

(F) Expressively Defensive (e.g., is vigilantly guarded, alert to anticipate and ward off expected derogation, malice, and deception; is tenacious and firmly resistant to sources of external influence and control).

(F) Interpersonally Provocative (e.g., not only bears grudges and is unforgiving of those in the past, but displays a quarrelsome, fractious, and abrasive attitude with recent acquaintances; precipitates exasperation and anger by testing loyalties and searching for hidden motives).

Phenomenological level

(F) Cognitively Suspicious (e.g., unwarrantedly skeptical, cynical, and mistrustful of the motives of others, including relatives, friends, and associates, construing innocuous events as signifying hidden or conspiratorial intent; reveals tendency to read hidden meanings into benign matters and to magnify tangential or minor difficulties into proof of duplicity and treachery, especially regarding the fidelity and trustworthiness of a spouse or intimate friend).

(S) Inviolable Self-Image (e.g., has persistent ideas of self-importance and self-reference, perceiving attacks on one's character not apparent to others, asserting as personally derogatory and scurrilous, if not libelous, entirely innocuous actions and events; is proudly independent, reluctant to confide in others, highly insular, experiencing intense fears, however, of losing identity, status, and power of self-determination).

(S) Unalterable Objects (e.g., internalized representations of significant early relationships are a fixed and implacable configuration of deeply held beliefs and attitudes; is driven by unyielding convictions which in turn are aligned in an idiosyncratic manner with a fixed hierarchy of tenaciously held but unwarranted assumptions, fears, and conjecture).

Intrapsychic level

(F) Projection Mechanism (e.g., actively disowns undesirable personal traits and motives and attributes them to others, remains blind to own unattractive behavior and characteristics, yet is overalert to and hypercritical of similar features in others).

(S) Inelastic Organization (e.g., systematic constriction and inflexibility of morphologic structures, rigidly fixed channels of defensive coping, conflict mediation, and need gratification create an overstrung and taut frame that is so uncompromising in its accommodation to changing circumstances that unanticipated stressors are likely to precipitate either explosive outbursts or inner shatterings).

Biophysical level

(S) Irascible Mood (e.g., displays a cold, sullen, churlish, and humorless demeanor; attempts to appear unemotional and objective, but is edgy, envious, and jealous, and quick to take personal offense and to react angrily).

Note. (F), functional attribute; (S), structural attribute. Taken from the *Millon Clinical Multiaxial Inventory–III Manual,* by Theodore Millon, 1994, Minneapolis, MN: National Computer Systems. Copyright 1994 by Theodore Millon. Reprinted by permission.

References

Ackerman, J. J. (1995). *Clinician's guide to child custody evaluations.* New York: Wiley.

American Psychiatric Association. (1980). *Diagnostic and statistical manual of mental disorders* (3rd ed.). Washington, DC: Author.

American Psychiatric Association. (1987). *Diagnostic and statistical manual of mental disorders* (3rd ed., rev.). Washington, DC: Author.

American Psychiatric Association. (1994). *Diagnostic and statistical manual of mental disorders* (4th ed.). Washington, DC: Author.

American Psychological Association. (1974). *Standards for educational and psychological tests.* Washington, DC: Author.

American Psychological Association. (1986). *Guidelines for computer-based tests and interpretations.* Washington, DC: Author.

American Psychological Association. (1992). *Ethical principles of psychologists and code of conduct.* Washington, DC: Author.

American Psychological Association. (1994). Guidelines for child custody evaluations in divorce proceedings. *American Psychologist, 49,* 677–680.

Antoni, M. (1993). The combined use of the MCMI and MMPI. In R. Craig (Ed.), *The Millon Clinical Multiaxial Inventory: A clinical research information synthesis* (pp. 279–302). Hillsdale, NJ: Erlbaum.

Archer, R. P. (1992). *MMPI-A: Assessing adolescent psychopathology.* Hillsdale, NJ: Erlbaum.

Bagby, R. M., Gillis, J. R., & Dickens, S. (1990). Detection of dissimulation with the new generation of objective personality measures. *Behavioral Sciences and the Law, 8,* 93–102.

Bagby, R. M., Gillis, J. R., & Rogers, R. (1991). Effectiveness of the Millon Clinical Multiaxial Inventory validity index in the detection of random responding. *Psychological Assessment, 3,* 285–287.

Bankston v. Alexandria Neurosurgical Clinic, 583 So. 2d 1148 (La. Ct. App. 1991).

Bard, L. A., & Knight, R. A. (1987). Sex offender subtyping and the MCMI. In C. Green (Ed.), *Proceedings of the first conference on the Millon clinical inventories* (pp. 133–137). Minneapolis: National Computer Systems.

Barefoot v. Estelle, 463 U.S. 880 (1983).

Barton, W. A. (1985). *Recovering from psychological injuries.* Washington, DC: Association of Trial Lawyers of America.

Becker, S. (1994). *Memorandum re New Jersey state board of psychological examiners* [Forensic Committee]. Livingston, NJ: New Jersey Psychological Association.

Black's Law Dictionary (6th ed.). (1990). St. Paul, MN: West.

Blaney, N. T., Millon, C., Morgan, R., Eisdorfer, C., & Szapocznik, J. (1990). Emotional distress, stress-related disruption and coping among healthy HIV-positive gay males. *Psychology and Health, 4,* 259–273.

Blau, T. (1984). *The psychologist as expert witness.* New York: Wiley.

Bonnie, R. J. (1994). Lorena Bobbitt, "moral mistakes" and the price of justice. *Developments in Mental Health Law, 14*(1), 20–23.

Briner, W., Risey, J., Guth, P., & Norris, C. (1990). Use of the Millon Clinical Multiaxial Inventory in evaluating patients with severe tinnitus. *American Journal of Otology, 11,* 334–337.

Brodsky, S. L. (1989). Advocacy in the guise of scientific advocacy: An examination of Faust and Ziskin. *Computers in Human Behavior, 5,* 261–264.

Brodsky, S. L. (1991). *Testifying in court: Guidelines and maxims for the expert witness.* Washington, DC: American Psychological Association.

Brooks v. White, 1993 U.S. Dist. LEXIS 2560 (S.D. Ala. Jan. 27, 1993).

Butcher, J. N. (1990). *The MMPI-2 in psychological treatment.* New York: Oxford University Press.

Butcher, J. N., Dahlstrom, W. G., Graham, J. R., Tellegen, A., & Kaemmer, B. (1989). *MMPI-2 manual for administration and scoring.* Minneapolis: University of Minnesota Press.

Cattell, R. B. (1967). Suggested restructurings of the concept of reliability. In D. A. Payne & R. F. McMorris (Eds.), *Educational and psychological measurement: Contributions to theory and practice* (pp. 59–66). Waltham, MA: Blaisdell.

CDI v. McHale, 848 S.W.2d 941 (Ark. Ct. App. 1993).

Choca, J. P., Shanley, L. A., & VanDenburg, E. (1992). *Interpretative guide to the Millon Clinical Multiaxial Inventory.* Washington, DC: American Psychological Association.

Cicchetti, D. V. (1994). Guidelines, criteria, and rules of thumb for evaluating normed and standardized assessment instruments in psychology. *Psychological Assessment, 6,* 284–290.

Cohen, J. (1994). The earth is round ($p < .05$). *American Psychologist, 49,* 997–1003.

Committee on Ethical Guidelines for Forensic Psychologists. (1991). Specialty guidelines for forensic psychologists. *Law and Human Behavior, 15,* 655–665.

Craig, R. J. (1993a). *Psychological assessment with the Millon Clinical Multiaxial Inventory (II): An interpretive guide.* Odessa, FL: Psychological Assessment Resources.

Craig, R. J. (1993b). *The Millon Clinical Multiaxial Inventory: A clinical research information synthesis.* Hillsdale, NJ: Erlbaum.

Dahlstrom, W. G., Welsh, G. S., & Dahlstrom, L. E. (1972). *An MMPI handbook* (Vol. 1, rev. ed.). Minneapolis: University of Minnesota Press.

Daubert v. Merrell Dow Pharmaceuticals, 113 S. Ct. 2786 (1993).

Dawes, R. M. (1989). Experience and validity of clinical judgment: The illusory correlation. *Behavioral Sciences and the Law, 7,* 457–467.

delRosario, P. M., McCann, J. T., & Navarra, J. W. (1994). The MCMI-II diagnosis of schizophrenia: Operating characteristics and profile analysis. *Journal of Personality Assessment, 63,* 438–482.

DeWolfe, A., Larson, J. K., & Ryan, J. J. (1985). Diagnostic accuracy of the Millon test computer reports for bipolar affective disorder. *Journal of Psychopathology and Behavioral Assessment, 7, 185–189.*

Dusky v. United States, 362 U.S. 402 (1960).

Dyer, F. J. (1985). Review of the Millon Adolescent Personality Inventory. In D. J. Keyser & R. C. Sweetland (Eds.), *Test critiques* (Vol. IV, pp. 425–433). Kansas City, MO: Test Corporation of America.

Dyer, F. J. (1991). Trauma, trauma everywhere. *New Jersey Psychologist, 41*(4), 30–32.

Ewing, C. P. (Ed.). (1985a). *Psychology, psychiatry, and the law: A clinical and forensic handboook.* Sarasota, FL: Professional Resource Exchange.

Ewing, C. P. (Speaker). (1985b). *Ten commandments for the expert witness* [Cassette Recording]. Sarasota, FL: Professional Resource Exchange.

Exner, J. E. (1991). *The Rorschach: A comprehensive system* (2nd ed., Vol. 2). New York: Wiley.

Faust, D., & Ziskin, J. (1988a). The expert witness in psychology and psychiatry. *Science, 241,* 31–35.

Faust, D., & Ziskin, J. (1988b). Response to Fowler and Matarrazzo. *Science, 241,* 1143–1144.

Federal rules of evidence. (1992). Boston: Little, Brown.

Finney, J. C. (1966). A programmed interpretation of the MMPI and CPI. *Archives of General Psychiatry, 15,* 75–81.

Flynn, P. M., McCann, J. T., & Fairbank, J. A. (1995). Issues in the assessment of personality disorder and substance abuse using the Millon Clinical Multiaxial Inventory (MCMI-II). *Journal of Clinical Psychology, 51,* 415–421.

Fowler, R. D. (1965). *Purposes and usefulness of the Alabama program for automatic interpretation of the MMPI.* Paper presented at the annual meeting of the American Psychological Association, Chicago.

Fowler, R. D., & Butcher, J. N. (1986). Critique of Matarazzo's views on computerized testing: All sigma and no meaning. *American Psychologist, 41,* 94–96.

Frye v. United States, 293 F. 1013 (D.C. Cir. 1923).

Garibaldi v. Dietz, 752 S.W.2d 771 (Ark. Ct. App. 1988).

Gilberstadt, H., & Duker, J. (1965). *A handbook for clinical factorial MMPI interpretation.* Philadelphia: Saunders.

Goldberg, L. R. (1965). Diagnosticians vs. diagnostic signs: The diagnosis of psychosis vs. neurosis from the MMPI. *Psychological Monographs, 79*(Whole No. 602).

Goldberg, L. R. (1970). Man versus model of man: A rationale plus some evidence for a method of improving on clinical inferences. *Psychological Bulletin, 73,* 422–432.

Graham, J. R. (1990). *MMPI-2: Assessing personality and psychopathology.* New York: Oxford University Press.

Green, C. (1982). The diagnostic accuracy and utility of MMPI and MCMI computer interpretive reports. *Journal of Personality Assessment, 46,* 359–365.

Greene, R. L. (1988). Assessment of malingering and defensiveness by objective personality inventories. In R. Rogers (Ed.), *Clinical assessment of malingering and deception* (pp. 123–158). New York: Guilford Press.

Grisso, T. (1988). *Competency to stand trial evaluations: A manual for practice.* Sarasota, FL: Professional Resource Exchange.

Gualtieri, J., Gonzalas, E., & Baldwin, N. (1987). The accuracy of MCMI computerized narratives for alcoholics. In C. Green (Ed.), *Proceedings of the first conference on the Millon clinical inventories* (pp. 263–268). Minneapolis: National Computer Systems.

Gudjonsson, G. (1992). *The psychology of interrogations, confessions, and testimony.* Chichester, England: Wiley.

Gustafson v. State, 854 P.2d 751 (Alaska Ct. App. 1993).

Guyer, M. J., & Ash, P. (1985). Law and clinical practice in child abuse and neglect cases. In C. P. Ewing (Ed.), *Psychology, psychiatry, and the law: A clinical and forensic handbook* (pp. 305–330). Sarasota, FL: Professional Resource Exchange.

Halon, R. L. (1990). The comprehensive child custody evaluation. *American Journal of Forensic Psychology, 8,* 19–46.

Hamberger, L. K., & Hastings, J. E. (1986). Personality correlates of men who abuse their partners: A cross-validation study. *Journal of Family Violence, 1,* 323–341.

Hamberger, L. K., & Hastings, J. E. (1988). Characteristics of male spouse abusers consistent with personality disorders. *Hospital and Community Psychiatry, 39,* 763–770.

Hamberger, L. K., & Hastings, J. E. (1989). Counseling male spouse abusers: Characteristics of treatment completers and dropouts. *Violence and Victims, 4,* 275–286.

Hart, S. J., Webster, C. D., & Menzies, R. J. (1993). A note on portraying the accuracy of violence predictions. *Law and Human Behavior, 17,* 695–700.

Hawton, K. (1987). Assessment of suicide risk. *British Journal of Psychiatry, 150,* 145–153.

Haywood v. Sullivan, 888 F.2d 1463 (5th Cir. 1989).

Heilbrun, K. (1992). The role of psychological testing in forensic assessment. *Law and Human Behavior, 16,* 257–272.

Hendin, H. (1986). Suicide: A review of new directions in research. *Hospital and Community Psychiatry, 37,* 148–154.

Herron, L., Turner, J., & Weiner, P. (1986). A comparison of the Millon Clinical Multiaxial Inventory and the Minnesota Multiphasic Personality Inventory as predictors of successful treatment by lumbar laminectomy. *Clinical Orthopedics and Related Research, 203*(2), 232–238.

Hess, A. K. (1987). The ethics of forensic psychology. In I. B. Weiner & A. K. Hess (Eds.), *Handbook of forensic psychology* (pp. 653–680). New York: Wiley.

In re A.V., 849 S.W.2d 393 (Tex. Ct. App. 1993).

In re Arrigo, 503 N.Y.S.2d (N.Y. Fam. Ct. 1986).

In re Cheryl H., 153 Cal. App. 3d 1048, 200 Cal. Rptr. 789 (Cal. 1984).

In re Donald C.H., Jr., 1994 Wis. App. LEXIS 7 (Wis. Ct. App., Jan. 6, 1994).

In re Marriage of L.R., 559 N.E.2d 779 (Ill. Ct. App. 1st Dist. 1990).

In re Subpoena Issued to L.Q., 545 A.2d 792 (N.J. Super. 1988).

In re Woodward, 636 A.2d 969 (D.C. Ct. App. 1994).

Inwald, R. E., Knatz, H., & Shusman, E. (1982). *The Inwald Personality Inventory manual.* Kew Gardens, NY: Hilson.

Iwanski v. Streamwood Police Pension Board, 596 N.E.2d 691 (Ill. Ct. App. 1st Dist. 1992).

Jackson, D. N. (1985). Computer-based personality testing. *Computers in Human Behavior, 1,* 255–264.

Jackson, M. A. (1989). The clinical assessment and prediction of violent behavior. *Criminal Justice and Behavior, 16,* 114–131.

James, B. (1994). *Handbook for treatment of attachment-trauma problems in children.* New York: Lexington Books.

Jay, G. W., Grove, R. N., & Grove, K. S. (1987). Differentiation of chronic headache from non-headache pain patients using the Millon Clinical Multiaxial Inventory (MCMI). *Headache, 27,* 124–129.

Joffe, R. T., & Regan, J. J. (1989). Personality and suicidal behavior in depressed patients. *Comprehensive Psychiatry, 30,* 157–160.

Johnson v. Sullivan, 1649 Unempl. Ins. Rep. (CCH) §16,516A (C.D. Ill., May 5, 1992).

Kassin, S. M., & McNall, K. (1991). Police interrogation and confessions: Communicating promises and threats by pragmatic implication. *Law and Human Behavior, 15,* 233–251.

Kilburg, R. R., Nathan, P. E., & Thoreson, R. W. (Eds.). (1986). *Professionals in distress: Issues, syndromes, and solutions in psychology.* Washington, DC: American Psychological Association.

Krug, S. E. (1987). Microtrends: An orientation to computerized assessment. In J. N. Butcher (Ed.), *Computerized psychological assessment: A practitioner's guide* (pp. 15–25). New York: Basic Books.

Langevin, R., Lang, R., Reynolds, R., Wright, P., Garrels, D., Marchese, V., Handy, L., Pugh, G., & Frenzel, R. (1988). Personality and sexual anomalies: An examination of the Millon Clinical Multiaxial Inventory. *Annals of Sex Research, 1,* 13–32.

Lanyon, R. I. (1968). *A handbook of MMPI group profiles.* Minneapolis: University of Minnesota Press.

Litwack, T. R. (1993). On the ethics of dangerousness assessments. *Law and Human Behavior, 17,* 479–482.

Litwack, T. R. (1994). Assessments of dangerousness: Legal, research, and clinical developments. *Administration and Policy in Mental Health, 21,* 361–377.

Lohr, J. M., Hamberger, L. K., & Bonge, D. (1988). The nature of irrational beliefs in different personality clusters of spouse abusers. *Journal of Rational-Emotive and Cognitive-Behavioral Therapy, 6,* 273–285.

Lowman, R. L. (1989). *Pre-employment screening for psychopathology: A guide to professional practice.* Sarasota, FL: Professional Resource Exchange.

Malec, J. F., Romsaas, E. P., Messing, E. M., Cummings, K. C., & Trump, D. L. (1990). Psychological and mood disturbance associated with the diagnosis and treatment of testis cancer and other malignancies. *Journal of Clinical Psychology, 46,* 551–557.

Maloney, M. P. (1985). *A clinician's guide to forensic psychological assessment.* New York: Free Press.

Marks, P. A., & Seeman, W. (1963). *The actuarial description of abnormal personality: An atlas for use with the MMPI.* Baltimore: Williams & Wilkins.

Matarazzo, J. D. (1986). Computerized clinical psychological test interpretation: Unvalidated plus all mean and no sigma. *American Psychologist, 41,* 14–24.

Matarrazzo, J. D. (1991). Psychological assessment is reliable and valid: Reply to Ziskin and Faust. *American Psychologist, 46,* 882–884.

Mauet, T. A. (1988). *Fundamentals of trial technique* (2nd ed.). Boston: Little, Brown.

May v. Southeast Wyoming Mental Health Center, 866 P.2d 732 (Wyo. 1993).

McCann, J. T. (1990). A multimethod-multitrait analysis of the MCMI-II clinical syndrome scales. *Journal of Personality Assessment, 55,* 465–476.

McCann, J. T. (1991). Convergent and discriminant validity of the MCMI-II and MMPI personality disorder scales. *Psychological Assessment, 3,* 9–18.

McCann, J. T., & Gergelis, R. E. (1990). Utility of the MCMI-II in assessing suicide risk. *Journal of Clinical Psychology, 46,* 764–770.

McCann, J. T., & Suess, J. F. (1988). Clinical applications of the MCMI: The 1-2-3-8 codetype. *Journal of Clinical Psychology, 44,* 181–186.

McCormack, J. K., Barnett, R. W., & Wallbrown, F. H. (1989). Factor structure of the Millon Clinical Multiaxial Inventory (MCMI) with an offender sample. *Journal of Personality Assessment, 53,* 442–448.

McGee v. Bowen, 647 F. Supp. 1238 (N.D. Ill. 1986).

McNiel, K., & Meyer, R. G. (1990). Detection of deception on the Millon Clinical Multiaxial Inventory (MCMI). *Journal of Clinical Psychology, 46,* 755–764.

Meehl, P. E. (1954). *Clinical versus statistical prediction: A theoretical analysis and a review of the evidence.* Minneapolis: University of Minnesota Press.

Melton, G. B., Petrila, J., Poythress, N. G., & Slobogin, C. (1987). *Psychological evaluations for the courts: A handbook for mental health professionals and lawyers.* New York: Guilford Press.

Millon, T. (1969). *Modern psychopathology.* Philadelphia: Saunders.

Millon, T. (1981). *Disorders of personality: DSM-III: Axis II.* New York: Wiley.

Millon, T. (1983). *Millon Clinical Multiaxial Inventory manual* (3rd ed.). Minneapolis: National Computer Systems.

Millon, T. (1985). The MCMI provides a good assessment of DSM-III disorders: The MCMI-II will prove even better. *Journal of Personality Assessment, 49,* 379–391.

Millon, T. (1986a). A theoretical derivation of pathological personalities. In T. Millon & G. L. Klerman (Eds.), *Contemporary directions in psychopathology: Toward the DSM-IV* (pp. 639–669). New York: Guilford Press.

Millon, T. (1986b). Personality prototypes and their diagnostic criteria. In T. Millon & G. L. Klerman (Eds.), *Contemporary directions in psychopathology: Toward the DSM-IV* (pp. 671–712). New York: Guilford Press.

Millon, T. (1987). *Manual for the Millon Clinical Multiaxial Inventory–II (MCMI-II).* Minneapolis: National Computer Systems.

Millon, T. (1990). *Toward a new personology: An evolutionary model.* New York: Wiley.

Millon, T. (1993). *Millon Adolescent Clinical Inventory (MACI) manual.* Minneapolis: National Computer Systems.

Millon, T. (1994a). *Millon Clinical Multiaxial Inventory–III (MCMI-III) manual.* Minneapolis: National Computer Systems.

Millon, T. (1994b). Personality disorders: Conceptual distinctions and classification issues. In P. T. Costa & T. A. Widiger (Eds.), *Personality disorders and the five-factor model of personality.* Washington, DC: American Psychological Association.

Millon, T., & Davis, R. D. (1996). *Disorders of personality: DSM-IV and beyond.* New York: Wiley.

Millon, T., & Green, C. (1989). Interpretive guide to the Millon Clinical Multiaxial Inventory (MCMI-II). In C. S. Newmark (Ed.), *Major psychological assessment instruments* (Vol. II, pp. 5–43). Needham Heights, MA: Allyn & Bacon.

Millon, T. Green, C. J., & Meagher, R. B. (1982a). *Millon Adolescent Personality Inventory manual.* Minneapolis: National Computer Systems.

Millon, T., Green, C. J., & Meagher, R. B., Jr. (1982b). *Millon Behavioral Health Inventory* (3rd ed.). Minneapolis: National Computer Systems.

Miranda v. Arizona, 384 U.S. 436 (1973).

Mnookin, R. H., & Weisberg, D. K. (1989). *Child, family and state: Problems and materials on children and the law.* Boston: Little, Brown.

Monahan, J. (1981). *Predicting violent behavior: An assessment of clinical techniques.* Beverly Hills, CA: Sage.

Monahan, J. (1992). Mental disorder and violent behavior. *American Psychologist, 47,* 511–521.

Monahan, J., & Steadman, H. J. (1994). Toward a rejuvenation of risk assessment research. In J. Monahan & H. Steadman (Eds.), *Violence and mental disorder: Developments in risk assessment.* Chicago: University of Chicago Press.

Moreland, K. L. (1993). Computer-assisted interpretation of the MCMI-II. In R. J. Craig (Ed.), *The Millon Clinical Multiaxial Inventory: A clinical research information synthesis* (pp. 213–234). Hillsdale, NJ: Erlbaum.

Moreland, K. L., & Onstad, J. A. (1987). Validity of Millon's computerized interpretation system for the MCMI: A controlled study. *Journal of Consulting and Clinical Psychology, 55,* 113–114.

Mossman, D. (1994). Further comments on portraying the accuracy of violence predictions. *Law and Human Behavior, 18,* 587–593.

Murphy, W. D., & Peters, J. M. (1992). Profiling child sexual abusers: Psychological considerations. *Criminal Justice and Behavior, 19,* 24–37.

Musetto, A. P. (1985). Evaluation and mediation in child custody disputes. In C. P. Ewing (Ed.), *Psychology, psychiatry, and the law: A clinical and forensic handbook* (pp. 281–304). Sarasota, FL: Professional Resource Exchange.

Nebraska v. Tlamka, 511 N.W.2d 135 (Neb. Ct. App. 1993).

New Jersey State Board of Examiners. (1993). *Manual for members of professional boards of the state of New Jersey.* Newark, NJ: Author.

New Jersey Statutes Annotated (West), § 2C:2-9 (1982).

New York Criminal Procedure Law, § 730.10 (Consol. 1983).

New Jersey v. Cavallo, 88 N.J. 508, 443 A.2d 1020 (N.J. 1982).

Ngai v. United States, 79 U.S. 440 (1979).

Nunnally, J. C. (1967). *Psychometric theory.* New York: McGraw-Hill.

Ownby, R. L., Wallbrown, F. A., Carmin, C. N., & Barnett, R. W. (1990). A combined factor analysis of the Millon clinical multiaxial inventory and the MMPI in an offender population. *Journal of Clinical Psychology, 46,* 89–96.

Pendleton v. Commonwealth, 685 S.W.2d 549 (Ky. 1985).

People v. Ruiz, 222 Cal. App. 3d 1241, 272 Cal. Rptr. 368 (1990).

People v. Stoll, 783 P.2d 698 (Cal. 1989).

Peters, J. M., & Murphy, W. D. (1992). Profiling child sexual abusers: Legal considerations. *Criminal Justice and Behavior, 19,* 38–53.

Piersma, H. L. (1987a). Millon Clinical Multiaxial Inventory (MCMI) computer-generated diagnoses: How do they compare to clinical judgement? *Journal of Psychopathology and Behavioral Assessment, 9,* 305–312.

Piersma, H. L. (1987b). The MCMI as a measure of DSM-III Axis II diagnoses: An empirical comparison. *Journal of Clinical Psychology, 43,* 478–483.

Quinsey, V. L., Arnold, L. S., & Pruesse, M. (1980). MMPI profiles of men referred for a pretrial psychiatric assessment as a function of offense type. *Journal of Clinical Psychology, 36,* 410–417.

Reik, T. (1948). *Listening with the third ear.* New York: Rinehart.

Repko, G. R., & Cooper, R. (1985). The diagnosis of personality disorder: A comparison of MMPI profile, Millon inventory, and clinical judgement in a worker's compensation population. *Journal of Clinical Psychology, 41,* 867–881.

Retzlaff, P. D., & Sheehan, E. P. (1989). A response consistency statistic for the Millon Clinical Multiaxial Inventory (MCMI). *Journal of Psychopathology and Behavioral Assessment, 11,* 143–151.

Retzlaff, P. D., Sheehan, E., & Fiel, A. (1991). MCMI-II report style and bias: Profile and validity scales analyses. *Journal of Personality Assessment, 56,* 466–477.

Retzlaff, P. D., Sheehan, E. P., & Lorr, M. (1990). MCMI-II scoring: Weighted and unweighted algorithms. *Journal of Personality Assessment, 55,* 219–223.

Rogers, R. (Ed.). (1988). *Clinical assessment of malingering and deception.* New York: Guilford Press.

Rogers, R., Bagby, R. M., & Perera, C. (1993). Can Ziskin withstand his own criticisms? Problems with his model of cross-examination. *Behavioral Sciences and the Law, 11,* 223–233.

Rogers, R., Dion, K. L., & Lynett, E. (1992). Diagnostic validity of antisocial personality disorder: A prototypical analysis. *Law and Human Behavior, 16,* 677–689.

Roid, G. H. (1985). Computer-based test interpretation: The potential of quantitative methods of test interpretation. *Computers in Human Behavior, 1,* 207–219.

Roid, G. H. (1986). Computer technology in testing. In B. S. Blake & J. C. Witt (Eds.), *The future of testing: Buros–Nebraska symposium on measurement and testing* (Vol. 2, pp. 29–69). Hillsdale, NJ: Erlbaum.

Rubenzer, S. (1992). A comparison of traditional and computer-generated psychological reports in an adolescent inpatient setting. *Journal of Clinical Psychology, 48,* 817–827.

Sandberg, M. L. (1987). Is the ostensive accuracy of computer interpretive reports a result of the Barnum effect? A study of the MCMI. In C. Green (Ed.), *Proceedings of the first conference on the Millon clinical inventories* (pp. 155–164). Minneapolis: National Computer Systems.

Sawyer, J. (1966). Measurement *and* prediction, clinical *and* statistical. *Psychological Bulletin, 66,* 178–200.

Shapiro, D. L. (1984). *Psychological evaluation and expert testimony: A practical guide to forensic work.* New York: Van Nostrand Reinhold.

Shapiro, D. L. (1985). Insanity and the assessment of criminal responsibility. In C. P. Ewing (Ed.), *Psychology, psychiatry, and the law: A clinical and forensic handbook* (pp. 67–94). Sarasota, FL: Professional Resource Exchange.

Shapiro, D. L. (1991). *Forensic psychological assessment: An integrative approach.* Boston: Allyn & Bacon.

Siddall, J. W. (1986). Use of the MCMI with substance abusers. *Noteworthy Responses, 2*(2), 1–3.

Snyder, D. K., Widiger, T. A., & Hoover, D. W. (1990). Methodological considerations in validating computer-based test interpretations: Controlling for response bias. *Psychological Assessment: A Journal of Consulting and Clinical Psychology, 2, 470–477.*

State v. Galloway, (N.J. Super. 1993).

State v. Hurd, 432 A.2d 86 (N.J. 1981).

State v. Shearer, 792 P.2d 1215 (Or. App. 1990).

Strack, S., Lorr, M., Campbell, L., & Lamnin, A. (1992). Personality and clinical syndrome factors of MCMI-II scales. *Journal of Personality Disorders, 6,* 40–52.

Taylor v. Heckler, 605 F. Supp. 407 (D. Me. 1984).

Tisdale, M. J., Pendleton, L., & Marler, M. (1990). MCMI characteristics of DSM-III-R bulimics. *Journal of Personality Assessment, 55,* 477–483.

Tyler v. State, 618 So. 2d 1306 (Miss. 1993).

United States v. Banks, 36 M.J. 150 (CMA 1992).

United States v. Dennison, 652 F. Supp. 211 (D.N.M. 1986).

United States v. Hearst, 424 F. Supp. 307 (N.D. Cal. 1976).

United States v. St. Pierre, 812 F. 2d 417 (8th Cir. 1987).

Van Der Linden, W. (1994). Fundamental measurement and the fundamentals of Rasch measurement. In M. Wilson (Ed.), *Objective measurement: Theory into practice* (Vol, 2, pp. 3–24). Norwood, NJ: Ablex.

VanGorp, W. G., & Meyer, R. G. (1986). The detection of faking on the Millon Clinical Multiaxial Inventory (MCMI). *Journal of Clinical Psychology, 42,* 742–747.

Watkins, C. E., Campbell, V. L., Nieberding, R., & Hallmark, R. (1995). Contemporary practice of psychological assessment by clinical psychologists. *Professional Psychology: Research and Practice, 26,* 54–60.

Watson v. Rinderknecht, 84 N.W. 798 (Minn. 1901).

Weiner, I. B., & Hess, A. K. (1987). *Handbook of forensic psychology.* New York: Wiley.

Widiger, T. A. (1985). Review of Millon Clinical Multiaxial Inventory. In J. V. Mitchell (Ed.), *Ninth mental measurement yearbook* (pp. 986–988). Lincoln, NE: Buros Institute.

Widiger, T. A., & Corbitt, E. M. (1993). The MCMI-II personality disorder scales and their relationship to DSM-III-R diagnosis. In R. J. Craig (Ed.), *The Millon Clinical Multiaxial Inventory: A clinical research information synthesis* (pp. 181–201). Hillsdale, NJ: Erlbaum.

Widiger, T. A., & Frances, A. (1987). Interviews and inventories for the measurement of personality disorders. *Clinical Psychology Review, 7,* 49–75.

Widiger, T. A., Williams, J. B. W., Spitzer, R. L., & Frances, A. (1985). The MCMI as a measure of DSM-III. *Journal of Personality Assessment, 49,* 366–378.

Wiggins, J. S. (1973). *Personality and prediction: Principles of personality assessment.* Reading, MA: Addison-Wesley.

Wrightsman, L. S., & Kassin, S. M. (1993). *Confessions in the courtroom.* Newbury Park, CA: Sage.

Ziskin, J., & Faust, D. (1988). *Coping with psychiatric and psychological testimony* (4th ed.). Los Angeles: Law and Psychology Press.

Ziskin, J., & Faust, D. (1991). A reply to Matarrazzo. *American Psychologist, 46,* 881–882.

Index